My Father, My Son

Max Cohen, M.D. and Donald Cohen Ph.D., 1996

"In reconstructing their relationship, the authors have accomplished for fathers and sons what Dan Levinson's, *The Seasons of a Man's Life* and Gail Sheehy's, *Passages,* have been able to achieve in providing a structure for the various phases of male and female development."

"The basic relationship between a father and son is the essence of healthy living. These letters echo the importance of what that means."

—**Rollo May, Ph.D.**, author of *Love and Will*

D1516154

Praise for **The Inside Ride**

A Journey to Manhood, Letters Between Father and Son

"An intimate look into the power of reflections of two psychotherapists, a father and son. In a time of revolutionized modern communication, they invite the reader to hear the poignant story through thoughts expressed in responsive letters. Your heart will embrace your own child or parent as meaningful moments of revelation jump off the page."

—**Janis Abrahms Spring, Ph.D.**, author of *After the Affair, How Can I Forgive You?: The Courage to Forgive, the Freedom Not To, Life with Pop: Lessons on Caring for an Aging Parent*

"*The Inside Ride, A Journey to Manhood* offers a window into a complex and caring relationship between father and son. Set over a lifetime, these powerful letters permit us to participate in the evolving ties between two thoughtful and loving men."

—**Jeffrey Werden, Ph.D.**, *Psychoanalyst, Former President National Psychological Association for Psychoanalysis*

"This series of letters between Donald Cohen and Max Cohen serves as a dialogue over the years from Donald's early childhood to adulthood. The reader may be touched by the genuine mutual caring and respect, which enables them both to seek and offer understanding and compassion. Reminiscences from both father and son facilitate warmth and reconciliation. The symbolism of the Coney Island Ferris Wheel serves as a metaphor for *The Inside Ride* of their rich, evolving relationship. This book may offer a template for readers as we reflect on our own parent-child experiences."

—**Joseph P. Wagenseller, D.Min., LP**, *Jungian psychoanalyst, Former Chair of the American Board for Accreditation in Psychoanalysis, Former President of the C.G. Jung Institute of New York City*

Books by Donald Cohen

Poetry Collections
Memory Man Volume 1
Memory Man Volume 2
Memory Man Volume 3
Gathering Seasons
Writings From The Ferris Wheel

Childrens' Books
Milo, My Stray Cat

Books co-written by Max Cohen and Donald Cohen
My Father, My Son

The Inside Ride

A Journey to Manhood

Letters Between Father and Son

Max Cohen, M.D.
Donald Cohen, Ph.D.

Nicolas Hays
Lake Worth, FL

Published in 2020 by Nicolas-Hays, Inc.
P. O. Box 540206
Lake Worth, FL 33454-0206
www.nicolashays.com

Distributed to the trade by
Red Wheel/Weiser, LLC
65 Parker St. • Ste. 7
Newburyport, MA 01950
www.redwheelweiser.com

ISBN: 978-0-89254-191-1
Ebook ISBN: 978-0-89254-682-4

Library of Congress Cataloging-in-Publication Data available upon request

Cover art:
Plaza Mexico, USA—Mimi Gross
(From author's private collection)
Photo of authors on back cover by Emily Cohen

Book design and production by STUDIO 31
www.studio31.com

Printed in the U.S.A.

Dedicated to my grandchildren

May they continue their inside ride with joy.

When I was a boy of fourteen, my father was so ignorant I could hardly stand to have the old man around. But when I got to be twenty-one, I was astonished at how much he had learned in seven years. —Mark Twain

If your son suddenly begins to fall at a headlong rate, you must, through the agency of love and greater age, throw him a line and haul him back. —Richard Ford, *Independence Day*

Contents

The Inside Ride

Starting slowly
I ride the roller-coaster
Faster and faster
People, places and things
Views passing by
Drifting, stretching
Staring out
Transitory, like a locomotion
The way of motion
In emotion
Speeding by
Furiously
Moving images
Purposely
Whirling all around me
Everyday life
Faded photographs
Windows of nostalgia's wonders
Crowding my solitude
Sensing the sameness
Surrounds me on all sides
Everywhere my eyes seize
Merging into one neutral circle
Ups and downs, leveled off
Unexplainable
Why it all condenses down to one
I ponder the me, he, and we
Of it all
Stitched up
Alchemized, alike in substance
A molten rock

Of interior remains
Off the roller-coaster
My soul stretched wide
See outside
On the inside ride

Poem by Donald Cohen
From *Writings From The Ferris Wheel* (2019)

Foreword

by

Jared Cohen

It's a funny thing to realize you are just like your dad. For me, it's been a journey to get there. For years I was in denial about it. He fixates on things, takes on a project and makes it the theme of every conversation, insists on making his various collections a living museum for all to see, and is master of the tangent for his latest stream of consciousness thinking. That couldn't possibly describe me.

The more I saw his reflection in the mirror, the more I projected, which meant creating distance between us. I wouldn't call, I'd get frustrated when he didn't understand something I was talking about, and when he would ask if I received his messages, I would get annoyed and explain that nobody uses voicemail anymore. In truth, this was part of my own identity crisis.

But all of that changed when I had kids. A few sleepless nights, some exploding diapers, and the sheer responsibility that comes with raising a child made me quickly realize that being a dad is hard. It's also humbling to think that as a parent, I haven't even caught up to my own memories yet. I have photos, but my recollections begin in elementary school. I expected my dad to be present for all my baseball, tennis, and soccer games. Even though I was a terrible saxophone player and never really learned to read music, I would have been devastated if he missed me march in the Memorial Day Parade. I believed I was the center of the universe, so thought nothing of it when he was in a bad mood, stressed out, or wanted me to stay at the dinner table long enough to have a family dinner. I remember all of this.

I'm now getting a taste of my own medicine. My three girls drag bedtime out, leave their clothes all over the place, at times mark up the walls of my newly renovated apartment, and it seems that on days when I really need them to lighten my mood, they decide to snub me. But I am also experiencing the power of a single smile, a cute gesture, a moment of comfort, all of which evoke a string of emotions that I didn't know existed.

I never got this as a kid. But I'm getting it now and, in many respects, I feel that I am reliving my own childhood through my dad's eyes. It's one of the most powerful experiences that I've ever had. When he comes over to play with my daughters, it is as if I'm watching chapters of my life that I don't remember. He makes the same jokes, plays the same games, and has the same endearing qualities with them that he must have had with me when I was a toddler.

These are powerful emotions, but they also fill me with guilt. I find myself wondering what life challenges, hardships, and stresses he was forced to endure and hide while I threw a temper tantrum about someone leaving me out at recess or because I didn't get a toy I wanted. Were there moments he felt his life was falling apart? Did he ever cry in the other room to avoid exposing me to his emotions? Were there moments when he wanted to be completely present but something happened to get in the way?

If he ever felt these things—and he must have—he never showed his hand, instead choosing to parent in the most selfless way possible. I sometimes feel tempted to ask him to take me back to these moments, but truth be told, I don't think I could handle hearing it.

I'm late to the game, but find that at this stage of life I'm trying to draw as many comparisons to my dad as possible. Now that I want it, it seems harder to live up to his example and that irony is not lost on me. He worked out of the house, never traveled for work, and didn't have the kind of job that required him to be out for dinners all the time. We played baseball against the garage, once raced to New York City from Connecticut so that I could meet Mickey Mantle, chased my favorite basketball stars around Madison Square Garden, made snowmen together, and played endless sets of tennis.

I struggle to reconcile my life with the impossible standard that he has set. It's strange for me to write all of this. My dad loves to reflect on and relive the past. I don't mind doing this when the experiences are positive. I suspect I would not enjoy or feel comfortable having this conversation verbally and it takes the publication of his book for me to find the will to write it down. As I write this, I wonder if it will be followed by probing questions and a desire to go deeper. But that is not what I want.

My dad is a constant reminder of what matters in life. I often get distracted by superficial metrics for success and it is when I am around him that I realize the true metric is the investment we make in our children. I suspect parenting will get both more fun and harder at the same time. The vast majority of my life will be as a parent and I believe the greatest gift he ever gave me was an ambitious playbook for how to live that experience to its fullest.

It's a wonderful feeling to have three of my own children and to have them ask me about my hero. I tell them with pride that it is my dad. I suspect they will go on their own journeys in our relationship, but I hope they arrive at the same destination. Today they like to joke and say, "Daddy's myyyyyy heeeeero." The lesson I learned from my dad is that it is up to me to earn that status. Fortunately, he showed me the way, which I suppose is my understanding of the "Inside Ride".

Letter to Dad

Jared Cohen

(Age 11, 1992)

Dear Dad,

I loved and really enjoyed spending time with you in Israel. It is great that we can spend so much time together. A lot of my friends' fathers never seem to be home and I feel I am very lucky that we have so much time together. As I get older, I feel that our relationship is getting stronger. I also feel that we have a lot in common. I am proud of you for doing your television and radio shows just as you are proud of me for the things I do like getting good grades and sports.

As I get older, I am aware that I am asking you more and more questions. I have been asking you for answers to questions about who shot John Kennedy to questions about our existence as human beings. You are always there to answer them and are rarely too busy for me. Some of these questions do not even make sense to me, but are probably normal for my age. What is life? What does our relationship mean to you? Why do people die? How is it possible to die and just not be here anymore?

As for working in the house, it makes me feel so happy and lucky especially when my friends say how lucky I am to see you every day. With you as my dad, I feel like the luckiest person in the world. Even if you get angry or even yell a little that makes me happy because it shows you really care about what I do.

I think I have some weird and complicated dreams. I dreamt that you were being inaugurated as president. I also dreamt that you were the brother of Henry VIII. What does that mean? You have also shared with me some of your dreams about me such as when you dreamt that I scored a hockey goal.

There are three provinces of your mind that I focus on. The first one is your taste in art and talent for sculpting. The second is your sense of humor. The third is your appreciative attitude. I thought also I would add a fourth, your lust to have fun. When I was younger,

I thought about being an artist, but now as I study your work, I am thinking about psychology and becoming more interested in the mind of other humans and their problems. I know one thing, when I grow up I want to be just like you. Whenever my kid needs me I will be there for him. You are a great role model as a father and I will be a good father to my children because of it. I am very lucky to have a terrific father who really cares about me a lot and would really depend on me as I depend on him.

This book you and Poppy are doing is a great way to communicate with other adults. I feel your relationship with Poppy is strong just like ours is. I love the fact that we have always stuck together as a family. Dad, I just want you to know that I think you are the best dad a kid could have.

Love,
Your Son,
Jared

Personal Note
by
Donald Cohen

Thirty-eight years ago, my father and I wrote a series of letters to one other. We published these letters in our book *My Father, My Son*. There was a strong desire to explore our relationship, and document the stages of development between a father and son. The writing of these letters enhanced and brought an understanding and acceptance of each other. We both felt that it could be helpful to us and sharing these personal letters would benefit other people as well. Over the years our journey, has inspired many people and hopefully provided a model for others to do the same. Our hope was that our book would encourage communication. Letter writing allows one to provide a history that can be recorded for future generations' understanding of their own origins. Sadly, it has become a lost art. The written word gives one the chance to express what was previously unspoken and it allowed us to break that silence.

After the publication of the original edition of *My Father, My Son*, many readers came forward to share their personal experiences with us. I realized how much I missed the process of written interaction with my Dad. My father had become a proud great-grandfather, and now I am a matured father and grandfather. Our own mortality was becoming an obvious destination. Approximately one year after our book was published, we made an attempt to resume this letter writing dialogue. Three years after that, we had a critical exchange. Those letters set the stage for the "Coney Island Boys" chapter of our new book.

Seven years later, when my father's eighty-third birthday arrived, I decided to take him back to his roots and we went on a pilgrimage to his childhood home in Coney Island. This was our new ride into late and later adulthood. We embraced that experience and it led to the correspondence which is now contained in the "Coney Island Boys" letters. This dialogue holds the essence of our history and highlights the journey we took together. The book goes back to where it all began. As my father was rapidly aging', the stage he referred to as his "extra innings" ("Donald, I got old so quickly"), there became a stronger need for me to resume another series of letters.

Two years passed, and when my father was eighty-five, we renewed our process. I wrote to my father, inviting him to take another quest with me, being aware that it would be our last opportunity to engage each other in this way. Several weeks went by with no response and he tentatively and sadly acknowledged that due to his failing health he couldn't write anymore. He really struggled with having to share those feelings with me. Of course this was a disappointment, but that reality became an inspiration for me to move this process onward.

I knew that I had to find a new way to reach him to pursue our journey. Each time I wrote, I would drive the letter from Connecticut to Long Island for his reply. In his glass-enclosed back porch, on the white chair that was formerly my mother's cherished spot, he would dictate his thoughtful response. This time together provided a safe structure of space that was disarming, and allowed us to become open and vulnerable during a difficult period in his life. After my father read his letters to me, I would carefully read each one back to him, making sure it was an accurate account of what he wanted to say. There was a reluctant acceptance to our new reality together. This enabled us to stay connected in a deep and meaningful way. We continued our conversation as long as it was possible. This became our "later adulthood to manhood" together. This concluded our conversations of a lifetime.

I am forever grateful that my father and I had a chance to dance the last dance. This new book *The Inside Ride: A Journey to Manhood* is a tribute to him and to our relationship. It was a true honor to have a father willing to take this voyage to the end—a voyage beginning in early childhood and ending in later adulthood. It traces all developmental stages between father and son. For those of you who know our journey through the original book, I hope these letters will provide an opportunity for you to witness the later years. We were fortunate to document our full life cycle, without regrets. I would like to think that this will inspire others towards closure with their loved ones. Even though this is a book about a long-running dialogue between father and son, and the vital role men play in child rearing, its essence transcends gender. We can all view our lives from the Ferris wheel of life. Included is a foreword by my son and an afterword by my daughter. Engaging the next generation keeps the ritual and importance of letter writing alive.

These letters can be read in many different ways. Time shifts from past to a more recent present, back to a more distant past and to the future. However, you might choose to begin with a chapter that parallels a particular point in your own life—or your parents' life, or your child's life. Take the ride on the carousel with us and know its intention is to be a vehicle for your memories.

There is great sacred understanding in sharing your very own "Coney Island."

Forever,
Donald Cohen,
March, 2020

Initial Exchanges

January 20, 1997
Dear Dad,

When I hear of death interfering with the connection between father and son, my heart grows heavy. Suddenly, I feel vulnerable and become aware of the fact that this is a possibility, or rather an inevitability, for us as well—a sad day waiting to happen.

A close friend of mine just lost his son in a tragic plane crash. I began to look for answers as to why this was happening. When I reach down inside myself, there seems to be no rhyme or reason for any of this. Sons are not supposed to leave this earthly world before their fathers. One can never take what one has for granted, and how dare we think we can control our destiny?

By sad coincidence, I just heard of a celebrity who also lost his son. Reading about their relationship made me think of how much I cherish the way we've grown together. I hope our world sees how important it is for two people, a father and son, to make a relationship work. We need to embrace models who inspire us and from whom we can learn.

Dad, it makes me appreciate our love, and I want, more now than at any other time in my life, to hold on to what we have. Life is transitory, and I find myself seeking to hold on to the sense of certainty that exists for me now, finally, as I feel secure in the embrace of what we have discovered together on our respective journeys.

Love,
Don

* * *

January 27, 1997
Dear Don,

Your recent letter evoked a nostalgic reminder of our extended correspondence. I'm glad it's not over; it was just interrupted.

I can think of nothing more tragic than a parent living to mourn
the untimely and premature death of a child. Among the most painful experiences of my life have been the couple of times I've paid condolence calls to friends who have lost a child. There is almost nothing
of a consoling nature to say to someone who is grieving such a loss,
and I shudder at the mere thought of ever having to grieve such a loss
myself. I can say with complete conviction and without hesitation that
I never want to live to experience such a tragedy.

Death, of course, is inevitable and awaits all of us, but as you poignantly comment, the natural order of things is for children to survive
their parents. I truly believe that this is one of the things that makes
coming to terms with our mortality easier. I've sometimes wondered
how childless people address their issues of mortality: the fact that we
are going to die someday. For me, it is a significant comfort that part
of me will live on in my children and grandchildren and that, in this
sense, I can sustain the illusion of my immortality. This is the endless
spiral of existence, which we experience throughout our lives in the
perception of circadian rhythms, the cycle of light and darkness, the
endless alternation of seasons, and ultimately the repetitive experiences of birth and death. One can imagine that death is prelude to
new beginnings, and I believe that this is as it should be.

But having said this, how does one come to terms with the fact of
a child dying before his or her parent? Such an occurrence makes it
seems as if the fundamental system of existence has been disrupted
and that the cycles of day and night, winter and summer, have become
chaotic and unpredictable. I know it may seem that I'm getting a bit
carried away, but emotionally, I am heavily invested in and reliant
on the predictable order of things, personal as well as cosmic; and I
believe that we all tend to be so invested.

I could go on, but I'm tempted to interrupt my train of thought to
ask for your response. Am I suggesting that we resume our journey?

Love, Dad

Three Years Later

* * *
April 24, 2000
Dear Dad,

America is over the Y2K scare, referred to as the "Millennium Bug." Users and programmers feared that on December 31, 1999, all computers would stop working. Now we have a "Father/Son" scare.

I am writing this letter because it seems that has been my easiest way to communicate when we get into a difficult place with each other. Saturday night became one of those difficult moments. We were celebrating Mom's seventy-fifth birthday and peacefully embracing all our wonderful family accomplishments. The kids are growing up and getting along so well. My sister and I seem to have found a way to be together, and you and I have found a way to learn to accept each other for being the different people that we are.

I keep wanting to feel we are finally at a place where there is a mutual respect for each other. Unfortunately, that is perhaps an unfair and unrealistic expectation for me to have. I struggle with that as I am writing this letter. At this moment I am struggling with many different feelings. At one moment pain and sadness, with some guilt, and then of course there is the disappointment and anger at what took place Saturday night. As you know, I am aware of how proud you are of your grandson, as I also share that pride and joy over his accomplishments. You know that I am never shy about expressing positive feelings toward the people I care about. When it comes to your grandchildren, you are very demonstrative and vocal about your loving and proud feelings. I feel wonderful about that, and at times— although I know you feel it is a given—I wish, as I have before, that you could just as easily tell me directly how proud you are of me for being the father who raised these wonderful children. I try to accept that this is your way and not take it personally. Then we have Saturday night where everything seemed loving and positive—everyone seemingly getting along with each other, celebrating. I thought you had observed my sharing with Jared how proud I was of all his accomplishments, with his success in soccer just being one of many. I don't know if you have ever recognized what a special time soccer has been for us. I have tried to share that with you.

Late in the evening, with my wife and brother-in-law sitting with me, suddenly and completely out of the blue, you coldly and critically blurted out "you should get off Jared's back about soccer!" I admit that I was stunned and taken off guard, not able to stand back and detach myself from your comment, unable at that moment to wonder where you were coming from. This I regret, but I am human and I was so hurt and angry that this could happen at this time in our relationship. I felt not only surprised but it was as if a knife had been turned inside of me. I found it disrespectful and tactless, most importantly insensitive. What also made me angry was the timing of it—doing it in front of my wife and brother-in-law. I found it humiliating—weren't you the one who taught me to be aware of what you say and how it affects the other person? Remember your quote: "Tactlessness often masquerades as honesty." Didn't you think about how that comment might affect me at that moment? You know that I am sensitive and feel deeply about my relationships.

As a result of all of this I reacted in an angry way, stating "it was none of your business and I didn't ask for your opinion." I am sorry if that hurt you and you experienced it as an attack, but the suddenness and insensitivity of your comment took me off guard. I was trying to defend myself while feeling under attack. For many years I feel I allowed people to put me down and question my character, and I will no longer allow that. I have worked hard on myself. I hope you can understand this.

In retrospect, I wish I could have just had the presence of mind to have explored where you were coming from and why you chose to do it when you did. When I got a little grip on myself and finally asked for your opinion, you left the table, appearing very angry with me. Of course, I felt badly about that and knew it would filter down and affect the rest of the family. I think what hurt most is that I assumed you knew that Jared and I have a warm and honest relationship. If he were having a problem with me regarding soccer he would tell me. My understanding is that he feels great about what we have shared together and has no problem.

After dinner, I asked him if he felt I needed to get off his back and his reply was one of disbelief, saying if anything I have been nothing but the extreme opposite. Whatever goes on between Jared and me is our relationship as father and son. I wish I could have calmly stated that to you, but I was too hurt. I have always wanted your respect and love. What more can a son want from his father? That will always be there, even though we continue to see the same movie through two very different lenses. For that I am sad, but I need to accept this. I wish it could be different. I do need to defend who I am at this point in my life, yet still want to try to understand who you are and your motivations. I admit it is hard when I feel judged and attacked. Isn't that just a son wanting his father's respect? I leave you with that thought, assuming you want the same in return.

Love,
Donald

* * *

May 2, 2000
Dear Donald,

I am writing to you in hopes we can find some way to be civil to each other for ourselves, but more importantly for the sake of the people we both care deeply about. I'm referring to Mom, Dee, your wife and my daughter-in-law and beloved friend, and your children. Needless to say, our alienation, in addition to being a great loss for both of us, would impose an awkward hardship on all of them. I choose a letter because I believe I can be less emotional than I would be in a face to face encounter with you at this time.

Although we once again saw different movies at the same place and time, I believe there are a few basic facts on which we can agree:

1. I said something to the effect that I thought it would be better if you backed off on the subject of Jared and soccer. This was said after Jared had left the dining room, and only Dee and Ron were present with us.
2. You got very angry at me and accused me of being critical and judgmental of you, and that you hadn't asked my

opinion. You said it was none of my business and that I
was just putting you down.

3. I got angry at what I perceived to be a totally unwarranted
    reaction to what I intended as a constructive suggestion.
    As the argument proceeded, I got so angry at what I per-
    ceived to be your abusive tone that I left the dining room.
4. The next day you were still so angry that you hardly inter-
    acted with anyone, or so it seemed to me.

As I understand your position, you refuse to be judged, criticized
or put down by anyone, and that what I intended as a constructive
suggestion, you interpreted as a criticism and a put down. Of course
a suggestion inevitably implies that there is a preferable way, but I
can't believe that you seem to think that all suggestions are hostile. At
least you seem to believe that my suggestion was hostile.

If this is the way you want it, then I accept your condition, but of
course I insist that it be mutual and that you refrain from criticizing,
judging, or making suggestions to me as well. We're not talking about
feelings or thoughts, but only manifest words and actions because that
is all we control. We could naturally avoid controversial issues, and
confine our interactions verbally and otherwise to bland and unemo-
tional issues. Do you think you can avoid doing or saying anything
that I might construe as a criticism? What if I were to say something
to one of my grandchildren that you felt was not constructive or that
you disagreed with? Would you remain silent? And last, you obviously
feel that it should apply to our father-son relationship but not to your
relationship with your children.

For everyone's sake, I am willing to try to have such a relationship
in which we both watch every word to be certain that we don't offend.
It seems to me that such a relationship will inevitably be quite anemic
and sterile. If this is the kind of relationship you are seeking, we both
can try. I'm already wondering though, was your perception that I
was being critical of you a criticism and judgment you were making
of me?

Love,
Dad

Coney Island Boys

(LATE ADULTHOOD–LATER ADULTHOOD)

Full Circle

I am glad we have become respectful of each others differences.

How our relationship has deepened and intensified and how much on that day in Coney Island our roles were reversed.

"Your past must connect with your present to create your future."
—Jacob Rilis

* * *

July 25, 2007
Dear Dad,

Remembering . . . Happy Birthday! You are eighty-three today. That's many years of life experience. It's been over seven years since I wrote you a letter, and after visiting Coney Island this past Sunday, I feel compelled to document my experience with you. What a day, and so many feelings I want to express to you. Who knew after that critical exchange seven years ago we would be here today. I almost hid that letter but realized its part of our journey together. It would have been dishonest to leave it out. Despite how much we have resolved, we exposed lingering imperfections and mortal concerns. It is important to move forward becoming more aware of our vulnerabilities and differences, with an acceptance of who we are. It was time to take you back home to Coney Island. Now we can look back and be present in your past.

We live in a post-911 world. I know not to put things off and to pursue my dreams. First, I was going to write you a poem, but as time passed I thought, why not go back to expressing myself to you via letters? We have come so far, and we've talked for so long about visiting your past together and taking in a Brooklyn Cyclone baseball game. I had always longed to experience Ebbets Field and to relive with you that feeling you and other Brooklynites have described when you'd go to see the Dodgers play in the old neighborhood. Sadly, those days are over. We kept putting off this experience. Upon reflection, perhaps there was a piece of me that assumed you'd prefer to wait for the next generation than to spend this time alone with me. How foolish; that was just me not having enough confidence in our relationship. You might have felt that I didn't want to be alone with you either. That was not the case; I was simply letting my insecurity and discomfort get in the way. How misguided that was! We have waited too long.

Many years ago, after I graduated college, you wanted to enjoy Israel together as father and son. I just wasn't ready. Life is about timing, and this past weekend I finally realized that this was our moment waiting to happen. There's been talk in the news about plans to redevelop Coney Island and I didn't want to put off our going there together any longer. Interestingly, there was a *New York Times* article in the Sports Section this past Thursday. The article mentioned that Don Newcombe (the famous retired pitcher for the Brooklyn Dodgers) was going to visit Brooklyn on Sunday, and it was his first time back since the Dodgers moved to L.A. Somewhere this registered in my mind, but it took what happened on Saturday night for me to make the symbolic connection between the two returns to Brooklyn, Don Newcombe's and yours.

We were at your girlfriend Betty's birthday party out in Oyster Bay, the place (speaking of a return to beginnings) where my high school basketball career began. Being in Oyster Bay, not far from the house I grew up in, provided us with the perfect opportunity to go to Coney Island and take in a ballgame. All I needed to do was find out if there was going to be a game and if we could get tickets: the details that tend to make us put off opportunities. Incredibly enough, as I was leaving the party, I made a connection with a man sitting at the table next to yours, who turned out to be Saul Katz—the president of the New York Mets! Not knowing who he was, I mentioned that I wanted to take you to a Cyclone game for your eighty-third birthday. He asked me my name and when I said "Donald," he smiled and said "that was my close friend's name." At that moment, I realized that Betty's deceased husband and Saul's friend were the same "Don."

And I also thought of Don Newcombe, having just read about his return home to Brooklyn. So many "Don's," and so much synchronicity—or am I simply making these connections because that's what we humans do?

Although I miss Mom at these kinds of celebrations, I am comfortable with and pleased to see you are living a full life with Betty. It makes me value her. It was poignant for me to share a table with Mom's brother and his girlfriend, one of Mom's closest friends, and to also be next to a table at which so many of Mom's other friends were sitting. We were all celebrating with a family that obviously feels very close to you. In Mom's noticeable absence, I had a great deal to absorb during this night of celebration. I felt my own mortality being mirrored back at me in many ways.

Back to Saul Katz—whose name, by the way, seems apropos, too, given how much I love cats. When I mentioned wanting to go to a game, but not having a ticket, he said he thought there must be a game tomorrow (the Cyclones are the Mets' farm team). He told me to call him tomorrow and handed me his card, which was when I found out who he was. How lucky/incredible was that?! When Saul mentioned how impressed he was with my son, it dawned on me that he also was the guy you'd told me about whose friend in California is on the Rhodes Committee. His friend had interviewed Jared and had all those kind words to say about him. What a wonderful moment of connection with this man, Saul Katz.

Then, as I was leaving the restaurant, your friend, Bernie Tannenbaum, reminded me of how much he enjoyed our first book. He'd found it warm and felt we had done something important. I felt very validated. He also expressed interest in my poetry and told me about an experience he had had with the late poet Allen Ginsberg. I had a strong feeling that this was going to be a big weekend. The signs were all out there. Even when, ironically, my brother-in-law's computer crashed that same night while he was checking to see if there was a game and if any tickets were available, this too, seemed oddly as if meant to be.

Staying at your house Saturday night I'd felt particularly excited, as I anticipated our next day together. I hadn't had that feeling in our house since childhood. It felt to me like the eve of something special—like Christmas or Chanukah.

Sunday morning was a sunny day. Clear skies invoked for me a feeling that something memorable for the ages was about to happen. Of course, Saul Katz came through for us when I called him that morning. There was a game scheduled for 5 o'clock—a perfect time—and he told us to go to the park; we would find our seats waiting for us. He also said that Don Newcombe was going to be honored. Then, Steve Cohen, the GM of the Cyclones, called your house to confirm the plans. There we go with the names: Don Newcombe, Steve Cohen, everyone seems related. We were going back to the old neighborhood. The Cohens were going to Coney Island. I was like a kid jumping up and down in your kitchen.

We went outside to take our first picture. My first sighting was that old black sign in front of the house, Max Cohen, M.D. I had a strong desire to document the day. Across the street was the site of my old friend Steve Lanskey's house, which conjured memories of the night when I was a little boy and thought you and Mom had gone missing. I remember looking in your bedroom and panicking when I didn't see you. I remember running across the street and knocking on Steve's door in the middle of the night, scared that I was all alone in the world—clearly signs of the separation anxiety I had as a child. Sadly, all that was left of that house now was a big hole in the ground. Redevelopment was taking over my street of memories. Steve Lanskey was gone and so were the touch football games that took place on the lawn next to his house. I remember the emotional letter he wrote me after he'd read our book.

Next door to him was the girl I fantasized about and remember playing on our street, Pebble Lane. Many weekends were spent with her cousins Leslie and Stephen. They were Humphrey Bogart and Lauren Bacall's children. We had so much fun together.

We were on our way to Coney Island, to visit your childhood—just in time before they started to tear it down. I loved the idea that you were going to have the opportunity to do this on your birthday—with your son. The weather was magical: perfect temperature, bright sunshine, beautiful sky, a day for the "Boys of Summer." The drive was fun, as we anticipated the pleasurably mysterious unknown and a day of discoveries. We were so relaxed we couldn't stop talking to each other. It felt to me like I was also going home. The awkward silences of our past were gone. We missed the exit and it didn't even matter. Imperfection was okay, was to be celebrated. You even mentioned how beautiful the sky looked. I don't remember you ever sharing this kind of a moment with me before. Nor do I remember ever having shared my own aesthetic moments with you in this way. I loved how we did that together. We even talked about the Rolex watch you had given me. I was so relieved that you understood why I wasn't wearing it. It impressed me when once again you showed me your understanding of who I was when you said I was a guy who had never seemed able to wear a watch. I was never one who liked to be bound by time. Coincidentally, my watches always stopped. That was always a difference between us: I was the less formal one. I'm glad we've become respectful of each other's differences.

Ironically, as we arrived in Coney Island, time just about stopped. You could smell the aroma of the sea. I was so excited watching you seem to become a little boy again, looking forward to meeting your past. There we were, walking along Neptune, Mermaid, and Surf Avenues. How much more magical can street names be? You felt where you were and it all came back. Then we approached Sea Gate, your childhood community. The guard asked for your ID. We told him you had grown up here and it was your eighty-third birthday, and as if he were the Wizard of Oz, he responded (if not in so many words) with, "Why didn't you say so? Come on in." Watching you and feeling connected to my history and yours was like *being* in Oz, and then we found 48th Street, where we drove to that dead end I remember visiting as a child. There was that fence, and behind that, the wide open sea, just as it was back once upon a time. The seagulls were flying around and you were speechless. We got out of the car and the camera just started flashing, documenting the moments.

For one awful moment you thought your childhood house was gone. We quickly realized they had just added two more houses at the end of the block. Confusion turned to relief. Then you saw your old home and you got excited. The entrance was outlined in brick. You started to free associate, recalling the names of your neighbors. Your nostalgia button had been pushed. Suddenly, we noticed a Hasidic Jew in the old park across the street from your house, meditating by the water. We walked into the park. Echoes of your past were calling and I enjoyed watching you embrace them.

When I noticed two young Polish girls taking out the garbage in front of your old house, I realized this was our chance. We had to seize the opportunity. I asked them if we could come in. We walked upstairs. It was the way we both remembered it—I hadn't been there since I was a small child—although the two-family house seemed smaller to our adult eyes. You showed me the small patio off your bedroom where you and your brother slept on summer nights. It was the first time you'd ever shared that with me. At that moment I really got what your childhood was about, and knew where your love of the water had come from.

Your once neatly kept backyard was gone; things appeared run-down and overgrown; new houses crowded the area. The landscape of my childhood memories had changed. Hasidic Jews now lived in the house next to yours. The current owner was surprised when you told him how old your house was. You'd spent the first seventeen years of your life there. We walked around the corner, where you showed me the lighthouse and pointed out the haunted house. This prompted an outpouring of memories, as you recalled for me the things you used to do in the neighborhood, the names of your friends, and the houses in which they lived. I enjoyed watching you transform into a little boy on your eighty-third birthday, embracing the past, which lives inside you.

Next, we drove to the Sea Gate Pool Club and walked together through another part of your past. It felt like we were in *This Is Your Life*. We saw the beach and the old handball courts, which had become paddle ball courts, and the lockers which had become cabanas. I just wanted to be inside your head to know what you were thinking. You remembered we'd left the car running, so we went back to it. On the way, you gestured excitedly across the street to show me where the Boy Scouts used to meet.

It was time for lunch at Nathan's. First, we parked your car at the ballpark—Key Span Park. I found someone to take a picture of us in front of the statue of Jackie Robinson and PeeWee Reese. I was struck by the parallel between our trans-generational bond and the bond between these two men whose friendship transcended racial difference: Jackie Robinson, the black man who broke the color barrier, and PeeWee Reese, the white man who stood by his side; you and I, walking arm and arm, having journeyed so far together as father and son, bridging our own divides.

We walked over to Nathan's, which reminded you there used to be an old movie theatre across the street. You started to tell me about it. Then came the memories of you and Pop going to the movies on Saturday afternoons, of evenings spent hanging out in Steeplechase Park, the funhouse of distorted mirrors, and of days spent walking the boardwalk and going to the beach at the Sea Gate Pool Club … what a great place to grow up! I became aware of how much you'd loved your childhood. It helped me understand why you wanted us to grow up in a similar neighborhood and why you picked Roslyn with its Country Club to raise us. It only cost one hundred dollars for the summer—Sam's Snack Bar not being part of the deal. What was significant to me was watching their teenage son, Stew, working behind the counter with his Mom and Dad making me a charcoal-broiled hamburger. All my friends would gather around and it felt very cozy looking down at the pool area. Thank you for that, because I did feel like I grew up in a community that gave me a wonderful childhood, with sidewalks and street lights, and great times playing hide-and-seek and stickball in the street.

The ballpark, built on the side of the old Steeplechase Park— memorialized by a sign right over the boardwalk behind the stadium—was quaint and cozy. Towering over the park in right field was the old parachute jump. It looked just like a sculpture made from an erector set. Behind the left field wall, in the distance, the Wonder Wheel could be seen, and beyond that was a glimpse of the legendary, iconic wooden Cyclone roller coaster. We had entered the amusement park. It was a magical sight, and it took you back to an old, lost world, stirring up intense nostalgia. This was a moment to embrace a time before a post 9/11 world. We arrived at Nathan's, which was crowded with others who were also trying to recapture their pasts, while waiting endlessly on line. It was the original Nathan's and although the hotdogs had gotten thinner, nobody cared. The crowd had one shared goal: to experience a piece of history. I loved treating you to lunch, watching the "little boy" in you gobble up two hot dogs with sauerkraut. Nathan's is now commercial and not original, but still wanted a memento. Although she couldn't speak English, the waitress understood, and smiled as she handed me the receipt, which I still have.

You were tired and had trouble walking. That was hard for me to face. Our roles had become reversed, and now I found myself taking care of you. It felt good to do this, although doing so also made me aware of the passage of time and our mortality. There were moments of sadness, wishing time could just stand still. These cherished memories were what would become our future. And, in a sense, they are already doing so; as I write of our day together, it feels timeless to me now . . . Dad, I want you around and always will. I so value our moments together. I'm not taking anything for granted now, as I know I often did in my earlier years.

At the gate, we gave them our name, and they let us right in—like VIP's. I think you enjoyed the special treatment. Thank you, New York Mets and Saul Katz, and my newly-adopted cousin, Cyclones General Manager Steve Cohen. When we entered the stadium, you needed to sit. At the "will call" window, I asked the guy who gave us our tickets what kind of seats we had, and he smiled saying, "Who do you know?" I felt honored and proud to have our day acknowledged by larger forces. I knew I had to contain my excitement somewhat, as I was wary of pushing you too hard physically. Your physical limitations made me sad, but also made the experience all the more precious. We spent a short time in the Museum of the old Brooklyn Dodgers as we surveyed the inside of the stadium. Then off to our seats taking the elevator, poignantly bringing to mind for me how you had always been the one to take the steps when possible.

We got to our seats—the first row behind home plate! You realized we must be sitting in the owner's seats, because the tickets had no price on them. This seemed magical to us both, and you seemed amazed. I had always been the mystic and you the skeptic. For a moment it seemed like the gap had been bridged. Everything seemed to fall into place. I looked down and saw a white feather at my feet, which reminded me of the seagulls we'd seen earlier on the beach by your house. I couldn't help but imagine Mom was orchestrating the day, sharing our joy and watching over us. I shared this mystical thought with you, looking up into the sky again, the way I had that morning. I entertained the thought that some small part of you believed this to be possible.

Suddenly, Don Newcombe was standing right in front of us on the field, as he was introduced over the loudspeaker. I experienced a series of associations. Newcombe was one of the first black players in major league baseball, which made me think of Jackie Robinson and his breaking of the color barrier in baseball. In turn, this triggered a memory of you taking me to a special dinner honoring Jackie Robinson when I was ten-years-old. That autograph from our night forty-six years ago still hangs upon my office wall. What a remarkable chain of memories and feelings! I'm so excited to be making all of these connections. It brings tears to my eyes and I feel chills. I want to document it all.

In the third inning, an announcement came over the loudspeaker, welcoming Donald Cohen and his father, Max Cohen, on his eighty-third birthday. Two Don's in the house, actually three, Betty's deceased husband. I thought you were going to pass out. You gave me a startled look and asked how this could be happening. I smiled and pointed to the sky and whispered, "Mom." Again, I saw that gleam in your eyes. Of course, then I fessed up that I'd told Saul it was your eighty-third birthday, which must have set things in motion. We were having our *Field of Dreams*. Like everything else that had happened on this magical day, the weather cooled down just in time for the game. A magnificent breeze hugged our souls and we enjoyed a couple of innings, then got ready to move on. I put the feather I found in my bag and we both left the ballpark with our Don Newcombe bobble heads. You surprised me on the way out by asking me to get you a Brooklyn Cyclone hat. Of course, I was happy to oblige. We left the stadium together in our new hats. I never remember you asking me for much: Dad, that made me so happy this was my treat.

There was one more thing I wanted us to do—visit the amusement park—but as we walked over to the boardwalk behind the stadium, you confessed you were too tired for the walk. So, we lingered instead on the boardwalk, where I enjoyed watching you sit on a bench looking out at the ocean, staring into infinity. Again I had that warm feeling towards you, only imagining where your thoughts were taking you, as you looked out at what must have been a familiar sight from childhood. Knowing full well how you wished you could have taken the walk with me—another dose of mortality's realities.

I left you for a while and walked down the boardwalk. Seeing the sign behind the ballpark as a memorial to Steeplechase Park was emotional for me. It sparked another memory of a birthday party you held for me there when I was ten years old. That turned out to be a traumatic day, as I watched all my friends go down that slippery wooden slide, too afraid to try it myself. I had a lack of confidence; I knew even then that you felt bad for me. Just like Mom, I was never a lover of heights. And yes, despite the pain of that experience, I cherish my memories of Steeplechase Park. The boardwalk had a lot of color, clusters of families and friends, vendors, cotton candy; it was one big carnival. People were swimming, picnicking, enjoying themselves, as if nothing had changed over the years. It was Coney Island 2007. On the walk, I spotted a reggae band and people from all different backgrounds enjoying the music on a beautiful Sunday afternoon. I couldn't help wondering how much longer Astroland, this landmark from the past, would remain part of our history. I wanted one more close-up glance of the people riding the roller coaster. I listened to the familiar screams of excitement and fear, the sound of the Cyclone going up and down and moving at different speeds, and I thought about how many times this scene has repeated itself over the years.

Now I slipped away to buy two T-shirts: a "Coney Island" one with a picture of the Cyclone, and one of "Steeplechase," which had that funny face that used to smile at you as you entered the amusement park. You must have wondered what had happened to me. When I got back, it tickled me to add them to your birthday goody bag.

It was time to go home. We passed the sign to Flatbush, and you pointed out the exit for your old high school, Abraham Lincoln. You became nostalgic again, Dad, and I was enjoying it all. I knew we'd had a full day and both of us acknowledged how special it was. I felt so good about the two of us being able to do this together, and that it was just us. When we got home, I looked at the top of the garage and, for a moment, imagined the old basketball hoop still up and my friends being on their way over for a three-on-three game beneath the lights. We hugged and kissed each other like never before and told each other how much we loved our day. We both seemed to know our relationship would never be the same. I watched you carry your goodie bag into the house after we said good-bye and it felt good.

When I called Saul that night to thank him, he told me he was going to visit the new Cyclone Stadium tomorrow, and I thought to myself, how fitting. I woke up the next morning in a panic. I had accidentally forgotten to take the white feather out of the bag that I'd thrown out. Thankfully, I was able to find it in the garbage. All I could think of was rescuing the memory of Mom and her white hair and finding a place for her to sit in the miniature model of Ebbets Field recently made for me by a good friend before he died. Later that day, the same friend's wife called to arrange for delivery. The model will be here tomorrow. Also that day, I saw, of all things, a headline on the front page of the *New York Times* Arts section about a singer on the Coney Island Boardwalk. I have enclosed the article. Another moment of connectedness: the place of our special day made the front page. We were there. How cool is that? Now, I have to dig up that Don Newcombe article to send you. Dad, there are no accidents, just meaningful coincidences. If you are open to it, you will see the synchronicity.

Finally—although when you are on a magical, mystery ride, taking the journey, there is no such thing as "finally"—remember you asked me for the name of the person who wrote the book *Coney Island?* It dawned on me that I had given you that book a few years ago for your birthday. The author's name is Charles Denson. Last night at a party, a friend, who like many other people had heard our story, gave me a copy of that book. My first reaction was to politely decline, as I already have it, but then I realized having another copy might be just the thing. So, I bit my tongue and accepted the gift graciously, which was in any case, the respectful thing to do. It occurs to me that maybe your "Coney Island" has been lost, but now another has been found.

Happy Birthday, Dad.

Love,
Donald

* * *

October 15, 2007
Dear Donald,

I just re-read your letter for at least the tenth time, and it still chokes me up and gives me the chills. It really was a magical day on my eighty-third birthday and I am forever grateful to you for it. The only way I can respond to it is to free-associate to the feelings and thoughts it provokes.

The memories that were stimulated by this visit to my childhood still reverberate in my head even though two and a half months have passed. It felt as if you were guiding me through a kaleidoscope of my early life and it rekindled my memories of those years and the people who inhabited them with me. These days I'm now living are like extra innings, and the people who have become so important to me since those years, didn't yet exist for me.

I'm eighty-three years old and I've led a full and extremely rewarding life. My birthday in Coney Island did make me aware of my mortality and the fact that these are my declining years. I'm not afraid of dying as I inevitably will in the coming years because I can see myself returning to the place I was before I was born of which I have no memory. It's like dreamless sleep. I will live on in the memories of the people who have been important to me, just as Mom lives on in your memory and mine. As you so keenly observed, she was with us on our magical day.

The other powerful stream of memories concerned our evolving relationship from your childhood, through the years we documented in our first book to the present day. How our relationship has deepened and intensified and how much on that day in Coney Island our roles were reversed. It felt so good, and it still chokes me up. These are not easy feelings to identify and describe, but they are so deeply satisfying that it almost hurts physically.

You, of course, know what I'm feeling because you're now the father of two wonderful kids. What pride and pleasure we feel about how successful Emily and Jared are as young adults who have their lives unfolding ahead of them. You and Dee certainly did a great job.

Finally, I want to comment about your references to the fact that in life's journey there is no finality, on the continuation of the journey. There will be more birthdays, and surely we'll visit the past again as we continue our personal journey.

I love you Donald. Thank you for many wonderful days, but especially my eighty-third birthday celebration.

Love,
Dad

The Perfect World

(EARLY CHILDHOOD–MIDDLE CHILDHOOD)

Oedipal Son to Oedipal Father

People seemed to expect me to be the perfect son with the perfect father.

Is it the curse of parents who genuinely love their children, that their love becomes the inescapable vehicle for inculcating guilt?

* * *

February, 1982
Dear Dad,

I began to write this letter four years ago when your granddaughter Emily was born, but somehow the words just would not come. Then last year I found myself, at thirty-one, the father of a son. We now share that same experience of having sons. It's a different feeling being more than just your son now, and maybe I can begin to understand what you went through raising me. I will probably do all the positive and negative "fatherisms" to my son that you did to me. History has a tendency to repeat itself. It seems to be one of those givens that comes with being human.

During Dee's pregnancy with Jared, I remember people constantly making me feel as if I had to have a son. There was all this pressure around me with people telling me they were convinced that Dee and I were going to have a little boy. The nine months of pregnancy were difficult enough without this additional anxiety over the gender of our child.

I have a recollection of resisting people's various comments by responding with the classic line, "I do not care what sex my child is as long as he or she is healthy." How pretentious can you get? And not very convincing to either myself or the others. I acted as if it concerned other people more than me, and at times I am sure my denial of my own needs was successful. You always had the ability to see through my facades and I remember you calling me on this one.

Perhaps this was my way of coping with a potential disappointment. It seems as if most men want to have sons they can live through vicariously. Why should I be any different? With it comes the expectation that through Jared I can come to terms with my own unconscious resolution of my difficulties with you. It's an awkward transition from Oedipal son to Oedipal father.

I remember you sitting in the car with me one day telling me that you hoped I would have a son. At that moment I became aware of the fact that I really wanted a boy. There was always a part of me that wanted to please you and make you proud of me. There were moments when I felt that you would have been disappointed if we didn't have a boy.

It was important to gain your approval. That need to receive acknowledgment from you continues to be important to me. When you told me how special it was for you to have a son, it came to me as never before how important I really was to you. That moment meant a great deal to me. I felt wanted and needed. Over the years l would have difficulty knowing where I stood with you. That feeling seems to be dissipating. I felt it was difficult for you to express your love to me in words. Mom would always communicate to me how much you loved me. Being demonstrative seemed difficult for you. Your kindness, warmth and love for me would come through in other ways, but sometimes I just needed you to say, "I love you." When you shared your feelings with me about how it was important for me to have a son, I suddenly realized that this was your way of letting me know that I was loved.

This need for recognition from you seems endless. I have always felt like the more demonstrative one in our relationship. There were many times when I felt foolish for being that way, like the time I threw you a kiss across the dinner table at a restaurant. I remember a look of judgment from you. The disapproval was more than I could handle.

You seemed to be the more private one, always being "appropriate," and I was the exhibitionist seeking attention and seeming to cause you embarrassment. You were "Apollonian" and I was "Dionysian" when it came to our respective personalities.

The one early memory I have of our displaying emotions to each other physically was under difficult circumstances. I remember being twelve years old and sleeping over at a friend's house and spending the next day there. You came over and grabbed me away. You were furious and ordered me into the car. I hated what you were doing to me at that moment. I felt embarrassed in front of my friends and my first girlfriend. We went home and you gave me one of your infamous lectures, á la *Father Knows Best,* because I was not home studying for my finals at school. We both ended up crying and embracing each other in the backyard.

For some reason, I have never forgotten that moment and maybe it was because we were so open with each other. I want that feeling back between us. So often I have had regrets about the fact we have not been more physical with each other through the years. Those wrestling matches we had together always seemed so precious, a time when we both simply let go of our inhibitions toward each other.

How ironic that the very backyard where you and I embraced was to be the place where I celebrated my Bar Mitzvah. How absurd when you realize that after my Bar Mitzvah, we considered it a healthy transition in our relationship for me to have the privilege of shaking your hand. I remember you commenting to me, "Now we can shake hands and not kiss each other." This seemed to become a ritual for our expression of love toward each other for many years.

It makes me sad just writing about this, and thinking of our loss— that for such a long time we remained physically distant from each other. I was not ready to become a man and face the problems of growing up. (There was an enormous need for that hug and kiss.)

Our relationship for some time became one in which you would say black and I would say white. You said study and I said baseball. As we got older it became more complex. You said Freud, I said Jung. You were the realist, I was the idealist. You wanted me to be you, and I wanted you to be me. We went through the motions, tried to do the right things for each other; you did Cub Scouts and Little League, and I went pre-med.

I felt that you wanted me to be someone important, to make something of myself. Those expectations intimidated me and seemed to contribute to my fear of competition and success. There was encouragement to be my own person, but sometimes I felt that you had an agenda for who I should be. This would often get in the way of my being able to pursue my own dreams. Whenever I would do things your way, it seemed to please you. Perhaps you wanted to create me in your own image and I wanted to create you in mine. This all appears to have biblical overtones.

Writing letters to you and expressing my feelings this way gives me a sense that I am completing a part of my destiny with you. The night before I started writing, I went to a colleague's house for dinner, a doctor in the town where I now live. He discussed with me how, at age forty-six, he was an accomplished doctor who had achieved material success but still felt he had not completed his destiny. I found myself identifying with his feelings of incompleteness. Then he began to talk about how his father was a great man who never seemed to do all the things in life that he wanted to do.

As we continued to talk, I became more absorbed in the conversation and we started to share personal feelings about our fathers. My friend told me about how he always wanted to write a novel about his life but something always seemed to get in the way. It soon became clear to both of us that we had a fear of failure and a strong need to succeed. We both wanted to reach a certain potential within ourselves.

I began to think about writing letters to you, particularly when my friend said that he had a need to go beyond his father's dreams for himself. He wanted to achieve all the things that his father would have wanted to do. Here was a man with no end of impressive credentials. Looking at his life from the outside, one could easily assume that there would be no reason for discontent; but he still had not accomplished what he had always wanted. He had become a successful doctor, but not the writer he had aspired to be.

I am starting to gain a better understanding of why I decided to undertake this dialogue with you. It has also become clear why it has been, and still is, so hard for me to write anything that I feel would be meaningful. I am anxious about the possibility that it will not be interesting and then I will have failed. I know you have always wanted to write and now this gives both of us the opportunity to live out a dream together.

There is a great deal of excitement and apprehension about what the outcome of this experience will be. We come from different generations, and mine was one that seemed to encourage openness between people. I figure if Freud and Jung could correspond in letters about their relationship, so could we. Their relationship was indeed similar to that between a father and son.

Until recently I felt that it was just you who needed more out of life than simply being the successful professional man. But now I sit here writing and find myself a psychotherapist in private practice with an empty and restless feeling within me, a feeling that seems to be driving me to create more meaning in my life.

Somehow it appears as if these letters will help me get over the hump. Can we do it, Dad? We can both have the satisfaction of expressing ourselves and growing together as people. The risks make it exciting but I feel as if I have to be the inspired son who motivates his father. An interesting switch and a far cry from when I was your little boy, whose only goal at twelve-years-old was to play ball for the New York Yankees and watch *Bonanza* on Sunday nights. I feel some resistance about getting into my feelings knowing that you will respond to whatever I write.

As I write, I know there is the possibility of my appearing self-righteous in order to protect myself. There will be feelings that we have never shared with each other. I am aware that some of those feelings may have already come out. At times during the course of our relationship it seemed as if we had a need to protect each other from our own imperfections.

I had a tendency to be preoccupied with always trying to do the right thing and feeling I had to watch what I said. People seemed to expect me to be the perfect son with the perfect father. It was an image that at times we both seemed determined to protect. That is the price one has to pay for being the son of a psychiatrist. Maybe the psychiatrist has to be more concerned about what kind of image his son projects to the community.

Whenever I felt pain, you were there to protect me. As a result, I had a false sense of security. I began to believe that you could always make everything better for me. Even my own sister felt reassured about getting on an airplane as long as you promised her it would not crash. That reassurance helped alleviate my anxieties about flying as well. Whatever would happen to me, I felt that you would bail me out.

Surprisingly, I also felt protective of you, although I don't know if you ever knew that. When I saw you hurting about something I would hurt too. Your failures and disappointments became mine as well and I am sure the same holds true for you. I never wanted you to fail at anything and that was manifested in my burning desire for you to be as good an athlete as my friends' fathers were. When you could not save the boy from Mexico from drowning at the bottom of the pool, I felt bad for you. I did not want you to feel a sense of failure, yet at the same time I had to confront the reality that you could not always save the world. It was hard watching you try to give him CPR and breathe life back into his young lungs. You were indeed mortal and my virtuous concern for your feelings was clearly mixed up with my neurotic selfish need to see you as perfect. It was my first direct encounter with death and the realization it could happen to me. Fortunately, Mom picked up Joe DiMaggio at the beach that same day and befriended him. I remember him taking us to his private club so I could hear the Giants play in the NFL Championship game on a Trans-Oceanic radio. A good diversion at the time. We both need to stop protecting each other and learn to let each other be fallible. In the past, neither of us was really comfortable even when beating each other in tennis.

This experience presents different challenges. I'm forced to be the intelligent writer that I always felt came so naturally to you; and you have to be a more open, uninhibited person, which always seemed to come more easily for me.

This conversation will force us to confront what I feel have been two major issues between us over the years. I have always felt intimidated by your intelligence and success, and you have always commented on my casualness and lack of inhibition. The writer in both of us will have to come out, in addition to a great deal of self-disclosure. We will each have to confront our vanity, becoming both participants and observers in the re-creation of our experiences growing up together. Clark Blaise, in his book *I Had a Father,* states, "memory is a guide to the future as well as a recollection of the past."

My concern is that you will have a more difficult time being public about your life than I will, but you may feel the opposite concern. I am going to fight within myself not to protect you and hope that you can do the same with me. We have to be honest. This is something that has been a constant dynamic and controversy in our relationship. Who cares more about what people think? We both care a great deal and it is about time that we admit that we are not so different on that score. Let's get on with it even if it gets sticky at times.

People are so surprised when I tell them that you thought about journalism as a career. I get off by telling people that you are a good writer and seeing how they react. It is difficult for me to completely understand my investment in this. Perhaps I have always admired the writer in you and could not understand why you have always been so private about it. We are so different that way. You never seemed to need to tell people how well you could write and I wanted everyone to know how brilliant my father is. There is also a need now for me to feel more closely connected to that creative side of you. Writing seems to be such an excellent vehicle for creative expression.

Our relationship seems to be a major preoccupation for me at this time in my life. I have gone from wanting nothing to do with you to a desire to have everything to do with you. I never want to be the son who says that he wishes his father and he had worked out their relationship and said the things to each other that always needed to be said. Unfortunately, for many fathers and sons, it is too late and time has run out for them. I don't want that to happen to us.

As time passes by, I have become increasingly aware of your mortality and limitations as a person as well as of my own. In my earlier years, I had a need to idealize you and my feelings were mixed with love, fear, and worship. I wanted to deny anything that would interfere with my god-like image of you. When your father died many years ago, I remember how upset you were and I wanted to avoid dealing with the reality of what was happening. I was not accustomed to seeing you vulnerable.

There have been times when I have felt cheated because there was never an opportunity for me to get to know your father and see the kind of relationship you had with him. I feel a strong need now to know more about your relationship with him as well as with your mother. At this point I want any dimension of you that will help give me a keener understanding of your being.

Writing about your father's death evokes feelings of terror in me; I think back to how I felt when you became ill some years ago. I have trouble imagining what my life would be like without you around. It disturbs me and I do not like to think about it. Death feels so final and cold, and I am not ready to have you be gone. It's now 1982, my son was born in 1981 and I suddenly realized John Lennon was murdered in 1980. There is that inevitable life cycle of birth and death—like a crack in the cosmos.

Separation and being alone has always been very uncomfortable for me. You know that as a young child I was literally afraid of my own shadow. I remember when we took a vacation to Jamaica and I went into a panic thinking you had disappeared from the hotel. There was just no tolerance for being alone. It gave me the unsettled feeling that you were going to leave me. If T.S. Garp could lose his father in a plane crash and the little boy Elliot in *E.T.* was forced to live accepting an absent father, then why couldn't the same thing happen to me?

Sometimes my only sense of security was to sleep in your bed at night. I felt so foolish for being that insecure but I couldn't help it. At times I felt there was something seriously wrong with me. Whenever you would leave me alone the fear was too much to take. It felt as if you were abandoning me and would be gone forever.

Whenever you and Mom would have an argument, the same kind of fears would start to come back. I suspected that if you ever got divorced, I would never see you and I would grow up without a father. What a disturbing thought and it happened so often.

Our family seemed to represent the image of the All-American Family, so whenever things got shaky at home I never felt prepared for it. Somehow it appeared that conflicts in our house would come and go, but I tended to suffer with an exaggerated view of perceiving us as the perfect family. I always felt Mom helped to perpetuate that myth for me when she would say we were more "open" than other families. My interpretation of that was we could do no wrong and therefore negative feelings at home always made me feel severely uncomfortable. I had the naive belief that nothing should ever go wrong in my life. Perfect sons should never lose perfect fathers. That was really the way I thought life was supposed to be as a child—*Leave it to Beaver* and *The Mickey Mouse Club.*

There is a yearning in me to immortalize our relationship. Working through my fears of death has been one of the driving forces behind writing letters to you. Just writing about my feelings makes me feel more alive. I have needed to resolve my feelings of emotional separation from you and still there is difficulty in accepting the concept of death in either a literal or symbolic way.

Would you believe that as a young child I used to lie in bed during the night preoccupied with thoughts of dying? My imagination would take me to the battlefield and pretend I was on the ground dead so the enemy wouldn't come after me. I was gullible enough to think that I could actually live forever and control my mortality. It always concerned me and I wondered if other people my age had the same preoccupations. These seemed to go on during the early years of my life when I first started to go to camp and school. Being different from everyone else was something I feared. Ironically, later in life I would have an investment in wanting to be different from other people. I actually believed that all of my childhood heroes would remain alive forever. When John Kennedy was assassinated, I remember walking around in a daze. It was as if the world has stopped and I was all alone; later it was John Lennon. Pinky Lee and Howdy Doody seemed so far away. Again, I did not want to be left alone without my gods around me. The thought of someday having to be completely responsible for myself and the other important people in my life was very threatening. But that inevitable day will come when you won't be around to help me carry the responsibilities that come with being an adult.

It is a great comfort to me knowing you are still the elder statesman in the family. As a child, my fears were so desperate that I convinced myself I could control my breathing. My fantasy life was my escape, and it kept me going. I would do anything to fill the void and emptiness that came with confronting my inevitable mortality. There was always a way to defend against despair. There was something safe about being sick and staying home from school, crawling into bed to watch *The Little Rascals* and, of course, *Make Room for Daddy*. I would also have my Wonder Bread with peanut butter.

People made comments to me about the fact that I believed in Santa Claus longer than most children. That need to idealize men seemed to dominate my existence. Finally, when I ripped that false beard off your face one Christmas, I had one of my first confrontations with reality. Santa was not real and boy was that a disillusion! My expectations of the world seemed shattered. Santa was as make believe as Dorothy's Wizard of Oz. I remember seeing your eyes and hearing your voice through the beard. There was so much anger and disappointment in my voice when I told you (while you sat in your Santa's chair) how much you looked like my father. Indeed, you were dressing up as Santa Claus, and while other people found the moment amusing it was embarrassing to me. It was as if you had betrayed me and were taking my fantasy away. Of course I was too young to articulate it so these feelings were kept inside. Up to that point my need to believe in Santa Claus had served a purpose. It was now gone and there had to be a new meaning for me.

I always seemed to have the need to search for meaning in my life and you seemed so content all the time—another idealization, because now I know that was not an accurate perception of you. I have been curious over the years about how you felt when I stripped you of your god-like image for the first time. Since then there have been many disillusionments and confrontations with reality. Little did I know that this was just the beginning.

It was comforting as a kid knowing that I could go back to my room and crawl into my fantasy life. There was always pressure to keep this side of me private because I was afraid you or someone else would make me give it up. Being idealistic was more appealing than anything I perceived as realistic. You always seemed so damn realistic to me and I wanted no part of it.

You were beginning to become a rival in my eyes. People thought you were the greatest. It was so difficult for me having you be everyone's Santa Claus. Sometimes I did not want to share you; I needed you all for myself. It seemed that my friends, Mom, and my sister viewed you as the all-knowing one. Later on, all the professionals I knew felt the same way. You were god and everyone said so. Still later on, when I got my Ph.D., you were perceived as the real doctor and final authority.

Mom always promoted you and I would spend a great deal of energy wanting to get her to respect me as much as you, if not more. This was the case especially when it came to professional issues. I was afraid to be interested in things you were involved with for fear that I could not measure up. There was a great deal of resentment toward you for being so important to other people.

My fantasy life in my room and interest in sports were my only means of feeling important. This was how I could separate from you and not feel a need to compete. Playing with my toy soldiers, cowboys, and other little men gave me a world that I could control and dominate. I could determine who would win the war or game. But I feared that you would open my door and discover my little world.

I enjoyed talking to myself as well as playing with myself. There is nothing like that first ejaculation. It sure made me feel like something very strange was happening to me. I did not want you or anyone else to interfere. There were moments when I felt guilty for giving myself pleasure and I thought something was wrong with me. Those *Playboy* pictures were fun to masturbate over and it made me feel so powerful. I had a mad crush on actress Jane Russell whom I later realized resembled early pictures of my mom. This was part of my emerging boyhood wrapped in my first desire.

My room was like a refuge and it seemed as if that was all I had. If you discovered what I was doing there it would be as if there would be nothing left of my own. You might even think you were the stereotypical psychiatrist with the crazy son who liked to talk to himself. Continual concern with what you thought of me just seemed to stay with me. I could not get away from it. Those footsteps up to my room threatened my self-pleasures. I felt that you were going to be ashamed of me for not being like other sons my age. My Sunday evening activity was curling up in my bed and listening to the Ranger hockey games on the radio, when I was supposed to be doing my homework. Before bed I was reviewing my interactions at school analyzing how many times I might have said something foolish. This became a neurotic evening habit of mine. I was relieved later on to find out my sister did the same thing. The pillow at night was my safe haven that allowed me to chase my personal demons away.

My only interest in life was being the world's greatest lover and a professional baseball player. There was absolutely no interest in what you were reading or doing. I felt as if we had very little in common during my early years.

Sometimes I felt you would have been better off with a different son. You tried to reach out to me and I would reject you. We would go fishing and I would get seasick. You would take me sailing and all I would want to do was watch a Yankee game. Then there would be the man-to-man chats and I would only want you to go away so that I could watch the ball game. You even went out and bought me a dog named Lucky that you tried to get me to enjoy. There was within me an inadequate feeling and a fear of never being able to live up to the image of what I thought you wanted in a son. Whenever I failed at something, my main concern was that it would embarrass you. I remember when Jared bravely went down a big water slide in Hawaii years ago. I couldn't let him down when he pleaded with me to join him. All these people were watching, waiting to see what I would do. It was like déjà vu. The Coney Island slide all over again. Well, I did it and what a relief! I don't know if I ever told him about that. Nothing like unfinished business. Now I don't want to embarrass my son.

Our common ground seemed to be crossing swords together, riding on the bike for two, throwing the baseball around, and watching boxing matches in the movie theatres. I remember how special it was going to the Calderone Theater to see the heavyweight championship fight between Floyd Patterson and Ingemar Johannsson. Those drives to Adelsteins, the local store for baseball cards and sports magazines were something I always anticipated. And what about going to Baker Field to watch Archie Roberts play quarterback for Columbia University? Later on it was spring training and going into the Yankee dugout. Then, of course, you would make me breakfast, even though we would hardly talk to each other. I was attached to my Sara Lee chocolate pound cake.

I used to question whether you really wanted to do some of those activities. Maybe you were just doing them because I enjoyed it. Did you want to please me as much as I wanted to please you? The difference here is that I did not like to admit to you that I felt a need to please you.

Our best moments of all seemed to be the midnight snacks in the kitchen in our underpants. They were relaxed and informal. You know how to whip up some creative dishes before bedtime!

I had a gnawing impression that you wanted me to broaden my interests in life, but I did not want to. My fear of having you catch me masturbating and playing with my little men was now being replaced by a concern that you would come into my room at night and discover me reading numerous sports books. How I craved those Chip Hilton books. I would dread your questions and judgments about it. All I wanted to do was hide the books from you when those footsteps approached my room. That familiar feeling of letting you down and feeling embarrassed endured.

Part of me felt defensive and needed to justify what I was doing.

It bothers me that I had to do that. I've gone from my early years of worrying about where you were all the time to my pre-adolescent and pubescent years of wanting to avoid and hide from you. Now I'm trying to go the opposite extreme in sharing my deepest feelings with you instead of hiding from you.

Dad, I'm eager to receive your reaction and response to all of this.

Love,
Donald

* * *

Dear Donald,

Last year, soon after Grandma Jennie died, your sister Ellen asked me about my relationship with my parents. She said that it was hard for her to think about my having been a child with feelings about my parents comparable to her feelings about me. I asked her to elaborate and she said that for as long as she could remember I seemed like more of a parent to my mother than a son insofar as she seemed so dependent on me. As for my father, she said she remembers very little of him since he died in 1958 when she was only ten years old, and she knew him only from occasional visits. You have mentioned remembering almost nothing about him except that I was very upset when he died. You were seven years old at the time.

It occurs to me now that it is probably true of the perception that many people have of their parents. Were they really ever children themselves, with the same fears, insecurities and dependent yearnings that the relative helplessness of childhood inevitably inspires?

You grew up during a period of time when there was a tendency for parents to feel very responsible for their children's failings. Do you remember the song in Leonard Bernstein's *West Side Story* about Officer Krupke, which facetiously attributes guilt to the parents of delinquent youngsters leaving them depicted as innocent victims? This attitude was wrongly attributed to Sigmund Freud and his psychoanalytic wisdom. In fact, I'm sure Freud never intended to be so interpreted. But ours was a generation of guilt-ridden parents who often lost sight of the fact that we had also been relatively innocent victims of our parents' limitations. The result for you and your contemporaries, I believe, was that you grew up with more feelings of entitlement than generations before you and fewer feelings of obligation and responsibility toward your parents.

We all tend to take for granted that the way things are is the way things have always been, and that it is supposed to be that way. In a child-oriented environment, children are bound to feel that their needs and sensitivities are the first priority whereas the needs and sensitivities of parents are less important. It wasn't until later in your adolescence that I remember emphasizing to you that our relationship is a two-way street, that I too have feelings that can be hurt.

I would like to tell you something about my relationship with my parents and especially my relationship with my father so that you will better understand where I am coming from. You don't really remember Pop, as we all called him. He was a very warm and gentle man who rarely displayed anger toward his three sons. (I am the youngest, seven years and five years younger, respectively, than my brothers.) We all adored him, and paradoxically, we were all afraid of him.

I can clearly remember the few rare occasions when he became angry with me, and even at that, he was never violent or abusive. Only once do I remember him spanking me and not very hard at that. I was very young, about five or six, and I asked him for two dollars. I wouldn't tell him why I needed it, but it was very important to me. I wanted to buy something for him but wouldn't tell him because I wanted to surprise him. He gave me one dollar; when he refused to give me another, I angrily flushed the single dollar down the toilet.

Pop worked very hard and long hours, but when he was home in the evening and on his one day off, he was almost always with his sons. I remember waiting eagerly for him to come home at night and especially looking forward to his day off on Saturday. He was a marvelous storyteller and the other kids in the neighborhood would huddle with us around him as he told his stories which, unfortunately, I can no longer remember.

The highlight of my week in those days was Saturday evening when he took my brothers and me to the movies and to Nathan's Famous for hotdogs. Grandma would sometimes come along, but somehow this became established as our weekly excursion with Pop. As each of my brothers got older and preferred being with their friends, it was eventually just the two of us. By the time I got old enough to prefer being with my friends—who were by then more interested in being with girls—it was hard for me to abandon my father. I continued to go with him for a long time because I was afraid his feelings would be hurt if I didn't. This continued, except that I began to occasionally skip a Saturday for one or another reason when I had to be with my friends, and especially when a particular girl, one whom I had a crush on, was likely to be somewhere and I might be able to see her.

I felt so guilty about abandoning Pop that I can still remember how hard it was to tell him. As for the girl, I never told her how I felt and only once did I force myself to call her and ask for a date. I was very timid with girls and so scared that I'm sure I was relieved when she told me she couldn't go out with me on that occasion for some reason or other. Very likely, I was also relieved because I wouldn't have to tell Pop that I couldn't be with him on that particular Saturday.

By the time I was sixteen or so, my father must have perceived my struggle and made it easier for me somehow, though I can't remember how he did it. It was subtle and I just realized he understood. Maybe he always understood and the entire drama I've just described was in my own mind.

The main thrust of what I'm trying to tell you is that here was a warm, gentle and loving man whom I wanted very much to please. I was afraid to displease him, not because he might angrily punish me or strike out at me, but because I was afraid he would be hurt or disappointed.

Understand that at this time I had not thought any of this through. I only knew that he was the most important person in the world to me. Somehow I knew, or at least I believed, that I could always count on him, that he would be there to pick me up if I fell. But I also knew that I was afraid of his slightest displeasure because it filled me with agonizing guilt.

Somehow this fear of his displeasure contributed to my timidity with girls during adolescence. I somehow got the idea that men are diminished by virtue of a weakness for women, like Sampson and Delilah. A woman would exploit a man's passion for her as if this passion rendered him helpless and without strength.

Years later, when I was beginning medical school, I was driving my first car and my father was sitting next to me. When he reached to get something out of the glove compartment, I was so startled and panicked that he would see the contraceptives I knew were there that I reached over quickly to intercept his hand by getting him what he wanted. In the process I lost control of the car and smashed into a lamppost. I awoke from my mild concussion to find my father slouched next to me, unconscious and bleeding profusely from a gaping head wound. It was several days before we were assured that there was no skull fracture and no evidence of serious internal injuries.

For reasons difficult for me to specify, I obviously felt my father disapproved and was disdainful of man's weakness for woman. Yet he was clearly always shy and timid with women himself. As for his attitude toward my mother, he always required of me and my brothers that we respect her and try to please her, though he never seemed able to please her himself. I recall her frequent haranguing of him and his quiet efforts to assuage her.

I often wondered why he loved her, or whether he loved her, or if he didn't love her why he stayed with her. To the day she died, a year and a half ago, my brothers and I also tried to assuage her and we certainly were attentive to her as you observed. I think we were so good to her more because my father required this of us (or so we thought), than because of affection we felt for her.

All of this is prelude to what this letter is all about. I wanted to convey some of the feelings with which I approached fatherhood, especially as pertaining to a son. My fantasy was that I would be all the good things I believed my father was and that my son would love me the way I loved my own father. But even beyond that, I could be even more to my son because I had the advantages of a fine education and my son would also admire me and want to share my interests. My father's hobbies consisted mostly of doing things with his hands, primarily building or fixing things around our house. A weekend treat was helping him as he rebuilt the fence around our backyard or some other handy venture. Similarly, you were going to grow up and help me think great ideas.

So what went wrong, if indeed anything did, during those early years? I tried, or thought I tried, and even succeeded at being all the things I imagined I would be to you. Against the landscape of your entire childhood, you recall only a couple of instances of my behaving harshly toward you. If these were the only occasions, and I believe there were only a few, you very likely remember them because they stand out in such sharp contrast to the way I usually behaved toward you.

In spite of that, you apparently felt that your mother and I were intrusive, somehow threatening the privacy of your secret world. I remember all the things you describe, but I frankly never even entertained the possibility that you doubted that I loved you. But you know, I remember feeling the same doubts about my own father's love for me. Personally, I think it was just another aspect of my tremendous desire to please him.

I do recall your intense involvement in fantasy and at times feeling some concern about the extent of it. I knew you were expressing a yearning for heroic achievement, even omnipotent mastery in war games or ball games. I even appreciated that your rejection of other interests somehow reflected fears of competing with me. But how to deal with it was a problem I pondered in vain. Little did I realize that all I had to do was wait and be patient.

This is one point where the frame of reference with my own father breaks down. He had little formal education, and though he was bright, well informed and successful, there was never a question on his part or mine that I was expected to surpass him in education, scholarship, and even achievement. After all, I was the beneficiary of so many opportunities and advantages that were denied to him.

Obviously, Don, I couldn't offer you these same competitive advantages over me. I was always aware of the problem though, and in spite of my eagerness for you to admire me, I always tried deliberately to minimize my own achievements and to emphasize how much better you were in those areas of competitive sports where you did indeed excel. Maybe, in spite of my best intentions, my underlying desire for your admiration peeked through and frightened you.

Another thought I have is that my father never thought analytically about these issues. He just behaved spontaneously in response to impulses that were conditioned by his own experiences. Maybe as an analyst I lost some of the spontaneity that characterized my father's responses. But I honestly don't believe I did.

I genuinely enjoyed being a father, and I regard the years of your childhood and your sister's childhood as among the most gratifying and rewarding of my life. It's hard for me to believe that any of my behavior was postured. As for my suggestion that men don't kiss, as you know, I was merely repeating what my father had said to me. I'm sure you are correct in saying that I felt uneasy about physical affection between men, as I'm sure my father did. This must be a reflection of insecurities about manliness that I surely felt and I'm reasonably certain my father felt as well.

At least you never seemed as timid and fearful with girls as I remember being. Maybe having a sister helps a boy to view girls more realistically as regular people. Clinically I've noticed that men without sisters tend to be more fearful of women who thereby are easier to idealize.

Your observation that I seemed as eager to please you as you were to please me certainly seems valid, even understated. I was so eager for your love and admiration that I tried very hard to be everything I thought you wanted. You've surely noted that I could not tolerate your being angry with me or rejecting me. Even as you grew older, on the few occasions when we quarreled, as soon as my anger was spent, I felt an irresistible need to make up with you and reassure myself that you still loved me.

When as a child you seemed to distance yourself from me, I should have understood your need, but I found it painful. I guess it sometimes made me unfairly intrusive, though consciously I thought I always tried to respect your privacy. If you recall, I sometimes joked about the fact that in our family, no one was permitted to be unhappy. If ever you or your sister seemed troubled, I found myself driven to find out what was wrong. I now realize that what was wrong was my unwillingness to allow you the privilege of nursing your pain in privacy if you so wished.

You speak of being protective of me. This was certainly true of my feelings about my father, but I wasn't confronted by the pressure to confide my troubles to him. In that sense, my father certainly respected my need for privacy more than I respected yours. As I grew up, I would go to some lengths to conceal my disappointments, frustrations, or troubles from him. I always found it hard to ask him for anything, though he was very generous. Somehow I grew up feeling that asking for anything or asking for help was a weakness and that remains a flaw in me. This must have affected you. Years later, I would sometimes wish that you and your sister would spare me and your mother the knowledge of your every ache and pain, though I fully realize that I had always made this difficult for both of you to do that.

The stronger wish, I guess, is to always be there for you, even if there is nothing I can really do to help. This is a difficult frustration for every parent. In fact, it is difficult for anyone to come to terms with the realization that often there is little we can do to help the people for whom we deeply care. I like to paraphrase the Alcoholics Anonymous Serenity Prayer: "Try to do the things we can do something about, to accept the things we can do nothing about, and to strive for the wisdom that enables us to distinguish between the two."

You speak of feeling that you were intimidated by your perception of my expectations of you. I fell victim, no doubt, to the occupational hazard of being a parent, insofar as I undoubtedly cherished the opportunity of realizing and experiencing through you all of my own unrealized and frustrated ambitions and dreams. How can a father avoid creating a climate of expectation for his son that reflects his own values and ambitions, fulfilled and unfulfilled?

I certainly reveled in your success as an athlete but also shared your pain and frustration when your achievement fell short of your expectations. I also enjoyed your popularity with friends, boys and girls alike. I admired and was proud of your apparent ability to relate so comfortably to girls, a facility which I acquired to a much lesser extent only later in my own life.

Nevertheless, you were accurate in your perception that I was disappointed and frustrated when you so forcefully rejected any embrace of the · cultural and intellectual interests I valued. I felt thwarted when you rebuffed my efforts to expose you to music and literature, or when you disdainfully dismissed my efforts to engage you in conversations about serious subjects such as politics or world affairs which were so important to me.

I recall vividly buying you a microscope and trying to involve you in the mysteries of otherwise invisible things, but I don't recall that you were even minimally interested. The same thing happened with a chemistry set and a camera. I recall feeling that you were probably thinking that you wished I would leave you be and stop bugging you with things you considered irrelevant.

I knew you were reacting to competitive conflicts with me but I never stopped searching for the key to alleviating the anxieties I assumed you felt. You were trapped by an exaggerated conception of my success and achievements. The modesty you perceived was both genuine and even deliberately articulated to you in an effort to moderate your illusions about me. This was the more difficult to achieve because I obviously valued the admiration of friends and colleagues, and could hardly do other than try to live up to their expectations of me. I was always eager to be liked, admired, and most importantly to be needed.

The powerful desire to be needed probably was the dominant motivation for my choice of profession. It is not remarkable that many people perceived this need and my willingness to be helpful, and freely availed themselves of the help I offered. This was too important a source of my self-esteem, and I couldn't conceivably compromise it in order to make myself less intimidating to you. Equally important was my deeply felt need for you to admire me, but I never figured out how to accomplish this without also being an object of intimidating awe. Your need to idealize me undoubtedly conspired with my own need to perpetuate the myth of my omnipotence.

It has struck me that in some ways, children whose parents are less obviously involved with their children's well-being have an easier time of it. Clearly, children who can easily perceive their parents as cruel or insensitive can more easily rebel and assert their own individuality with less guilt.

Is it the curse of parents who genuinely love their children, that their love becomes the inescapable vehicle for inculcating guilt? Or is this a self-serving way of portraying my narcissistic investment in my children as a virtue? My guess is that it is a little of both. I wonder whether it is possible for parents to deeply care for their children and still not be concerned about and invested in the way their children feel about them. For me, the two seem to have been inseparable.

As for the separation anxiety that plagued you throughout your childhood, I can readily understand its origins. You were born at a time of considerable emotional turmoil in Mom's and my life. I was scheduled to go back into military service because of the Korean War. Mom felt threatened by my likely departure soon after you were born and we were both very concerned about her being left alone with two infants.

As it happens, I was finally called to military duty when you were about one year old, and when I returned after being away for two months in Alabama you were clearly angry and rejected me. Fortunately I was stationed for two years at Mitchel Air Force base on Long Island where I ran the Mental Hygiene Clinic, and we all moved to the house where you grew up, which was just a few minutes from the base. It was intended to be our home for just two years, but by that time, you, and especially your sister, seemed so unhappy about the prospect of moving back to New York City that we decided to remain. We still live in the same house. I should add that during those two years at Mitchel Field I was rarely home because I continued my psychoanalytic training in New York, traveling there every night after work.

You know how sensitive to separation infants one to three years old can be. In addition to my absence, Mom had a rough time during that period of your life, distressed and harried by the demands of two infants in a big house and mostly-absent husband. We always assumed that you were traumatized by the relative absence of enough loving attention during that critical phase of your development. I believe your separation anxiety during your childhood is attributable to these events.

I can go on, but I think I will be getting ahead of you. I know you will be writing to me again and there will be ample opportunity for me to respond.

Love,
Dad

Like Father, Like Son

It was hard to rebel against a father who cared.

God in his wisdom made old age painful so it's not so hard to say good-bye to life.

* * *

March, 1982

Dear Dad,

I was very excited to receive your first letter, and of course, a bit apprehensive. You really are a special man. What I was most impressed with was your capacity to be open and honest about yourself. We both had a need to please our fathers. I realize now that you do not view my early childhood feelings as being peculiar. It is comforting to know that you wanted to hide things from your father too. In the end, we both know how destructive that can be.

That accident with your father was something I never knew about. It is hard for me to imagine just what you were feeling during that time, but I can appreciate how difficult it must have been. You still have not told me how you felt when your father died. Did it make you think of your own mortality? Is it hard to go back to those feelings?

It's easy to forget that you were once a child with similar struggles, but now I feel more connected to the child in you. What do you think Pop would have done had he found that contraceptive? I am comforted by the fact that we had similar needs. You did not start your life at thirty-five and it is easy to lose sight of that reality. When you wanted to go off and be with girls, it made me think of how guilty I would feel leaving you behind if something better came along. I realize now that if I had let you inside more, as opposed to experiencing you as an intruder, you would have been able to understand so much of what I was going through.

You were right when you said it is easier for the child to blame his parents. These letters with you will help me understand and be more sympathetic with the fathers who come into my office. When they bring their sons with them I find myself wanting the son to appreciate the importance of understanding the father's relationship with his own parents. When the fathers share their personal histories with their sons, I have noticed that the sons become more sensitive to their father's needs. This experience with you has done the same thing for me.

It is so important to understand where another person is coming from before making harsh judgments about what they are doing to you. There is such a feeling of closeness that can develop if a father allows himself to be vulnerable with his son. You tried so hard not to impose on me that at times it made me uneasy. I did not feel you placed many demands on me, and when you did, I did not know what hit me.

At times it seemed you had trouble being direct with me about your feelings. I can't remember you ever telling me during my adolescence that a relationship is a two-way street. It seemed to come later on. My impression was that a father is supposed to do things for his son. Your difficulty with asking for things made it easy for me to take advantage of you and be insensitive to your needs. I find myself having the same problem.

I wish you had been more direct with me about sharing your own achievements. Although I was threatened by you, I had an enormous need to be proud of you. Your trying so hard not to intimidate me only created more of an air of mystery about who you were.

One of the more interesting parts of your letter concerned how you felt about your mother and its effect on your relationship with women. I always wondered why you did not have any women friends. At least it seemed that way to me. This was such an important dimension of my life. Your interpretation of how a sister can influence the way a man perceives other women has given me something to think about.

My sister and I were very close in my early years. I found her good company on a Saturday night watching the *Gale Storm Show* and professional wrestling matches—better known then as *Bedlam from Boston.* We both liked Pepper Gomez and his cast iron stomach taking on Haystacks Calhoun and Buddy (Natureboy) Rogers, later it was Bruno Sammartino. There were other times when we watched *Chiller*

Theater. One of my favorite privileges was being allowed to sleep in Ellen's room when it was Clara, the housekeeper's, night off. She and I would stay up for hours talking about all the problems I was having with my girlfriends. What a nice support system to have. This closeness allowed me to learn how to talk with a girl and gave me the opportunity to understand how girls feel. We also loved getting up early on Christmas morning. She would come into my room and we would open our stockings together. We shared so much joy together.

Unfortunately, as the years went on. I found us drifting apart and our sibling rivalry began to sabotage our early years of closeness. We grew apart but I never stopped looking up to her and wanting to please her. I have come to realize recently that my sister is important to me. Many of the women that I have been attracted to over the years have had the qualities that reminded me of her.

As comfortable as I appeared with women, I was always afraid of being rejected. As the years went on, I felt abandoned by my sister. I think my need for many women friends over the years has to do with a longing to re-establish a love and closeness with my own sister. The early advantages of having a sister later shifted and I often felt the loneliness of an only child.

I wonder if this will surprise you, because at times I have been curious about how you have perceived my relationship with Ellen. You must have had an investment in seeing us get along. I know I have such an investment with Jared and Emily. Coincidentally, the age difference between my two children is the same, and Emily is also the older child. To this day I am still trying to understand what happened between Ellen and me. It seems important for me to understand that now.

Another factor in my need to be close to women must have to do with the fact that Mom and I seem to have a better relationship than what you had with Grandma. I never perceived Mom as a castrating woman, although I had my moments. We were always able to talk and she made me feel so special. I never questioned your love for her, the way you questioned Pop's love for Grandma. Only for brief moments did I wonder whether you were happy with her. With whom did you have your first positive female relationship? Do you perceive Mom and Grandma as being complete opposites? I always felt you were kind to women, but I really never knew much about your relationships with other women previous to Mom. Did you feel Grandma dominated Pop so therefore you perceived men unable to hold their ground with women?

I must admit it seemed that Mom could get most of what she wanted from you. You appeared to derive satisfaction from pleasing her. Do you feel that you pleased her? I found myself invested in wanting her to express her appreciation to you. Interestingly, I have discovered from your letter that Grandma was not very good at that when it came to Pop. It seemed like he could never satisfy her. Somehow that makes me feel sad.

You seemed like such a giving husband and encouraged my sister and me to always respect Mom. Pop was obviously a good role model for you because he did the same thing when it carne to you and your relationship with Grandma. Was Grandma proud of Pop the way Mom seemed to be proud of you?

It was obvious that Grandma was proud of you and I felt she gave me special attention because I was your son. She used to refer to me as her "baby's baby." You were her son, the doctor. You always seemed proud of Mom but it isn't clear to me that Pop felt the same way about Grandma.

It was hard to rebel against a father who cared. Sometimes I wished that you had been a terrible father so I could justify my behavior. I imagine it was hard for you to leave me when I was young. When I am gone for one day, the guilt is enormous. You certainly taught me how to be a caring father.

Recently I have noticed that I am feeling closer to men and have a stronger need for close male friends. I never could understand why you did not have close male relationships. Your sharing with me has contributed to my desire to understand men more.

As I close this letter, I want to know that your response will, I hope, put a close to a lot of unresolved questions regarding my early years which I have held inside for a long time. Your last letter awakened them and served as a catalyst for new questions and answers.

Love,
Donald

* * *

Dear Donald,

After reading your last letter I realized that my portrayal to you of my mother was misleading. She certainly was not the unmitigated bitch you may have inferred.

A recurrent dream which dates back to childhood and pre-puberty will, I believe, reveal a great deal to you about my perception of my mother.

> **Dream**—I am being chased by a witch-like, ugly, fat and vicious looking woman who wants to kill me. I'm running away as fast as I can, but she overtakes me and I awaken screaming.

As I awoke, I realized that the woman resembled my mother, markedly distorted though she was; and comforting me at that moment was my actual mother, who by contrast with the witch in the dream, looked warm and lovely and loving. What makes this all the more confusing is the fact that Grandma so conspicuously favored me, even in childhood. In the years after Grandpa died, she would often call me Harry, my father's name, as if I now had become to her the protector my father had always been.

I felt guilty after reading your letter about having given an unfairly negative picture of my mother and I want to rectify it. We all have a tendency to oversimplify in our efforts to classify and define people to ourselves as well as to others. In the process, we do injury to the truth, since people, as you know, are complicated, multifaceted, and ever-changing in mood and outlook. Certainly this was true of my mother and is reflected in the ambivalent feelings I have about her.

As I write, another memory that may be pertinent springs to mind. When I was twelve or thirteen my mother became very ill with a severe urinary infection and there was danger of her dying. These were the early years of sulfa drugs and she was receiving such a drug. I vividly recall praying to God that she would be permitted to live, and vowing that if she lived I would never again masturbate. As you know, she did live, and I leave it to you to decide whether I kept my promise.

My portrayal of my parents' relationship was also oversimplified, though I remember it mostly as I described it to you. Pop treated her with a kind of benevolent tolerance, I believe, though it would not be accurate to say that she dominated him or that he dominated her. I mostly had the feeling that she felt more affection for him than he did for her. Looking back, perhaps his lack of affectionate display to her accounted for much of her anger toward him.

It's interesting to me that I feel as I do about my mother and father. My mother always seemed to regard me with favoritism over my brothers, and my father always seemed to favor my brother Carl, his second-born son. Carl was infected by some unpasteurized milk before I was born and suffered from tuberculosis of the hip. As a consequence of this infection, he had to wear a brace for years and the resulting disability left him lame with a stiff hip and a shortened leg.

In retrospect, it is easy to understand my father's over-protectiveness of Carl and the apparent favoritism he displayed toward him. Carl would bully me as a kid, frustrated as he must have been by his disability, and my father was unwilling or unable to protect me. I recall one of the few times Pop slapped me in response to my angrily calling Carl a "cripple." On another occasion, I had been given my first two-wheel bicycle, something I had wanted for a long time. After I had had it only a short while, everyone was pleased to discover that Carl was able to ride it in spite of his bad leg. Carl thereafter adopted my bike and no one seemed to care that I no longer had my cherished bicycle.

You ask about my feelings when my father died. I regarded it then, as I still do now, as a major loss. At the time, I was thirty-five years old and no longer materially dependent on him. In my adult life, I actually saw him infrequently, but he was nevertheless a very important person to me. I guess my thoughts about how he would feel about things I was doing was important, even though he mostly didn't know about what I was doing. This continued even after his death and must reflect an enduring desire to please him.

When Pop died suddenly, I suffered the usual grief, trauma and guilt. In one respect though, my reaction was less usual. I hated the condolence calls and visits that are part of the traditional ritual of mourning. I wanted to be with my wife and children, and I wanted to be alone. For me, the loss I felt was a private experience, and I wanted to nurse my wounds by myself. I asked Mom to call our friends and ask them not to come, and I returned to work after three days rather than the customary week. I felt that for me the best way to handle my grief was to return to my normally busy schedule.

Another dream, which I had numerous times in the years after my father died, informed me about another complex which I would not otherwise have thought about.

Dream—Although my father is supposed to be dead, I become aware that he is very much alive, living somewhere else, either alone or in another situation. I implore him to return, but though he doesn't explicitly refuse, he doesn't return. I feel rejected, as if he doesn't care enough for us or he's had enough of us.

I've spent much time trying to analyze this dream. I have on one occasion heard a similar dream from a patient. On its surface, it reveals a feeling that my father in his death rejects me, and I do experience this as valid. But it has other meanings for me as well, having to do with feelings of guilt and unworthiness on the one hand, and feelings that I'm. not being adequately rewarded on another. On another level, the dream deals with my conflicts about my own mortality. In one sense, it is dear to me in the dream that my father has found contentment and his reluctance to return expresses an unwillingness to again engage the pressures and stresses of life-as if to say, "Who needs it?"

My mother in her last years would sometimes say that God in his wisdom made old age painful, so it's not so hard to say good-bye to life. If the going is rough at any age, perhaps the same adage holds. If, "You don't have to be Jewish to enjoy Levy's Rye Bread," maybe you don't have to be old to find life so painful and difficult that it's tempting to think of being in another place which is peaceful and easy. Might that be heaven?

You comment at one point in your letter about my not having close female friends, which I'm not sure is true—though male-female friendships are inevitably constrained because they may otherwise be construed as sexual or romantic. After marriage, I would assume that we tend to develop relationships with other couples. Beyond these couple relationships, close relationships with other women would likely be romantic and therefore taboo.

As for your question about my early relationships with women, I must confess that in looking back there was no single one that I consider significant. I met Mom when I was eighteen, and though we didn't see each other exclusively for a year or two after that, she was always thereafter my "big number." Before eighteen, I had numerous infatuations, sometimes with girls I was dating and sometimes with girls I wished I could date. I remember being consumed as a young adolescent with a girl named Betty, but Betty may never have known she had an admirer. I recall thinking about her constantly, endlessly walking past her house in the hope of seeing her, even though when occasionally I did see her, I was afraid to speak to her. Otherwise there was the usual series of relationships in which I would lose interest if the girl seemed to like me more than I liked her, or vice versa. Your father's achievements as a Lothario, I'm afraid, are unimpressive.

Your comment that I had few male friends is puzzling to me because I believe the opposite is true. Over the years there have been many men whom I considered good friends, but as life proceeds time becomes a limiting factor. With the pressures of work, involvement with family, parents and brothers, as well as wife and children, and some interests which by their nature have to be pursued in solitude, the time available for friends is limited.

We tend at any point in our lives to spend time with friends who share with us some current interest. As these interests shift, we tend to develop new friendships and time spent with old friends is less. This is regrettable but almost inevitable. Even so, I have several very old friends with whom I still share a great deal.

Perhaps this is different in childhood and adolescence, when intense and intimate friendships can more readily blossom. I suspect that you also have lost track of some of your old and intimate friends, as you have increasingly become involved in your career, with your wife and children, and new friends with whom you now more immediately share common interests.

I think I have addressed all the questions you raised in your last letter but if I haven't done so adequately maybe you will raise them again in your future letters.

Love, Dad

The Rebellious Teens
Breaking Away

All I wanted to do was prove that my way was right and yours was wrong.

My guilt-ridden generation was brought up in the tradition of guilty devotion to parents on the one hand, and educated to believe that parents are ultimately responsible and blame-worthy for all of the ills and failures of their children.

* * *

May, 1982

Dear Dad,

Writing these letters becomes increasingly difficult as I reflect on my feelings during adolescence, that stage of life when a child inevitably struggles for his freedom. During this period of time, I became acutely aware of my male body parts, the world of athletics, girls, and fantasy. Many of my friends' fathers were sports-minded and not very oriented toward mental masturbation. In those days, being the intellectual son was the farthest thing from my mind. Your library seemed like a wasted space in the house. I was jealous of my friends with fathers who watched the ballgames on TV with them and discussed the sports page of *The New York Times*. It appeared as if you wanted to read only the front page of the paper and I just could not understand your indifference to the success of the New York Yankees. You genuinely tried to reach me and take part in my life, but something in me was resisting you. It was hard to pull away from such a warm and concerned father. The guilt surrounding my adolescent rebellion was enormous. You were the guy who turned me on to the bright lights of Broadway, once upon a time.

I was into my macho image and bullying people half my size with my big hairy body. You would never catch me picking fights with older guys who were bigger than I was. My friend's mother would hardly let her son associate with me. She felt I was a bad influence on him. That was ironically Steve Lanskey's mother; she lived across the street. That really hurt my feelings because in many ways I felt he was the real bully of the neighborhood. Ironically he was the boy across the street in my Coney Island letter. Although I felt terrible about giving a boy a black eye a week before his Bar Mitzvah, years later, I saw him at your country club. He read our book and his response was telling. He said, "I thought you were the guy who had everything going for you. I didn't know how vulnerable you felt as a kid." In retrospect, I went from being a bully to feeling bullied and during my high school years, I became empathetic. Interestingly now, I realize that my vulnerability made me more sensitive to the other kids that were being teased. I had felt teased but never admitted it. When I was very young, I was never in touch with the reasons for my anger and frustration so I took it out on others. I had low self-esteem and covered it up. Sometimes I was a self conscious and depressed kid.

And there was that one male rival I competed against all through my high school years. He was one guy I could never beat up. Whether it was sports or girls, he became the object of my anger. There was always a controversy over who was the better athlete or lover, yet I felt like he was the rock star, But I held that inside me. When we were playing kickball on the asphalt at recess and he came to the plate, the message was, "Kush is up—move back!" I waited in the wings, aware that it would not be exactly the same for me, knowing full well our girlfriends were watching on the sidelines. We even went to basketball camp together. I could never get away from competing with him. We shared MVP at Camp Scatico's Nate Holman Invitational Basketball Tournament in 1966. He too was big and hairy. Our peers were actually going to sell tickets just to see us have a fist fight in the sixth grade. The fight never took place and I was relieved. What made it even worse was that this male rival became an avid Dodger fan, while I was an obsessive Yankee fan. We spent our summers listening to Howard Cosell giving us the early morning scorecard, and I regularly had sleepovers at his house. Later on, it was the voice of Cousin Brucie on WABC-AM.

Despite adolescent complications, I needed his friendship, because underneath all my competitive feelings I cared for him. I needed that pass from him when I was under the basket to score my points. He always seemed to be looking for me. It was nice to be acknowledged. I liked the fact that people perceived us as "The Dynamic Duo." Whenever I needed encouragement during a game, he was there for me. When we were on the same team, no one could stop us. He always made me look good catching my touchdown passes playing touch football. It was a typical adolescent love/hate relationship and we had a lot in common. We were like *Butch Cassidy and the Sundance Kid.*

Being a conceited jock was a convenient way to cover up my insecurities. Underneath my facade was a fear that I would never amount to anything. I always felt you knew this about me and that gave me another reason to avoid you. Deep down, I still knew you were around to take care of me. Why finish a project if I knew you would finish it for me? There was always that ambivalence about letting you help me. But, as you noticed, I would always go for the help as long as it was on my terms.

I had so many fears, exemplified by the fact that I was convinced I would be the first person in history to forget his Bar Mitzvah lines and flunk out of school. You made sure that would not happen by giving me tutors. Going to the tutor was embarrassing and it was one of my best kept secrets. It was not only boring but inconsistent with the image I was invested in protecting. I wanted to believe that my independence was for real. Deep down I knew there was some kind of learning problem. There was no label for someone like me. I felt different from my friends; everything else seemed harder for me. Processing and understanding was difficult. I felt vulnerable, and so much shame. This was the secret I was hiding behind.

When the defenses were not working, I became conscious of the fact that my fear of girls was coming on strong, and every new expectation that developed with adolescence seemed insurmountable. One way to compensate for my fears was to hang posters of naked women all over the room. They replaced my sports heroes. This was easier than worrying about whether the girl at the movies with me would push my arm away as I was trying to put it around her or hold her hand.

It was becoming clear to me that I only liked things I was good at, and everything had to come easy for me. It disturbed me to reach out to you and show my vulnerability. I couldn't admit my difficulties with focusing and understanding when instructions were being explained. It felt as if my world was closing in on me. Reading comprehension became a problem. My mind would drift elsewhere. On some level I was anxious about possible rejection and humiliation, but I am sorry now that I deprived myself of those important man-to-man talks. I wish I had been able to express to you my concerns about girls and sex because these issues were so mysterious and frightening. How would I ever know where to put my penis that first time? I never could understand those dirty jokes at parties. Here I was, the son of a psychiatrist, and I could not even talk to you about my personal feelings. I didn't want you to know how lost I was and my struggle with learning basic principles. Maps and puzzles would baffle my mind. So often I couldn't organize my work and felt isolation because of my lack of confidence. All of this became overwhelming and frustrating. I had no patience. Math, foreign language, and the sciences where brutal for me. I often had nervous stomachs.

Now I strongly need to know what you went through as an adolescent. It was rare for me to seek this kind of personal sharing from you in the past, but it is hard to open up with someone who sees you as a threat and a rival. Or maybe it would be more accurate to say that it was hard for me to open up to you because it seems that I was the one setting up this whole dynamic.

I remember once discovering condoms in your drawer and being appalled by the idea that you had sex with Mom. It was extremely uncomfortable for me the first time I went into the pharmacy to ask for a condom. I wanted to make sure there was no one around because I was so embarrassed. My innocence was slowly being stripped away. It was terribly difficult to see you as an ordinary man with the same basic desires and instincts as everyone. I was very threatened by all of this.

Sex seemed like a taboo subject around the house, although in reality I know that was not completely true. You always seemed more modest about sex than Mom. She appeared unconcerned about covering herself up completely, but I knew that you were very protective about that part of your relationship. Sometimes I felt disturbed about this because it communicated to me that sex was very private. I feared walking in on you and Mom having sex, and indeed it almost happened once. I did not exactly burst in on you, but halfway down the stairs I knew it was time to turn around and go back. It was hard to imagine you having sex. You were ordinary people doing something that seemed extraordinary at the time. That's the stuff that makes for good legends. The bedroom was no longer the place to just hangout and watch Knick games together.

In general, I felt that Mom was the less inhibited of the two of you during those years. She and I were much closer than you and I. Mom built me up and I felt safe going to her with my feelings. She was my affectionate and most loyal fan. Every Saturday morning after my games, she would read the local box scores and fill up my scrapbook. When I was younger she had me convinced that my voice would eventually be heard in Carnegie Hall. Mom would always be the one to tell me how proud you were or what someone else might have said about me. She was the passageway for compliments. As a result of this, confiding in her was not a problem. We even liked giving each other head massages.

There were times when I felt guilty about my closeness to Mom, but my guilt was alleviated by my perception of you and my sister as having more in common. You both seemed more reserved and private. All of this makes Freud look like a genius. We really appear to have had all the ingredients of an Oedipal family. There were moments when I truly felt like Oedipus.

I also felt that I would never be on my own. Athletics saved me because I was talented in this area and my self-esteem was completely dependent on my being a basketball and track star. My track coach called me "Baby Steps" for my unusually short stride for a big guy. Although I hated to run, it was one of those things that came easy to me. Unfortunately the quarter mile, the toughest sprint in track was my specialty. I still regret missing the Penn Relays because of a pulled hamstring. Athletics was the one part of my life that made me feel superior to you. I liked being picked first in those choose-up games in the park, but of course there was that other boy who might be picked before me. He was that other bully in town. Having the best baseball card collection no longer provided status. Now my friends were competing to try and accumulate the largest number of trophies. At the time, it was the equivalent of having a Michelangelo sculpture in one's room. My friends and I would even hike up our scores at the bowling alley just so we could bring home another trophy. Then it was off to Wetsons for a hamburger and hoops in my friend's driveway.

I have this disturbing memory that when one of our moms drove us home, we would be asked to get out of the car and open the trunk with the keys to retrieve our bowling balls. There was always that dreaded fear that I would have trouble fitting the key in the hole and feel embarrassed. The anxiety about having to ask for help was unbearable. I felt like a failure.

I loved to show off for you and see that proud look on your face. You and Mom never missed a game and that meant a great deal to me. When I was hurt during a game, I liked it that you ran out to save me. Any way that I could get attention and be taken care of was all right with me. Even those cold days at the track meets never stopped the two of you from showing up. Although at times I may have appeared indifferent to your presence, I really cared. I truly appreciated the fact that you made compromises in your work schedule to come watch me perform. Now that I am in a similar position in my life, I realize what a sacrifice it was for you. It's very important to me that you know how much that meant to me.

Being a good athlete made me feel special and manly. During these years, I had to cope with my physical maturity and emotional insecurities. Being taller and hairier than my friends made me self-conscious at camp and during gym. While most of the guys were into bragging about their sexual prowess and penis size, I hid in a corner, embarrassed about my awkward, lanky body, and aware that my voice had changed. I was uncomfortable being so tall and hitting my head on the top of the school bus every day. This was not too good for my posture. Many of my moments were spent bending down trying to conform to a world that seemed more geared for short people. I can appreciate how Kareem Abdul-Jabbar must have felt!

I took to the short girls, I think, because being tall had such negative connotations. My first crush was on a four-foot, ten-inch girl who broke my heart. She liked the shorter guys. I felt so rejected and was afraid that I would go through life never being worthy of a woman's love. I was everyone's best friend. All I ever wanted was true love. There is nothing more humiliating than having your I.D. bracelet, symbolic during this time of going steady with a girl, thrown at you in the hallway at school. That happened to me when I broke up with one of the taller girls because I was more attracted to the girl who eventually rejected me. That Neil Sedaka song *Breaking Up Is Hard To Do* is ringing in my ears.

It was hard being attracted only to girls who were short and having to dance with them when they just came up to my navel. I felt very self-conscious. At one time I had trouble imagining myself ever being able to dance with a girl. I seemed to go after only those girls I couldn't get. It was tough to play the game of hard-to-get, particularly with girls I liked. They seemed to like the meaner guys who were not interested. Later I found out many of these girls had fathers that were distant. It was exciting to hang out, hoping to see the girl of my dreams walk by me in the hallway between classes just to get a glimpse of her. The only advantage of being tall, it seemed, was that I could always get a good view of what was going on. In the end, dancing in a bear-hug to a Lesley Gore song on a summer evening was the best show in town. Ironically, at a different time, she went to Camp Scatico and we both hung out at the canteen. I remember looking up in the audience in our schools gym admiring Ellen and Phil arm in arm. My dream was to be just like them, perfect love. I loved the song "Somewhere" from *Westside Story* and the romantic in me knew there was someone out there.

When we had to line up during assembly, the tallest person had to be first in line. I felt like the oddball, and whenever you told me that someday I would appreciate my height I looked at you like you were crazy. I had trouble believing you. Your reaching out to me seemed motivated by a need to say things to make me feel better. It was so hard to trust you. How could I trust you if I could not even trust myself? I am convinced that the self-confidence I derived in my fantasy world helped to prevent me from fighting with you more than I did. I always needed to find new fantasies to help me find my own validity in the world. There was nothing like taking my men and dinkey toys outside and building villages that I controlled. There was also dressing up as Wyatt Earp and Gene Autrey.

I loved the fact that people expected great things from me athletically, but unfortunately the pressure was too much for me. My guidance counselor, who happened to be the basketball coach, actually called Mom to make sure my schoolwork would not interfere with my basketball career. This was the year it counted for college. He wanted to give me an academic schedule that would suit my athletic needs. I felt like a child prodigy, starting on the varsity basketball team as a freshman. I liked it when the Oyster Bay coach came up to me after the game and shook my hand while telling me he thought I would make the big time. You never forget those special moments. That was an unusual accomplishment. Needless to say, the parents of the senior boys on the team did not like it much.

For me, losing a game was the equivalent of the whole world crashing down. I just couldn't take all the pressure and all the expectations being put on me. Basketball stopped being fun because it had become too serious. Becoming an All-American, which people told me I was going to be someday, became a weighty responsibility instead of a cheerful prospect. Worse was the fact that my terrible foul shooting was eventually one of the reasons we would lose some of our games. I already suffered enough guilt when the team had to spend part of basketball practice looking for my contact lenses. It seemed as if the spectators were going to have heart attacks waiting for the foul shot that I would throw up so high in the air. Even the great coach Nat Holman, better known as Uncle Nat at Camp Scatico, couldn't change my shot.

To add insult to injury I remember being the star of the play The Fantasticks. They pressured me to do it and I was afraid I would forget my lines. In the end I forgot a whole page and felt awful.

I so badly needed that one victory that made me feel special. When we lost, I became depressed and angry; I would often throw one of my famous temper tantrums. I resented your comments about how foolish it was for me to take losing a game so seriously. All I could see was you trying once again to take away my fantasy and my desperate need to feel special and significant. Behind all this was a feeling of helplessness and dependency on you. The only way for me to survive at this point was to believe that I was better than everyone else, or at least pretend that was the case. Could sports really be my ticket to independence from you?

My Bar Mitzvah just did not feel like a transition into manhood to me. It just seemed like it was what every Jewish thirteen-year-old boy was supposed to do. I found myself asking the same question as the boy in the movie *The Jazz Singer:* "If I was really a man, then why would I have to still listen to you?" Of course, I still depended on you both financially and emotionally. Then again, who really wanted all your responsibilities anyway? Although ritual and ceremony have always served an important function in terms of honoring and celebrating the various stages of one's life, all I had to show for it was being a horny teenager with acne, braces, glasses, and my competition with you.

My independence was taking a train on the Long Island railroad to the 1964 World's Fair in Flushing Queens with my friends. We were also allowed to ride our bikes around and take the bus to Roosevelt Field, a shopping mall on Long Island. Riding a bike gave me a freedom to explore, escape, and feel empowered. In addition to these concerns, I recall dreading during adolescence that my teacher would call on me to write something on the blackboard and I would have to leave my desk with an erection. It was almost as embarrassing as farting in elementary school and blaming the person next to you. This was a time when my vanity seemed to be functioning at a high pitch and going to the dermatologist became a way of life. One could only hope that no one would find out. Those early adolescent days of masturbating at my friend's house and deciding to go into our respective corners and agreeing to share our fantasies were over. When I was a kid, it was easy to be open and free with male friends.

It appeared as if people expected me to be perfect because I was your son, or crazy because all psychiatrists' sons are one or the other. There was no gray area and I truly began to look at life as an either/ or proposition. Both choices seemed unappealing to me. I was very self-conscious during this time of my life, feeling as though people were watching every move I made and constantly judging me. My resentment toward you was growing, too, and the burden of being your son at times felt enormous. High expectations of me and the pressure within me to never make a mistake were becoming harder to cope with on every level.

I hated school and found it completely irrelevant. Most of my time in class was spent fantasizing about the girl sitting next to me and mentally undressing her. The thought of *actually* undressing her scared me half to death but I did not want my friends to know that.

Being the class clown was another way to cover up my insecurities. I so didn't want the teacher to put me on the spot and ask me a question that I knew I would not be able to answer. I so dreaded that moment and the anxiety around it. Those were the moments I wanted to be invisible, similar to when I would have to duck under my desk in elementary school during one of those air-raid drills; anticipating an atomic attack by the Soviet Union. My dislike for school created a great deal of tension between us. Your lectures about my future bored me and I dreaded your helping me with my homework. Unfortunately, I needed it. Sometimes it seemed as if I could not write a school paper without you. I found it easy to become a passive recipient of your intellect. I hated those students who said they never studied and then got A's. Passing an exam was as hard for me as making a foul shot, and the pressure to do both about the same. The problem of a nervous stomach ache made the situation even worse. All I wanted to do was hide my report card and spend my evenings on the phone making sure I wasn't missing anything. One of the things that contributes to my fear of death is the idea that things will go on without me. I always had to make sure I wasn't being left out. There was that deep fear that I would be an island unto myself. Being me would be too much for anyone to handle if anyone knew my hidden deep dark secrets.

Every decision about my life seemed impossible and I would come to you to make them for me. What a hypocrite! Here I was, the big man wanting to rebel, and I could not make a decision without you, even when it came to completing a homework assignment by myself. You made everything look so easy and I felt so threatened by that. Your patience and self-discipline were overwhelming to me. Whatever the issue might be, it was you who had the last word on most things, and your judgments about my life were often hard to take. I often wondered if you came on as strong with your patients as you did with me. You seemed so rational to the rest of the world and at times so irrational with me. People came to you with their problems. Even my friends liked you, and everyone else had a great deal of respect for you.

During this time it was tough for me to understand why people seemed intimidated by you when they learned what you did for a living. I had no interest in your career and concerned myself only with how people perceived you. Part of me appreciated that so many people liked you, but another part of me felt threatened by it. I too wanted to be important. It was no accident that my friends at school came to me with their problems. This was my way of competing with you and it sure made me feel needed and important. Obviously, I was imitating and identifying with you, but I would not acknowledge it. That was the farthest thing from my mind. Watching you play the sensitive analyst to the world, who always did the so-called "appropriate" thing disturbed me, and made me feel inadequate. But on some level I also admired your strength. Asking for help felt like a weakness.

I still believed that you would always be around to make things okay whenever I was getting a raw deal. Like the time the coach did not put me on the All Star team in Little League—you were right there behind me. I admired the fact that you were, and still are, such a loyal person. Almost as if you were a voice from a higher source, you would always protect me and give me whatever I wanted. This conjures up an image of me standing at home plate in amazement as contact was made and I watched the ball sail over the centerfield wall. I can still hear Mel Allen saying "It's going, going, it's gone!" The reward was a slow trot around the bases savoring the moment and having you there to share it with me. This was a far cry from the days of my announcing make-believe ballgames in my childhood bedroom.

The rest of the world obviously felt the same way about you, or so it seemed. I remember the phone ringing late at night with emergency calls for you. People calling you with problems seemed commonplace in your professional world; someone always needed you. My nightmares had to compete for your attention but somehow you were there for me, although at times you did appear preoccupied. Unfortunately for me, I took that personally, but again would never mention it to you. I feared hurting your feelings or getting you angry at me. I did not like the feeling that you weren't listening to me. Maybe you were most of the time, but I certainly was sensitive about it and I am sure I will continue to be. I never wanted you to think of me as a person who talked too much and was a bore to be around.

During adolescence was the time when my relationships with authority figures became an important part of my identity. Although your sensitive, soft spoken, non-macho style was a refreshing change in comparison to the tough manner of my athletic coaches, you were a very demanding father in other ways. I felt you expected from me a great deal of emotional maturity and strong sense of responsibility. You were very forceful about what you believed was the right way to act or be. As a result, I hated anyone telling me what to do because it was difficult being dominated by another male. You were very different from my friends' fathers in that they seemed more concerned about winning or losing the games and how well their sons performed. I appreciated that you never embarrassed me the way some of my friends' fathers embarrassed them. Some of these fathers got so emotional they lost control and acted like teen-age boys themselves, living through their sons on the athletic field.

When it came to sports, you were clearly the sanest father around. When my coaches came down on me for my attitude, I experienced it as similar to the way I perceived your treatment of me at home. I remember having my coach refer to me as useless during one of my basketball games at camp. It felt humiliating but of course I shrugged it off. He came from the "School of Hard Knocks," better known now as "Tough-Love." My track coach once said to me, "If I stop getting on your back, then you might have something to worry about." What I think he meant was that he thought I had potential and therefore would push me. I just couldn't appreciate this at the time. You would tell me to fasten my seatbelt, wear my glasses, or cut my hair, and I was inclined to do the opposite. (Of course, now I make my own kids fasten their seatbelts and try to talk my son into having longer hair.) I felt that you were trying to control me by telling me what to do, especially when the tone in your voice came on very strong. All I wanted to do was prove that my way was right and yours was wrong. Sal's Barbershop wasn't the place to be with you anymore. I would rather have been with Holden Caulfield in *The Catcher in the Rye*.

I wasn't a coach's or teacher's favorite, and it is clear to me that our relationship was being reflected in all my dealings with male authority figures. There was even a controversy over whether I should be allowed into the camp honor society. They were probably still holding against me the night in the woods at the local canteen when my head counselor's flashlight caught my hand moving down my girlfriend's shirt. My coach at · camp did not want me in and that really hurt me. I never liked criticism, and I seemed to make myself vulnerable to it.

These were the early signs of what I call the "It's Not My Fault Syndrome," which really meant that I viewed the problems in my life as if they must be my fault. There was no grey area, no self forgiveness.

I did better with women. I enjoyed talking to girls more than guys. You were always kind to women. When it came to expressing feelings, I looked to talk with a woman. One of my closest friends was a girl in my class. She always made me feel good about myself. I liked the fact that she wanted to protect me. After basketball practice every day, I went to her house where she made me tuna fish sandwiches. On Friday nights, she was my cheerleader and loyal fan. Also, I still recall how kind and accepting my second grade teacher was. She believed in me and boosted my ego with her positive thinking. She was encouraging without being judgmental. She told me: "If you're driving by my apartment and the bird is in the window then you know I'm home and alive." For many years I would always look until it wasn't there anymore. That made me sad and I felt a great loss.

I would go sit nearby at the Roslyn Duck Pond and embrace my memory of Mrs. Gunderson. I was elevated by her. She and Clara always made me feel like I mattered. Clara was Mom's confidant and had a special place in our family. She came from West Virginia and loved when her sons would come over. They were football stars and it was as if they were my older brothers. When they would leave I would get into bed with Clara and watch the Mets games. She liked close low scoring games. I remember the days when TV's were small and black and white and there were limited channels. Life was simpler in the later fifties and early sixties. People were excited to watch *Million Dollar Movie*. Suddenly we had the *Wonderful World of Walt Disney* and color TV.

At times I heard your voice and expressions coming out in my behavior with my friends, and was uncomfortable to think that I could be a clone of you. Although I wanted to believe there was a difference in our personalities, it was clear to me that my ego was as large as yours, if not larger. Being loved by people was very important to me. I was too concerned with what people thought of me. Therefore, I kept my feelings in and tried not to let people know I was vulnerable. I liked to be "on" and to project a secure image, just the way you seemed to be able to do.

I used to be critical of you for not being able to say no to the demands of the world and put up your boundaries, but I am no better. There was always the feeling that this quality in me bothered you a great deal, almost as if perhaps you knew you might also have the same tendency. As you can now see, I believe that interpretation to be true, but I am interested in hearing your response.

You indeed became someone I began to take for granted. I continued to feel guilty for pushing you away, but I needed to, and in a typically adolescent style: arrogant and snotty.

Mom had a way of always letting me know what a great father, analyst, and person you were, and this probably contributed even more to my being threatened by you. I wanted Mom to worship me and forget about you, although it was nice that she was so proud of you. This could only be appreciated during one of my more mature and secure moments. How could I ever live up to what she perceived you to be? I would get tired of her quoting your opinions on life to me as if they were being handed down from Mt. Olympus.

You were, at least the way I perceived you, a modest man whose achievements seemed to be communicated to me through Mom. After reading one of your previous letters, I now know that part of your modesty was intended to minimize my feelings of competitiveness. I think you know that Mom's idealization of you made it more difficult for me. Then again, I must admit I never did express much of an interest and ask you directly. Furthermore I was so conceited that I could not understand how you could be so private about your success. Similarly, I couldn't comprehend how you could function with so few friends while I needed to be everyone's friend. We were so different; how could we be father and son? (I was busy being Peter Pan, not really wanting to grow up, and you were Captain Hook, getting in my way.)

I remember my friends being envious of my situation in that you always fulfilled my material desires. It became something else I would just come to expect from you, and it also kept you on the pedestal. If you did not buy me what I wanted, there was the feeling that Mom would in the long run. I was not someone who wanted very much at this time.

Sometimes I was embarrassed having more than my friends. There was no need to go to Hildebrandt's, the local candy and ice cream store. Our pantry was the local hangout with all its various assortments of junk food. Bazooka bubble gum was the favorite item. Those chocolate chip cookies from Horn and Hardart where not too shabby either. I had the satisfaction of turning my friends on to it. But I also had the feeling of not wanting to be labeled the spoiled rich kid. My public image was extremely important to me. I felt defensive and justified my material acquisitions by emphasizing to my friends how happy it made you to give me things. Although I think this was true, my real concern was my public image.

However, my good fortune came at a price, because I was always uneasy asking you for money or material things. How would I ever break away? Was it hard for you? You must have known how uncomfortable I felt. It is hard to be angry at someone who has been so good to you. Even though you never held money over my head, I felt you liked to have control over the kinds of things I would want to buy. Why not, you were paying for it. That's the point, and it definitely was not as satisfying having things I didn't buy for myself. This is probably why I asked for so little; it was meaningless if I could not do it on my own.

My material desires were not very conservative as I got older. You always seemed modest and somewhat sparing when it came to yourself, but generous when you would give to others. Your repertoire of cars and later interest in clothes seemed to be your only real extravagances.

I admired the fact that you enjoyed your life and would travel. We always went on great family vacations, but it's too bad I never appreciated them. You seemed to be able to do what you wanted and not worry about money. I could never imagine myself able to have that kind of freedom and security. It was not until later that I could appreciate that side of you. I marvel at how you love life and try to live it to the maximum, and still be such a thoughtful man.

When I was with some of my friends, I realized that not everyone was in my financial position. It was hard to understand why they had to worry about what to order in a restaurant. Even buying clothes was a chore for me, and to this day you are probably wearing those sweaters of mine that I have never worn. You always seemed more interested in how I looked than I did. It was embarrassing going to Bloomingdale's with my father because it was just another reminder of how dependent I was on you. The only thing I seemed to have over you was my height. Going shopping meant more time together and you telling me what I needed. My best friend seemed to appreciate my situation more than I, and he would come shopping with us and live vicariously through me. Again came that feeling that you might have the wrong son. It was all so tedious and I just could not tolerate anything that made me need you. Material things symbolized my dependency on you.

One of the things I liked about my relationship with my best friend at the time was that he needed me. He was the shy, domestic and meticulous one; I was the social butterfly who brought him out of himself. He was much shorter than I was and people often referred to us as Mutt and Jeff. It was important for me to have a sidekick. We were so close that we came up with our own private language. You and Mom even developed a friendship with his parents because of us and that relationship has continued.

My self-esteem was clearly enhanced by our friendship. It was nice having someone always telling me how great I was and wanting to take care of me, particularly when I felt inadequate. We were protective of each other and held our own secrets. When my back was bad after a basketball game, he was always there to help me get dressed. I needed a best friend who made me feel unique. There were times it was hard for me to share that with a third party without experiencing it as an intrusion. One could best summarize our relationship by the fact that he would make me lunch and do the dishes, while in return I helped him to feel more comfortable around other people. It's so nice to have someone rely on you for something. When we went ice skating at Skateland, I would embrace all the people and he loved watching me do that.

When I read the stock market page now, I chuckle because I remember finding it difficult to understand why a doctor would read Business Week. Money seemed like a subject having no relevance to real life. It had nothing to do with helping people. Easy for me to say, since I never had to worry about it. What a naive perception of life on my part. I regret that you sheltered me from this aspect of life as I didn't feel prepared to deal with the hard reality of being on my own in the world and managing my own money. Money always appeared so secretive in our house. You and my brother-in-law talked about it but I never felt like a valuable contributor. I never had an allowance as far as I can remember.

Because you were a permissive father it was hard to take advantage of you, as you put so much trust and responsibility back on me. And, of course, I did not always meet your expectations, particularly once when a girlfriend slept in my bedroom overnight and I made sure Clara, would not see her in the morning. You never knew about that little escapade. There were also the nights my friends would come over when you were not at home so they could have some casual teenage sex. If we could get a dry-hump, that was usually satisfying, but once in a while a girl might even let you feel her up—as long as you had the right lines at your fingertips. My favorite line would be, "Do you want to come up to my room and see my Buddha?" Remember that ugly thing that used to sit in my room?

I spent one whole summer hanging out in my bedroom with a girl, and she also made me lunches. You never did like her. Toward the end of high school when sex got more sophisticated, it was even more exciting getting a hand-job in the car. This sounds like *True Confessions*, but you might as well know I was not the perfect son.

I had trouble with our having a housekeeper because I was uncomfortable having someone else take care of me. It was undoubtedly easier that way but I could not even let her make my bed without feeling guilty about how dependent and helpless I was. Many times I would make my own bed and pick up my clothes. She was always part of the family and I had an investment in keeping it that way. When Clara said, "Turn the bed a loose," I knew it was time to get my ass out of bed. Everybody needs a Clara in their life.

It always hurt me to see the disappointment in your face each time I would get into trouble at school. We seemed to be growing further apart. Basketball was my life but you continued to try to discourage me from taking it so seriously by telling me that someday other things would take precedence. It was no different from your asking me if there could be anything else important in life other than sports and my response being, "Like what?" Let's face it, if your opinions did not conform to mine, then forget it. Basketball was the only thing that made me feel significant and shielded me from my failures in school. It became too important to me.

It seemed the only thing that mattered to me was how to get into the gym to play some basketball. Anything I could use to impress you was important to me and athletics seemed to be the thing I was good at. Let's call a spade a spade; I surely was not doing it in the classroom. Those feelings of being useless and incompetent continued, except for my athletic success. What would I have done without sports? It scares me to think about it. It is vital to have one thing you are really good at, yet dangerous to put all your eggs in one basket. There is greatness inside every child and their job is to figure out what that is, dig it out, and give it to the world.

One thing I definitely was not good at was working with my hands. This was a source of great embarrassment, so I would try to avoid any situation that could expose my clumsy hands. I never remember doing creative things with my hands or even expressing an interest in it. There was a time I worked on a construction job for my father-in-law and fell asleep on the job. I was better off collecting cardboard at the factory the summer before. Today my own children are better with puzzles than I am. I never had the patience or concentration. It also did not come easy for me and therefore I shrank from it.

Board games always intimidated me because I lacked the ability to comprehend the directions. In addition, I had trouble retaining the information and became distracted. If I had played football how could I ever learn the plays? I needed someone to walk it through with me to reduce my anxiety. My emotions always interfered with my performance and flooded my ability to function. To this day our relationship has been more cerebral. This has been a source of great sensitivity over the years. I always admired fathers and sons who could work on projects together that involved their hands. It never has been clear to me whether I didn't participate in this sort of activity because of lack of interest or lack of skill. Those two reasons are not really mutually exclusive. But we did have more of a gift for gab than other fathers and sons. I was surprised that you and Pop did things together that involved using your hands. Why didn't we?

All of this makes me wonder about Jared and me. What if he is mechanically inclined? Will we have things in common? I feel apprehensive about this. The thought of disappointing my son is an uncomfortable one. If he comes to me and asks for help I want to be able to come through.

You always seemed to know so much about everything and sometimes I really feel I did not take advantage of it. I just never asked enough questions. It was hard for me to admit that I did not have all the answers. That male ego can be impossible. I always admired people who could raise their hands in class and admit to not understanding the material. You could follow directions and do whatever you set your mind to do. At times it seemed you had the patience of a saint. I needed to develop that mental toughness. I hope some of it rubs off over the years. Here I am being the ambivalent son—one minute being very critical of you and the next doing just the opposite. I was torn between idealizing you and putting you down.

One of my most disturbing memories from high school centers on the night you got angry with me for being such an irresponsible student. In a fit of temper you said I would never make it to college with my study habits. To this day that comment lives with me. I was upset and hurt when you said that to me. It is not a meaningless coincidence that to this day I still have a recurring dream that I did not take the last class or exam to graduate from high school. I even have dreams that I never really finished my doctoral dissertation. That's probably why I was the first one in my class to finish it. Maybe I was afraid your prophecy about me would come true. I have been obsessed with staying ahead and always liked the fact that people would say I was so accomplished for my age. But also, Mom let me know that you were always seen as someone who had achieved a great deal for your age, so maybe I just had to match that. Both interpretations have their value.

Your initial threat about my never graduating may have been the primary motivation behind my ambition to make something of myself. It was probably exactly what I needed at the time. There is something to be said for a good kick in the ass. I certainly wanted to prove you wrong. Although it felt like a put-down at the time, on some level I knew it was true. One way to avoid failure is to stay ahead of yourself. I fear if I slow down, time will catch up with me.

That's what happened when it came to basketball; I was starting as a freshman and benched as a senior. How ironic that I became one of those seniors on the bench and had to watch a young sophomore take over my position. That was a painful time, particularly when

Dee, my girlfriend, brought her friends to watch me play and I sat on the bench. The only experience worse than this was in the early 1960s being out pitched by Chicky Strauss and having senior camp lose to junior camp for the first and last time. I felt like crawling into a hole and never coming out. The ghost of my basketball days ended too soon. Those experiences never leave you. My learning problems made the basketball too important. It all caught up.

The decline of my basketball career happened to coincide with the time all my friends started driving. I was one of the last to drive because I had failed my road test a couple of times. My earlier fear of blowing my Bar Mitzvah lines had turned into a deeper concern over whether I would spend my life being a loser, watching everyone else make it in life. I remember throwing things across my room after failing my driver's test. I was anxious the first time and I forgot to put on my eye glasses. My friends and other classmates were getting into college and I had no idea which, or even if any, schools would accept me. Those SAT scores were nothing to write home about. I was afraid of letting you down while all the other fathers would be proud of their sons.

You had the son with the undiagnosed Attention Deficit Disorder now referred to as ADD. I was clearly having post traumatic stress. One never gets over their ADD. You only learn to negotiate it. I felt like a failure at everything but lunch and sports.

You were a very intimidating force. When you felt strongly about an issue you were hard to deal with. There was a tone in your voice that sounded authoritarian and all-knowing. There was nothing worse than a lecture from you. This was one issue on which I was able to get Mom's support. At times it seemed everyone else was wrong and crazy. You came out smelling like a rose and it was hard to play you against Mom. Whenever she supported me, I would have a sense of power over you. But I always felt Mom went with the underdog, which was to my advantage because then I needed her and I think she liked that. For a change I was in control and she would not be idealizing you. It's hard to remember specific incidents and I may be exaggerating my perceptions so this could all be wishful thinking.

Sometimes I felt guilty about the attention Mom would give me. I was afraid you thought she was spending all your hard-earned money on me. At times, particularly around birthdays and holidays, I became aware that maybe you felt cheated and slighted. It always seemed as if I would get more than you, and I was not sure that was fair. What made it even worse was the fact that when you would get a gift, it was with your own money. You were the one working every day and maybe we all just took you for granted. It was uncomfortable for me sometimes to watch you, "good ole Daddy Warbucks," hand out money to various family members. I actually found myself feeling sorry for you.

Somehow I think you are going to be surprised by this, all of which, by the way, reminds me of a comment you made to me during this past year when you said half seriously, "What's the point in doing a lot of things with your kids when they don't remember them?" I took that seriously, and it made me wonder if you had many moments of feeling unappreciated over the years. It did seem as though you were being taken advantage of at times. How could I not feel some guilt about having negative feelings toward you, and at the same time let you buy me a car for high school graduation? First, you bought me a used white Chevy Impala, and later it was the sporty maroon-colored Firebird which I then drove to college in my sophomore year.

My basketball days were certainly numbered and my stardom was going by the wayside. I thought my problem was that I had become too comfortable being a star. I should have stayed with the cross country. It kept me in shape for basketball. The test of a true athlete, or true anything, is to be disciplined and follow through on your original goals. This lesson was probably a blessing in disguise. It's one thing to achieve a goal and another to stay there. The challenge is to maintain the same level of intensity. This is what separates the men from the boys.

As far as I was concerned there was nothing left for me. What would people think of me if I was no longer the basketball star? There would be no reason to know me. Who am I? The feeling is probably no different from the way a celebrity feels. I really felt people knew me only as Donald Cohen, the basketball player. It was becoming clear to me that everyone did not love me, and in fact, some people did not even like me. This was devastating and I felt I was going to be immobilized by this realization. I always identified with David Jansen, who starred in *The Fugitive*, feeling like the great imposter waiting to be exposed. If Superman could only have been Clark Kent, he would have been better off. This was my boyhood masquerade.

This time was a dramatic collapse of my identity, as the cover up for all my inadequacies came to the surface. I was at the height of my vulnerabilities. Hiding from my secret of feeling stupid was becoming more difficult. Life just felt too hard for me. It seemed easier for everyone else. I felt invisible and flawed. I finally let my guard down one night and burst into tears with you and Mom after coming home from a party where the "in" thing was to get stoned, to be a "freak." The times were indeed catching up to me and I did not know where I fit in. I was not a "jock" anymore but I didn't make it as a "freak" either. What does one do when one feels caught in the middle? Could I be at ease as a Protean personality living in such a culture of extremes? I wanted to be flexible because so many parts of me needed to be expressed, but I also wanted to fit in. I felt very alone, without an identity. The hippie movement was emerging and the new popular boy had come home from his summer at Berkley with blonde hair down to his shoulders. The Beatles had changed America. Times have changed, but what is now commonly seen as being a freak or a jock is not much different than when I was in high school. Being one of those in-betweens was a lonely feeling. (My whole dissertation, as you know, was about people in the gray area. And would you believe that I got a card today from the chairperson of my dissertation committee. My past is certainly coming back to me.)

So, I was not the "in" thing anymore. That night after the party was one of the few times I could remember letting you in. My need to be loved was very strong and you were there for me at that moment with no judgments. I cried and you held me. There was that need for you to hold me and listen to what I was going through. How I wanted to resist the idea that I couldn't always be strong. You and Mom were so empathetic.

I became tired of hearing you tell me that I cared too much about what people thought of me, but you were right. My concern was that my friends were talking behind my back. Something in me still could not completely trust and accept your love for me. I would begin to feel close to you and then fear something would happen to take it away.

Then came the night that the neighborhood "freaks" came into our house wanting to get the local has-been sports hero and psychiatrist's son stoned. This would be a monumental achievement for them. We made the careless mistake of not opening the windows. The house really reeked of pot and I will never forget the look on your face when you came home. You were furious and I was scared. All those feelings of your being there for me were gone. The self-fulfilling prophecy had taken its course. I do not know if I have ever seen you so hurt and angry. You seemed totally out of control. I could not believe that you were dialing the police station and that Mom had to stop you. I don't think you ever would have gone through with it anyway. Your reaction seemed so severe and it embarrassed me. My only immediate concern was that you were going to call all the fathers and tell them what happened. Well you did and that really turned me off.

After that, some of those guys never talked to me again and made fun of me. Now I really felt like I didn't fit in. You humiliated me in front of my friends. All I could think of was that your only concern about this was that your image in the community would be shattered. Could you actually have imagined a headline in the paper reading "PSYCHIATRIST'S SON GETS BUSTED IN HIS OWN HOUSE"? If that had happened, it would have been the ultimate humiliation for you. I began to feel more and more that you were not only caught up in what people thought of you but in fact what they would think of me as well.

It almost became a burden to be your son because I felt perfection was expected of me. Everyone expected psychiatrists to be open-minded, but maybe not when it came to their sons. I felt that people saw you as a liberal father, which you were, but you were conservative about certain things. If pot had been more accepted during this time, you would have been all right with it. At times you seemed bound and held captive by traditional morality.

The other side of this was that I was embarrassed for you because of the way you reacted to the situation. I was protective of your public image as the liberal psychiatrist. I was wondering how you could make such a fool of yourself. Being the doctor, you are supposed to have an investment in people seeing you as calm and rational. All I could think of was that you made yourself vulnerable and that people might not look up to you anymore. If they didn't like you, they wouldn't like me. I wanted my friends to think you were great because you were a reflection of me and I was used to all of them liking you. Of course, those particular people really were not my friends, but that didn't stop the feelings. If they thought you were a fool, then they would think the same of me. And even though they were not my true friends, I hated being left out.

Triangles were always hard for me because I always felt I was the one left out. First it was the triangle of you and my sister. In high school, it was the two guys talking about the girls they had sex with and smoking grass, while I sat and stared into space. And I remember those dreadful Friday night card games with me on the sidelines reading magazines. I never felt I could process and follow the rules of the game. Later on, it was you and my brother-in-law talking about business investments while I twiddled my thumbs. The forgotten son or misfit syndrome seemed to be hard to dismiss. When this whole incident occurred a part of me wondered how I could have let you down and been so suggestible. You never seemed to let other people influence you. Interestingly, I think you began to feel the same way about me later on.

It seemed I always had to be "on" and watch what I would say. You seemed so concerned about my image and whether I would embarrass you. You were clearly more concerned about my hair and my clothes than I was. There were times when you seemed obsessed with my physical appearance. I could not understand why you had such an investment in that. There was that time you would not let me go to an affair with you because the sports jacket did not fit right. If I had had it my way, my appearance at the affair might have been a little off, but so what!

There were moments in high school when I felt it would have been easier for me if you had done something else for a living. For all I knew, you were even treating some of my friends and acquaintances in your office. Sometimes it felt like I had no privacy. Our communication was becoming more restricted. There were certain people who thought it was intriguing to have you as a father, and others who felt sorry for me because I could not get away with anything. I remember a friend saying to me once that the only thing doctors are interested in is money. He sure didn't mind getting off on all your fun cars over the years. I'm still convinced he took money from our house. My generation had a tendency to be hypocritical anyway, preaching love and anti-materialism in the late sixties and into the seventies, but we were an arrogant bunch. Many of these people are now working on Wall Street. Look at me, getting defensive and wanting to protect you. It bothered me when people would think it was strange that you were a psychiatrist.

I was just as caught up with what people thought of you as you were about how people felt about me. If my friends thought you did something "cool," I would be proud of it. It was hard to accept being known as an oddball, or at the other extreme, as the son of a perceived god like a psychiatrist. I enjoyed the fact that my friends seemed to be able to relate to you as a regular guy. You became the ordinary father on Sunday mornings when you made breakfast for the family and made your special caviar mixed with onions.

Until I got to know my wife's family, I thought every family sat around at dinner and analyzed everybody and everything. In their family, the TV could be on and light conversation would be going around the table. It was actually refreshing. Often it felt as though everything was analyzed in our house and if I was quiet something had to be wrong with me. Sometimes I just wanted my space and a chair, and nothing more. Why couldn't a feeling just be a feeling?

There seemed to be little room for bad moods or depression without people in the family getting up in arms. My problems became yours and I ended up feeling like I had to take care of you. Whenever I considered putting up my boundaries, there was always that concern about your feelings being hurt. Sometimes I just wanted to be left alone, but I was afraid to say it. Our relationship during this time felt "heavy." You seemed sensitive toward all my moods and I was concerned that you would take what was going on with me personally. You were the man who was expected to understand everything. It was hard to keep my problems from you. I knew it was tough to fake it; you had a way of knowing what was going on with me. Sometimes I would ask myself how I got stuck in a house where everyone thinks so much about everything. What we did have was a lot of communication; I guess you could say we had something many other families did not have. It just seemed extreme at times.

I was getting ready to leave home and it felt like it was time. It was touch and go whether or not I was going to get into college, but I made it. You must have been pretty concerned about that. It was not until the last minute that I knew I was actually going. The thought of moving out seemed too good to be true, although transitions were difficult for me. I felt safer with structure and certainty.

While I write this letter, it's easy to understand how someone can lose touch with their past. Before the process of this book began to unfold, it was as if this time of my life was long forgotten. But ever since I started on this journey with you, many meaningful coincidences have come up. As I started this letter to you, about this particular stage of my life, the strangest thing happened. I was amazed to discover an envelope in the mailbox with my high school return address on it. Would you believe the director of the athletic department just invited me to play in an alumni basketball game, which coincidentally happens to fall on the same day we are scheduled to hear a talk on fathers and sons at the Psychoanalytic Convention? Let's do both, because I want you to come with the kids. I am so excited about the day we will have together. The next day we are going to a Freud/Jung symposium. What a weekend this will be. It's like bringing the past and present together.

How exciting, to the point where it almost feels overwhelming. This will be like living out one of my greatest fantasies. I have always wanted to go back to the high school gym on a Friday night one more time for that last hurrah. How ironic that my arch rival from high school will be playing on the team with me. It feels like an honor that I was asked to participate and was actually moved to tears opening up the envelope.

When I decided to take on this experience with you, it seemed fitting to shave off my beard, go back to wearing contact lenses, and lose weight to help me get back in touch with my past. Now it is literally going to take place. Coincidentally, at thirty-one, I look exactly like I did in high school. I could be anonymous to the people in my present and familiar to those in my past. This all seems too fantastic and borders on being psychic or fictional. But somehow it all feels very real to me. My body is vibrating just writing about it.

In addition to this occurrence came last week's meaningful moment. I met a man who is a psychologist in my hometown. We went to basketball camp together and he said he remembered me as being a fine athlete. My most recent friends have had trouble comprehending that this part of my past ever existed. Now I have a new friend who knew me during this time in my life and we are in the same field. There is now living proof of my past as an athlete. He came at a good time for me since I am seeking new male relationships that can be more open insofar as expressing feelings. I feel excited about the fact that something inside me is beginning to free up. Things seem to be happening at the right time. Timing is a crucial part of one's life. It seems at certain moments now that time never progressed. Maybe life is just feeling more timeless.

The move to college was just what I needed. I had to go forward. The best way to epitomize our relationship toward the end of high school is to cite the time I met Dee in my senior year. She was from a different high school and offered me a breath of fresh air. We would see each other at Howard Johnson's Restaurant after basketball games. I remember her in mini skirts and high knee socks. It separated me from my high school troubles and saved me from being lost at that time. I had to leave her abruptly late one afternoon because I knew you would be mad at me for driving in my sunglasses as the darkness began to set in. You had complete control over me and I was intimidated by you. It was as if I could not function without your constant approval. Would I ever experience my "coming-of-age?" I had clearly become this helpless, dependent adolescent with no mind of my own. What better reason to go off by myself to face the darkness and cruel reality of being in the world alone. I just had to get away from you. It was embarrassing being so dependent.

This seems like a good point to end this letter. Please respond soon.

Love,
Donald

* * *

Dear Donald,

After reading your last letter, I'm a little bewildered. It seems to me I dearly remember the teenage years about which you wrote, and I had thought that I was pretty well plugged into your feelings and experiences during that period. However, I had no idea that you felt so alienated from me as you implied. I knew, of course, that you avoided and resisted my efforts to involve you in the things I enjoyed and was interested in, and I knew that your obsession with sports was derivative of the self-esteem you so readily derived from your precocious excellence. Perhaps, I even contributed to your emotional investment in your athletic achievements because I genuinely shared your pride. It was a thrill to watch you play basketball so well, and more than hold your own with teammates several years your senior when you were just a freshman. I shared your success in an area in which I had never been very successful. My identification with you was gratifying to me and must have reinforced the enormous importance you gave to it.

Much has been written about the son's identification with the father as the vehicle which propels the boy out of the dilemma of his Oedipal rivalry with his father. In the classic model, the boy emulates his father and aspires to success and achievement in terms of the father's perceived values. This didn't happen to you until years later after you left home to go to college and athletics no longer offered you the easy road to distinction. Actually, your fantasies of athletic prowess collapsed while you were still in high school when your early promise faded into frustration and disappointment.

I vividly recall feeling and sharing your pain, anguish and humiliation when you failed to live up to your early promise. You were intimidated by your own grandiose fantasies which were fed by your friends, your coaches, and I guess even your parents. You heartbreakingly labeled yourself a "has-been" by the time you finished your sophomore season.

Herein lies one of the difficult dilemmas of parenthood. On the one hand, a parent is supposed to feel for, empathize with, and communicate a deeply-felt concern for the well-being of the adolescent, as much as for the child. At the same time, the parent is supposed to encourage a gradual process of separation, independence and individuation. To walk the narrow line between over-protecting, and thus inhibiting emotional growth and maturation, and encouraging separation without it being perceived as rejection, is an almost impossible task which goes on over a period of years.

In chimpanzees, this dilemma is rather crudely exhibited. The young chimp clings to the mother for several years but at some point the mother harshly pushes it away, as if to say, "You're old enough to be more independent now." As well as can be judged, the young chimp, so abruptly rejected, seems to handle it without lasting trauma. Alas, human children are presumed to be more delicate. I wonder . . .

In an effort to understand what happened to us during your adolescence, Donald, I've pondered long and hard about my own adolescence. Perhaps it is the distance of time and the fact that memory is so easily corrupted by self-serving needs, but what I recall most vividly about my adolescent perception of my father was his devotion to the well-being of his family and my eagerness to be worthy of his devotion. Of course l I'm talking about guilt.

My guilt-ridden generation was brought up in the tradition of guilty devotion to parents on the one hand, and educated to believe that parents are ultimately responsible and blameworthy for all of the ills and failures of their children. The latter, I'm convinced, gave rise to a "me" generation, relatively insensitive to the needs and feelings of parents, and convinced of the righteousness of the devotion to self. Like Dr. Frankenstein, we created a monster and now we're complaining.

You understand, Donald, that I am talking in generalities. I believe I was wise or strong enough to rebel somewhat against the inequity of what I am describing. In a variety of ways and on numerous occasions, I was able to insist that your mother and I had needs and feelings which demanded consideration. Compared to many of your peers, you were a good kid. But you and I both see many young adults professionally who are largely incapable of relating to other people's needs or are intolerant of them. When I grew up, such people were viewed. with moral indignation as selfish, self-centered, lacking in moral strength and character. Nowadays, these poor narcissistic souls are viewed as victims of unloving or neglectful parents. This is called "not being judgmental." Bullshit!

I have to emphasize that when I describe my recalled perception of my father, I'm now fully aware that my perception back then was naive. I have no illusions that my father was as selfless as I then believed him to be. He was behaving as people always have, in accord with his perception of his own appropriate or desired destiny. He certainly was governed by the same needs for self-aggrandizement and self-vindication that motivates us all. What is important in the context of the current subject is the fact that I, like many of my contemporaries, conceived of myself as having to please and be worthy of a virtuous parent.

An extremely successful businessman, sixty years old, recently consulted me because he felt shattered and bewildered by what happened between him and his thirty-six year old son. The young man, gay, flamboyant and expansive, worked for his father and was receiving compensation equivalent to one hundred fifty thousand dollars a year. As the father described it, his son had never been very productive at work, but was nevertheless overindulged by his father who was eager to seduce him into a more constructive lifestyle. Although their relationship had been very stressed for many years, the father was now overwhelmed by feelings of anguish and despair because the son was habituated to cocaine. And in a recent fit of cocaine intoxication, he threatened to kill the father for failing to give him a large sum of money to which he felt entitled. The father refused, he said, because of his unwillingness to subsidize his son's self-destructive habit.

In the course of describing these incidents and the background of his relationship with his son he spoke with tearful sentimentality about his reverence for his own very aged father. But he went on to elaborate that his father never demanded of him and pressured him the way he had with his son. As a consequence, he felt responsible for his son's problems and failures. He protested that he always meant well in spite of the fact, he guiltily acknowledged, that he was motivated largely by pride. He wanted to be proud of his son, and he wanted his son to perform in such a way that he could be proud of him. This, the young man obviously resents.

But what else can a father do? Can he do other than to encourage a son to try to succeed within the framework of the father's own values? Whatever your verdict about the particular values involved, people are enslaved by their own version of their culture's value system. Within each person's concept of good and bad, desirable and undesirable, good and desirable is believed to be consistent with happiness and well-being. Perhaps this man's values might be viewed by some as "too materialistic," too driven by the competitive need for the acquisition of money, status, and the illusion of power. He would probably acknowledge that from his present vantage point these are valid criticisms. But success is a relative term, meaningfully applicable only in a competitive context. Competitive means that there have to be winners and losers. This man was powerfully motivated from his childhood onward to be a winner. He now appears to be reproaching himself for wanting his son to be a winner too.

Of course I'm aware that the guilt I was hearing had much more complicated origins than I am elaborating. But the point is nevertheless clearly made that a parent can only apply his or her own values in bringing up children, and the benevolence of that parenting can only be judged from the frame of reference provided by those values.

On a recent weekend, Mom and I visited some friends in Palm Beach. It was a social weekend and we passed a great deal of time with a variety of people who spend their winters in this enclave of wealth and luxury. In one way or another, many of the men, all successful and wealthy, seem to be preoccupied with the age-old question, "What is life's meaning, what is it all about, and what is it all for?" These men are in their late fifties or sixties, they've all succeeded in building their own small empires, and they are all either retired, wrestling with the inevitability of retirement, or committed to avoiding retirement for as long as possible. These men are all "winners" as defined by society, insofar as they have acquired money, which after all is the way the score is kept in business.

But what is the point of accumulating money, unless like the traditional miser, there is ecstasy in counting it. People with money tend to want to spend it in ways that attest to their success. Having surpassed the point in the accumulation of wealth that provides for every creature comfort and pleasure, the field expands to include the demonstration of aesthetic superiority and display. This isn't cynical. These very men who are in the throes of what I am describing are freely able to acknowledge what I am describing.

I believe this all reflects the universal human condition. Human beings, by deeply rooted nature, are restless and dissatisfied. After all, are we not the species which is committed to the pursuit of the better way, the improved mousetrap, the more effective means to harness nature for our own pleasure and as the more effective means of destroying our planet? Maybe this restless dissatisfaction is what moved our forebears out of the trees, onto the savanna and ultimately into the cities of our contemporary civilization. Students of evolution tell us that organic evolution among homosapiens has been powerfully reinforced by cultural evolution in the history of recent centuries. Even our ape cousins are characterized by their remarkable curiosity, their apparent eagerness to learn new techniques of adaptation. Cultural evolution refers to the transmission of learned behavior from one generation to another.

For all of our arrogance, human beings have not overcome the humbling reality of our mortality. From the invention or inspired wisdom which enables some of us to believe in an afterlife, hopefully in heaven, or reincarnation in endless pursuit of the ultimate utopia, people find it hard to escape the confines of their limited life span. Don't "winners," after devoting a lifetime of tireless pursuit of competitive excellence, deserve a better fate than to just die like everyone else? For that matter, don't "losers" deserve a better break in the next round?

Fortunately or unfortunately, there is a way out of this dilemma. Doesn't the simple amoebae enjoy immortality; by endlessly splitting in half, it continues to live in the bodies of its offspring. Can it be that having children affords us the opportunity to emulate the lowly amoebae? Indeed it does. Anthropologists tell us that knowledge of paternity is a recent acquisition in human history, that some primitive cultures "discovered" in the twentieth century had no such awareness. They didn't even know that there is a relationship between coitus and procreation. How sad for those primitive men.

On the other hand, I was preoccupied with my evolving sexuality and my struggles to deal with my doubts about my virility. I was also exposed to much bragging among my peers about their sexual exploits. In high school, at least, I suspect that most of them were as virginal as I was. One incident stands out in my memory because the recollection of it for years afterward informed me of my tremendous insecurity in this area. I must have been seventeen because I was driving a car. A girl, whom my friends and I thought was beautiful, made it apparent that she liked me and wanted to go out with me. I was surprised and delighted. I asked her out and during the course of the evening I parked the car in an area overlooking the ocean that was the accepted locale for "making out." I still recall how scared I was. We necked and timidly petted, but she made it very apparent that she was eager and game for more. I remember being enormously aroused and confused by it. I hid behind a pretentious facade of respecting her and, after all, there were plenty of girls I could go out with if all I wanted was sex. She was cool to me thereafter and I somehow knew I had turned her off.

It wasn't until my first year at college that I lost my virginity with a girl whom I don't even remember now, but I recall running out so fast when it was over that I never even said good-bye. I felt guilty about having been so insensitive to her feelings and it bothered me for some period of time thereafter.

You don't mention, Donald, concern about the size of your penis during adolescence. In my experience and from my later work with adolescents, most teenage boys worry that their penis is smaller than other boys'.

In any event, concerns and insecurities about sex and ambition were private and alienating. Obviously, the sexual preoccupations were totally unacceptable and I think I would have done almost anything to conceal these secret thoughts and fantasies from my father. Even as a young adult, I was threatened by my father's possible discovery that I had a sexual life.

Nor would I have freely shared my self-doubts and fears of failure in other areas with my father because I would not have wanted to disappoint him. To be confident is to be manly; to be insecure is to be unmanly. I wanted for my father to be proud of me. I never realized this before, but I was indeed alienated from my father in those years to the extent that I couldn't share my deepest concerns with him.

I was unaware that my behavior with you during your adolescence conveyed the impression that I was unapproachable on the subject of sex. Actually, I recall numerous times when I would try to initiate discussions about sex but you seemed unresponsive. Assuming that you had started to masturbate early in your teens I remember trying to reassure you that it was a natural way for a boy to express his sexual needs when opportunities for actual sexual contact is denied. Of course, a father would hardly be likely to be open about his own sexual experiences in talking with his son, so why would the son assume that it is permissible for him to be open with his father about sex.

In all the years of our relationship, the one outstanding incident that I most regret was the one you describe concerning your "pot party." I wish I had known better, but I didn't. Though as a psychiatrist in the sixties I was much more aware of the spreading use of marijuana than most fathers, we were still governed by the traditional view that the use of pot, like other illicit substances, was exceedingly dangerous and addictive and a manifestation of serious personality disorder. Professionally, I was already dealing with the consequences of the use of other more potent hallucinogenic substances such as LSD and the growing popularity of hallucinogens among adolescents was terrifying. I had witnessed the experimental use of hallucinogens at the New York State Psychiatric Institute because of the early interest in the similarity of the effects of these drugs to some of the manifestations of schizophrenia. No one believed at that time that in a few years kids would be ingesting these frightening drugs for "kicks."

In addition, at the time this incident occurred, I believe I was uptight about other evidence of your rebelliousness, but I can't now recall specifics. I do remember being aware that some of the kids with whom you grew up were using these drugs and discussing it with you. I never suggested that you avoid them, but I did emphasize that they were not to smoke pot in our house.

I recall now with embarrassment, how frightened and enraged I was when your mother and I returned home that Saturday evening to find the house reeking unmistakably of that "dreaded stuff." Perhaps I felt guilty for having been too permissive. I consciously wanted to impress you with how strongly I felt about what I perceived was your betrayal of our trust. I was genuinely infuriated, but I never would have actually called the police. I was frustrated because you wouldn't tell me who the other boys were. I "pretended" to be calling the police in order to coerce you into telling me.

I felt an obligation to tell their parents, and if I succeeded in alienating them from you, that was okay too. Never before or since that incident have I felt so totally frustrated, inadequate, and infuriated with you. Needless to say if I knew then what I know now, I'm sure I would have reacted differently. So what else is new?

It was exciting to return with you to the Wheatley Gym last Friday night to the site of your high school glory and later heartbreak. Isn't it amazing how relaxed and effective you were on the basketball court, and especially at the foul line now that the pressure was off. Before the game started, and in retrospect, most of the afternoon before when we were in the city together, you were extremely tense and preoccupied. I guess the past harbors frightening ghosts for all of us.

Adolescence is usually defined as that period of life between childhood and adulthood during which those skills required for the responsibilities of maturity are acquired. This is viewed as a transitional stage between the dependency of childhood and the independence of adulthood. With the increasing complexity of civilization, this period of dependency is significantly prolonged because the skills required for maturity often take much longer to acquire. Although adolescence is often equated with the teenage years, it actually lasts much longer, especially when college and graduate education are pursued.

The Jewish tradition of Bar Mitzvah, roughly concurrent with puberty and sexual maturity, was conceived as a ritual to commemorate entry into manhood. Perhaps in primitive times, the teenage boy was able to take his place among the men who were engaged in tilling the soil or tending their animal herd. In recent centuries, the traditional Bar Mitzvah ritual has become an anachronistic symbol, commemorating the onset of sexual potency long before the young man has achieved social and economic maturity.

Effective participation in a technologically advanced society requires highly specialized skills which take many years to acquire, thus increasingly prolonging the period required for education and training. You and I were both married and young parents before we were completely financially independent. This enormously complicates our conception of adolescence and inevitably introduces conflicts and confusion as we struggle to reconcile our physical maturity and even our social maturity with continuing financial and economic dependence on parents. How can we feel that we are truly men as long as we are not yet fully able to sustain ourselves and our wives and children financially.

In view of the complexity of the problems and the prolonged duration of these inconsistencies, is it any wonder that these years are so often colored by intense emotional conflicts? You and I were fortunate, Donald, compared to many people we both knew in your generation and mine. My father must have been intuitively sensitive to these issues because he tried so hard to minimize the inevitable indignity of my financial dependence upon him. He was always generous, enabling me to continue my professional studies, even though I was married at a relatively early age and a father a few years later, without serious concern about financially supporting my family. As well as I can remember, he never reminded me of his generosity or my dependency or used it as a weapon or instrument of control in our relationship. To the best of my ability, I tried to do the same for you.

In spite of my father's best efforts, however, I vividly recall my enormous desire to be completely self-sustaining. This must have reflected the underlying emotional conflicts I felt about the incompleteness of my maturity. It was as if my adult facade was a pretense, concealing the underlying perception of myself as a boy.

Although it would appear that I've gone significantly beyond the teenage years about which you wrote in your last letter, I do so because I think that is the only way I can understand the emotional turmoil you describe in those years. There is a tendency to color our recollections of the distant past with the emotions of more recent and clearly remembered events. It occurred to me that perhaps this might partially explain the disparity between your recollection and mine of your teen-age years. The alienation you felt, I believe, was much more intense for several years after you left for college and this may color your recollections of the earlier period.

Having said this, I am probably already anticipating your next letter.

Love,
Dad

The Trials of Parenthood

A parent would say it is not easy being a parent and a child would say it is not easy being a child.

People naturally brag about their successes and minimize or rationalize their failures.

* * *

June, 1982

Dear Dad,

I have been thinking about my most recent letter to you and it is true that some of the perceptions about our relationship during this time were clouded by circumstances which occurred later in my life. My childhood Garden of Eden seemed to abandon me rather abruptly and all of a sudden I felt my innocence was being stripped away by the demands of adolescence. As a young child, my life was mostly here-and-now oriented and I expected my needs to receive immediate gratification. I resented having to shift myself into a future-oriented universe. Your presence as a "successful" man became an inevitable threat to my naive security. In writing letters to you through the eyes of an adult, it is possible to exaggerate perceptions, but I felt what was written was not meant to be an either/or commentary on the kind of father you were during my adolescence. Of course, some of my judgments about you were my own projections stimulated by anxiety about whether I could ever stand up on my own two feet. As the years progressed, so did the expectations of me. The decisions you make after early childhood begin to seem as though they involve higher stakes.

During my recent vacation, I had a dream about you which speaks to the more positive side of how I remember our relationship during my high school years. In the dream you were a bartender in the school gymnasium and just a regular guy taking part in my life with my friends. It reminds me of how you used to come outside and shoot baskets with all the boys. There were also many times when it was just the two of us.

Whenever you were in the arena where I was the star, you were never experienced as a threat. As in the dream, you were just a regular guy. The problem was what you represented to me when we were not playing ball. Yes, there were close moments between us, but you knew more than I did and you had already proven yourself in the world. As long as you were coaching my Little League team or being one of the den leaders for Cub Scouts, I could handle you.

One of the reasons my transition from early childhood was difficult is that I never considered life to be anything other than unconditional love, with me on the receiving end. I just expected that the world would revolve around my needs. Parents were there to make the child happy. After all, life was supposed to be fair as long as it was on the child's terms.

A child learns early on how to manipulate his or her environment to get what he or she wants. Even when you left me for those two months during my early years, I apparently was determined to not talk to you upon your return. The guilt inside of you had begun to take over. This gives the child the perfect opportunity to take advantage of that and the parent so often bends over backwards to please the child.

You probably overcompensated because of the guilt brought on as a result of the separation. It only took me thirty-one years to forgive you, Dad!

The problem with all of this is that it creates an unrealistic environment when it comes to dealing with the rest of the world. By the time I reached adolescence I couldn't cope with people, particularly coaches and teachers, telling me what to do, unless it was on my terms.

Of course, now that I am a parent, I find myself suffering from the guilt as well. When Dee and I took our vacation to Saint Barth's, I found myself feeling apprehensive about how our leaving would affect the children. Would Jared do the same thing to me that I did to you? (And you weren't even away on a vacation.) When we came back, Emily let me know that she forgot what I looked like while I was gone. But somehow children survive and the world goes on without parents.

Parents are not always needed by their children. What a blow for the ego, but also a relief. It is important to communicate that we don't always need them either. Anyway, a vacation preserves our sanity for ourselves and for our children. They also need a vacation from us.

It's easier to say now, but maybe we are better off if parents are more selfish and don't try to accommodate their children all of the time. Now that I am a parent, it is easier to recognize that I have needs too and have to find a balance between my own needs and those of my children. Maybe children aren't so delicate after all. I am convinced now that the more responsibility you give children early on the better off they will be in terms of self-esteem. This is particularly true when it comes to learning how to make decisions. One needs to feel one has some control, if not complete control, over one's own fate; we want that sense of mastery.

You identified so much with my pain and wanted to protect me from it. I had trouble learning to accept that. Naturally I find myself doing the same thing with my kids. When Emily is left out of a triangle with her girlfriends, it is as if I am going through the pain. I feel so helpless. When she called me from school today crying and asking to come home, I had to work very hard to make sure I didn't run to school. Seeing Emily hurting was tearing me up inside, but I knew she had to learn how to deal with her fears. I was glad that we had the chance to talk on the phone because I had a break in my day. When she came home this evening and I asked her what was wrong, naturally I had trouble getting much response, even though I spent the day hurting for her. What else is new, as you say? What more can a parent do? It is hard to find that balance between wanting your child to be happy and preparing them for the harsh realities of growing up.

In the Old World, the parents had control over their children and children had to obey. There was no other choice but to act on their instruction. Guilt was non-existent for the parent. Then your generation became parents and wanted to give us everything that you did not have. Was all that freedom good for us, or did it perhaps just reinforce our infantile narcissistic wishes. I must say that having parents with an Old World philosophy would have been very unappealing.

Having young children made me realize just how self-centered human beings can be. Did I ever consider the fact that maybe when you and I were out throwing the baseball around or going to a Cub Scout meeting, you might have had a rough day at work? I don't think you ever would have said "no" to me if I needed you because my needs seemed to come first. Maybe if you had said "no" more often, it would have given me permission to do the same thing with you and other people. Sometimes you just did not want to be with Pop and maybe he felt the same way about you.

I began to expect people around me other than you to give me the same kind of treatment. Perhaps I will do the same with my children, or maybe our generation will strike a balance between the last two. Can a relationship between a parent and a child reflect mutual respect? You really wanted me to be happy and make things right for me. I appreciated the fact that you wanted for me to have all the advantages that you didn't have. But was there a price?

The feeling of entitlement is so true for many of us. You also had needs, and looking back I feel it would have been in my best interest to have been reminded of that more often. I needed to know from you that you can't always get what you want. We are a generation which is restless and hard to satisfy. It's never good enough. We're motivated by extravagant desires for what we can do or get next. Maybe that's true of all people and has nothing to do with a generation gap.

So much of me wanted to believe that life was limitless and I should be able to do only what I wanted to do. In addition I felt that I should have whatever I wanted. Recently, I had to contend with the fact that Emily spotted a stuffed animal in the pharmacy that cost twenty-two dollars and she really thought I should buy it for her no matter what it cost. I actually struggled for a moment, and then as she carried on with her tears I realized how absurd I was being. There had to be some boundaries, and my guilt about not making her happy would only be a disservice to her later on. I just had to live with the fact that my own wish to be seen as "Daddy Wonderful" would have to go by the wayside for a while. One realizes that children get over their disappointments and life goes on for them, business as usual.

Just two weeks ago, Emily did not want to go to school because she did not feel like it. At that moment I was prepared to say to her that I had to go to a meeting that I didn't want to go to. We both ended up fulfilling our obligations. When Emily asks me to not go to work, halfway out the door, it becomes obvious to me that she actually believed I should do that and be with her. It becomes hard to say good-bye. How dare I disappoint my daughter.

You always felt that burdening a child with your needs was wrong. I agree with you up to a point, but you felt so strongly about it that I am not sure it was helpful to me. I needed to know that you had ordinary drives and that girls were once as important to you as they were to me. Even Santa Claus has sex and goes to the bathroom. We never seemed to joke about sex. I needed that personal connection with you. You did always give me sound advice about girls and sex, but I needed more of that personal sharing about all your fears and insecurities growing up. It was not important to know the intimate sexual details of your life with Mom, but how you felt during various stages of your sexual development would have been important to me.

At least now I can say there is a genuine curiosity about those experiences which were most important in shaping the way you viewed the world. Probably, as I look back, if you had tried to do this with me earlier I might have felt it was intrusive, but of course, not doing it gave me the option of saying you don't care. You and I both know it's hard for a parent to win when it comes to pleasing his child. "You're damned if you do and damned if you don't."

Dad, you talked to me about many things and we did a lot together, but I just don't remember enough of those heart-to-heart open discussions about being a man. In addition, I never knew when you might have needed your own space. That's probably the last thing on an adolescent boy's mind.

During my pubescent years, you seemed so separate from me. You were definitely the adult and I was the kid. Your assumptions about my not being able to handle your needs may have been a misconception. I am not saying I would have wanted a role reversal between us, but maybe I needed a little more of a balance. The sharing that we are doing now might have helped me earlier on to feel less afraid about being a man and could have alleviated those moments of feeling alone. Now I know that even my own father could feel many of the same things I did. It makes me feel closer to you.

Just last week, a father and his eleven-year-old boy were doing the same thing with each other in my office and it moved me to tears. The feeling between a father and son during that time of special sharing is similar to how I feel with a patient when we both reach that moment of sharing some feelings that we have in common. When a personal experience like that occurs, all of a sudden one feels less isolated.

I feel you were a wonderful father and had good intentions, but I always felt as though I was the more open one in the relationship. You appeared awesome and invincible. Remember, Dad, this was a perception through the eyes of an adolescent, not an adult.

Maybe it is time for a society in which neither parent nor child has complete control of the other's destiny. I feel badly sometimes that children today have so much control over their parents, particularly now that I am on the other side. Somehow that does not seem right, but neither does going backwards. There must be a middle ground between too much flexibility and severe rigidity. As I said before, the plight of a parent is a difficult one, but so it may be for a child as well.

I remember a man I worked with asking his child to do a chore for him on a Saturday. His son had agreed earlier to help him during the week. Something came up during the week for the parent, and he said that it could now only be done on Saturday. The child got upset and said, "That's my day off," to which the father replied, "From what?" The child responded by saying to his father, "You may get up to go to work every day, but I also get up at six every morning to go to school, and that is work to me." And then the boy said, "At least you get paid for your work."

One of the reasons I had trouble in high school is that I could never see how I would ever, later on in life, apply half of what was being taught to me. There was no incentive. You tell me, Dad, who was right in this situation between the father and son above? Not an easy solution, so perhaps some element of respect and compromise must be met.

Another example of this power struggle between parent and child occurred today in my practice. This had to do with the fact that the son did not like being threatened with the possibility of no allowance because he had not retrieved his own money that was owed to him by a friend. He felt a lot of time had gone on without asking for it simply because he had forgotten all about it. He had a problem asking for the money and resented the fact that his parents did not sit down with him to explore his fears. Instead he was hit with an ultimatum that made him feel infantilized and was more an act of control.

They accused him of being a spoiled brat with no values. At least those were his perceptions. Wouldn't it have been more helpful for the parent to have offered an opinion about the situation without coming on in such an authoritarian manner? He said he felt like defying them rather than concentrating on his problem about asking people for money. I feel sympathetic to this child's problem because, as you know, I never found it easy to ask you or anyone else for money. The other side of the relationship is that the father resented the fact that his son would say he was going out somewhere without even asking his parents for permission.

Neither the parent nor the child is right or wrong. Anyway, is that the issue? It seems to have more to do with the fact that neither one of them felt respected by the other. Can't there be equal rights for both parties involved? We all have opinions and values and the problem seems to be in the way we impose them on others. Must there always be winners and losers?

As for men questioning the meaning of their lives in their fifties, I find myself doing it all the time. We all ask ourselves what is the meaning of it all, only to come up with an assortment of answers that meet our needs at any given moment. Maybe family and children are what we live for, but it is important to keep in mind that we all share one thing in common and that is the fact that we are all mortal. With mortality comes vanity. We care what we look like and how the product of our hard work, either our material acquisitions or our children, turns out. We all want to feel that whatever it is that reflects our success will make us feel proud and remind us of how wonderful we are. Was all that hard work worth it? We all have a need to believe that what we did was right. The investment in time is enormous. One must find ways to justify that reality. Anyway what was it all for? Did I do the right thing? Could I have used my time better? Who knows, maybe what is important is that all we can do is what we feel is right and within our capabilities.

Shakespeare's plays brought him fame and immortality, but for me, I would have to say it would be my children. For they will, I hope, be around longer than I will and it is only fair to say that I have a desire for them to reflect an image that will preserve my vanity. Of course it would hurt me to see my son picked last for a choose-up game of football. How could I not want my children to adopt some of the values I lived by and the accomplishments I achieved? As you have said to me before, what more can a father do or expect from his child? It is important to be honest about that. How could I not impose that on them to some degree unless I had a strong dislike for what I stood for? One of my patients told me she felt her father was so in love with himself she felt the way to his heart was for her to make sure he knew how wonderful he was, and to have no opinions of her own. In this example lies the delicate balance between a parent and child.

So you see, Dad, I do understand your dilemma as a father now. But it would be a tall order to expect an adolescent to understand. However, maybe that is not a fair statement for the generation at large. I don't want to make that assumption. As I watched *The American Music Awards* last night, I could not help but be moved by the sight of Kenny Rogers accepting his award on stage while carrying his little boy on his shoulders. That really touched me and gave me a great deal of hope for future father and son relationships. It was so nice to see that little boy bask in his father's glory. You tried so hard not to intimidate me with your accomplishments and yet I longed for an opportunity that would allow me to be proud of you and make me feel honored to be your son.

I really identified with that little boy and his father, realizing how lucky they were to share that experience together. When push comes to shove, we both thrive on seeing each other get recognition. You were my hero as a child and will, I hope, always remain that for me. I was always sorry that I missed your talk at Hofstra when I lived in California. There was always a need in me to watch you be a teacher for other people. I always knew you had a lot to offer people. Just reading the letters written by you so far has made me so proud to have a father who can express himself in an articulate way with such sensitive material.

Whether it be John Lennon, Kenny Rogers, Max Cohen, or any other successful man, I would imagine that there would be a wish to have his son achieve things beyond his own successes, even if there is some degree of ambivalence about it. It was nice that Pop wanted you to make something of yourself and that he provided you with that opportunity. As a result of that, I have been fortunate enough to have been given the same opportunity. If I had not taken advantage of it, I would have had trouble living with myself, particularly because I am surrounded by men who did not have the same advantages. There was a time when I felt apologetic for my good fortune, but now I am just beginning to appreciate it.

Having you as a father was more difficult from the standpoint that Pop was going to give you the education that he never had. But you were right when you said to me that it would be harder for me to aspire to something denied to you. You were and are a tough act to follow, but I attribute a great deal of my ambition to that challenge. If you had been a failure, who would I admire?

The story you shared with me about parking with that girl reminded me of a similar story from my sophomore year in high school. There was a girl who was several years older than me and I had a mad crush on her. Apparently she felt the same way about me. I became a victim of my own Samson and Delilah complex. The attraction to her had made me feel very vulnerable. Although I was overwhelmed by her sensuality, I was trying desperately to keep it under control. I was double-dating with a friend because I did not yet drive. When I went to walk her to the door at the end of the evening, she invited me inside. Once I entered her living room, she started to take off her clothes and came on strong. I was a nervous wreck and could not deal with it very well. Naturally, I was pretending to be a perfect gentleman. The fortunate part is that my friend got impatient and started persistently honking the horn, so I was forced to leave. The unfortunate part of the story is that she never talked to me again. Now I know how Dustin Hoffman's character in *The Graduate* felt.

As I was growing up, I wanted to possess the women in my life. I had to please them and meet their standards, and liked to put on the charm to keep them from breaking my heart. You could have defined me as the romantic, vulnerable and innocent type. Whenever I was rejected by a girl, it was experienced as a tragedy. Behind all my bravado was a sense of sadness. Yet, I once ran out on a girl and never said goodbye. It still bothers me.

I learned as the years went by that one way to attract a woman was to get involved in her interests. In many ways, my cultural interests can be attributed to my passion for women and the need to please them. Sharing enthusiasm with another person was important for me. I felt a need to learn all the things she would teach me in order for me to get what I wanted. That connection to a woman was so important to me and still is. As I get older, I find myself having an unlimited curiosity to understand women. Although I run the risk of sounding politically incorrect, this has clearly helped me develop a strong inner feminine side. I was the guy in elementary school who crossed the tracks on his bike during lunch, hoping to bring a teen magazine back to my girlfriend for the week—something I knew she would cherish.

Every guy seems to have at least one experience that could be described as impersonal sex and which he never forgets. I remember my two closest friends taking me to a massage parlor for my bachelor's party before I got married. These were the same guys selling pretzels at Woodstock. As the woman was touching various parts of my body, there was an uncomfortable feeling within me. I couldn't look at her and something about the whole experience seemed demeaning. Although I did not admit it to my friends, I couldn't wait to leave. The highlight of my night was going to the bathroom where I overheard someone listening to the Knicks playoff game with the Los Angeles Lakers. It was a turn-on just hearing the swish of a Walt Frazier jump shot.

They got me drunk that night to the point where I vomited all over my clothes. Would you believe they dumped me off at my mother-in-law's driveway in my underpants? She was gracious enough to put me right to bed. So much for my sexual escapades.

Dad, for some reason I was so preoccupied with other parts of my anatomy that I never seemed to have the time to be worried about whether my penis was big or small. The only other thing I can say about this is that I was aware of the fact that it was unusual not to be worried about that. Then again, I prided myself on being different even to the point that wet dreams always took a back seat to masturbation. There was only one "Big Dick Rocky" and he hung out in Bunk Three at Camp Kennebec during the summer of 1961. He used to beat me in step-ball. It was impossible not to notice the size of his penis.

Isn't it nice that you and I are breaking tradition by sharing our deep sexual secrets with each other? It is good to find out we had so much in common even when it came to girls. Why do we deprive ourselves of exposing our innermost concerns to the ones we love? Your father would have been proud of you no matter what he knew about this part of your life, because I know the same holds true for our relationship. If you had disappointed him he would have gotten over it. We all disappoint the ones we love. I hope my children feel they can come to me and share their deepest concerns, and I with them. A father can't expect his son to open up with him if it is not made comfortable for him to do so.

That awful night of the pot party I wasn't sure whether you were going to call the police or not. You called my bluff and won. I buckled under the pressure because I knew you would call my friends' fathers. I remember hearing how one of them flushed all the pot down the toilet. This incident bothered me for a long time and I could not look any of the guys in the face at school. Those same guys were still talking about it at my first high school reunion. They wanted nothing to do with me; I felt like a real fool. At that point I could have benefited from my four-year-old daughter's words of wisdom: "Sometimes I feel foolish, but I am not a fool." You said that if you knew then what you know now you would have reacted differently. What would you have done differently?

You were accurate about my being anxious about that alumni basketball game. I seemed to regress to the things I used to do at that time. Would you believe that ten minutes before leaving your house for the gym I couldn't find my sneakers? Just like the old days. Mom found them sitting on top of the refrigerator. They say you can't go back, but this one evening refuted that theory. It was in this same gym that I remember hearing Judy Collins perform when she was just beginning her career. Number thirty-two on the back of my jersey lives on.

It was a magnificent evening. I felt it was special having the opportunity to relive this meaningful time in my life, particularly in light of the fact that I am in the process of re-experiencing my life through these letters with you. Here I was, living out what I had just been writing about. Life does imitate art. One could say this is profound but true. What made it more meaningful was that you rearranged your weekend plans just to be there. What a father will sacrifice for his son. Some things never change and I could tell you were as excited about this as I was.

As an adult, I had a second opportunity to appreciate you going through my adolescent routine. It was really special to look up in the stands and see you sitting there with your granddaughter. When I put in those foul shots, I could not resist seeking you out and smiling. There was still that thrill hearing the cheerleaders shout my name in the background.

One of the more moving moments of the night was when my old friend, the archrival, started to talk to me about the loss of his father several years ago. I had not seen him since I went to his house with you to pay a condolence call. It occurred to me at that moment how unfair it was that he was deprived of having his father take part in this great event, and I had the good fortune of having you there. He was the father who used to come into the locker room and talk to the reporters. Remember when the doctor used to make house calls carrying his magical black medicine bag. I crave that time of innocence so lost to us now.

I can't believe there was a time I thought life was supposed to be fair. What a classic childhood illusion. It is so easy to take your parents for granted. Suddenly, after not seeing this old friend for so many years, I felt a real closeness to him and began remembering how his father used to come to all the games too. When you got sick several years ago with a heart attack, I realized how much denial I had around the fact that I could have lost you, my greatest admirer. Thanks, Dad, for staying around to see me make it professionally and sink those foul shots that could never be made in the past. You always did tell me not to take it so seriously and just relax. I guess that finally on this night I could be realistic about my status as a basketball player.

Another significant part of the evening was when my old coaches and teachers commented to me that they couldn't get over the fact that after all these years I still looked the same. They should only know what I looked like just nine months ago-bearded, with glasses, and forty pounds heavier. Fittingly, the evening ended with my old friend and I alone in the locker room. Coincidentally, we just happened to be in there at the same time. That locker room was a place that brought back memories of my old dependencies and heroics. At that moment it was time for one of those old dependencies.

In the old days, it was a bad back which prevented me from bending down to get my clothes. Now it was just a stubborn knot in my sneaker lace. I needed his help to get it out. There was a moment of slight embarrassment. Not only did we team up on the court that night, but we managed to also get that knot out. I should say he got the knot out. At that point all I could say to him was, "Isn't it nice to be needed?" What made me feel positive about it was that in the past I might have felt uncomfortable about being dependent on another man to help me out, but tonight it felt like it belonged in the scenario.

After the game I went to a party and was discussing our book with an old friend who appeared as macho as ever. All he could do was yawn at the idea and not take it very seriously. Part of me started to get angry and defensive until I realized that he remembered me as the class clown who never took himself seriously. It was shades of my Emmett Kelly complex—formerly showcased on our mantelpiece but now buried in the attic, with other hidden gems.

You never did like the wise-ass in me. Now I could see why. How could I expect someone to switch gears on me when he has not seen me for so many years? How hard It can be to break an old image. What was important about it for me was the fact that I had no invest-ment in trying to undo that old image. After all, that image was what the evening was in part all about. The moral of the story for me was, "Before making judgments about other people, try to understand where that person is coming from." Not a bad New Year's resolution.

Finally, another emotionally striking thing for me that evening had to do with one of my other old companions. When I went to bas-ketball camp as a kid, where they tried to keep me out of the honor society, I was comforted by the fact that I had a friend who had the same thing happen to him. Several years ago, I heard he had an acci-dent which left him paralyzed. This shocked me, particularly because this guy was the All-American Boy who had everything going for him. Well, there he was sitting in his wheelchair at the game, watching a bunch of guys with whom he used to play basketball. I admired his courage and ability to share in the excitement. It was as if nothing had changed. The evening became not only a high school reunion but a camp reunion as well.

For years I had been having dreams about him and wondering how he was doing. Now I know he is doing fine; he came back into my life for a frozen moment, a moment I had trouble letting go of at the end of the night. I had a sense that he felt the same way because we said good-bye about six times. There is something special about a long Jewish good-bye between two old friends. I have the feeling that our paths will cross again sometime. A transitory moment in time will now become a fond memory. Years later we saw each other and found out the Beatles stayed at his friend's house in Miami after the Ed Sullivan Show in February, 1964. He gave me the photos that now hang in the foyer of my house, taken with the Beatles when he was a young boy. There were the Beatles taking a boat ride with him, his dad, and Murray the K, a well known DJ on the radio during that time.

My financial dependency on you certainly complicated my conception of adolescence. Interestingly, it was very similar for the two of us in respect to this issue. It is nice to know that you had trouble with it too. For some reason, I never realized how true that was. I seem to be deriving some comfort from knowing that you had help in getting started, as I did. If that were not the case, maybe it would have been that much more intimidating for me. The shame of my financial dependency on you seems to be gone now. If anything, I feel grateful for not having student loans on my head like my friends. I hope my children have the same opportunities I had. We finally have to realize that we don't have to apologize for being helped and can feel good about the fact that things were made a little easier for us. As a result, life could be more fun, and I feel good that I made the most of it.

The hardest part of the financial dependency had to do with the fact that I had always assumed that once you were chronologically out of adolescence and were starting a family, you should be completely on your own. It certainly bothered me, but why make life harder for yourself when you don't have to. I am not into being a martyr. Being professional students certainly delayed our transitions into adulthood.

I appreciated the fact that you never held money over my head and would try to create ways to enable me not to feel uncomfortable about my financial dependency on you. It was so hard asking you for ten dollars to go out. It sure was easier thinking about my goals without having to worry where my next meal was. Money may not be the ticket to happiness but it definitely gives one a certain freedom. I always liked the fact that you would sometimes give me money for no reason, even if it was what we have learned to call "the famous hundred." Dad, haven't you heard of inflation? (I hope you know I am kidding . . . just covering my bases.) Basically, all I mean is that for years you have been giving my sister and me the same amount of money on our birthdays and other special occasions. Maybe you are just hung up on tradition. You always have been the sentimental type and a creature of habit. You always got up at 7:15 in the morning and came home for dinner at 7:15 holding your briefcase. We were the fifties/early sixties sitcom family waiting at the dinner table for your arrival.

Well, Dad, we have both gone beyond the teenage years in our letters. But I have come to realize that this period of my life was very much connected to many of the same feelings that I experienced in my young adulthood, for obvious reasons. Although some of my recollections may be distorted, I have to re-state that the foundation of my later alienation from you was definitely occurring during this period of my life. Maybe you just never knew some of the things I felt, and as much as you thought you knew your son, there is a lot more to know.

Sometimes we just won't see things the same way. I am working very hard at not feeling invested in making us have to fall into that old dynamic. As you know, all perceptions tend to be subjective, for what else could they be? What it comes down to for me, Dad, is that we were close but yet so far away from each other.

Love,
Donald

* * *

Dear Donald,

I agree almost completely with your views about the need for parents to respect their own needs as well as their children's needs. Most children, I'm sure, possess more resilience than we tend to assume. Certainly a tense, frustrated and unhappy parent who feels painfully trapped by responsibility is not likely to be an effective caretaker. If the pleasure goes out of parenting, then the quality of parenting has to suffer.

Children differ in their ability to assume responsibility at a given age. Some infants and young children develop more rapidly than others as a function of varying rates of neurological maturation in the early years. But I fully agree that as a child's development proceeds, responsibilities should be assigned at a pace to match the child's ability to perform.

One area, however, is particularly sensitive during those very early formative years. The traumatic potential of separation from parents during these early years is too well-documented to be ignored. Actually, I would have had more concern about Jared's vulnerability when you recently went on vacation. As it turned out, from what you say, Emily was more troubled by the separation than he was, even though she is old enough to have a concept of time and old enough to know that you'd be back after an interval of time. Perhaps Jared's reaction to separation was effectively tempered because of his strong attachment to Michelle, the mother's helper with whom he spends a great deal of time and who provides for so much of his care.

I was not under the impression that I was such a permissive parent. If there was good reason to say no, it seems to me that I did that relatively easily. What I and others of my generation didn't do was to give sufficient importance to our own needs, if those needs conflicted with what we perceived to be the legitimate needs of our children. Of course, this is only apparently true most of the time because people are usually so adept at justifying their self-interest.

You described an incident from your practice involving a dispute between a father and son, and you asked me for an opinion about who was right. I believe that this is the wrong, or at least an unrewarding question. "What is wrong?" is, I believe, the more relevant question. Here is a boy who obviously feels put upon, abused and disadvantaged. He resents the authority and privileges that his father assumes are legitimate. I believe that the problem can only be understood if the boy's feelings of injustice are explored and illuminated. Perhaps this will enable him, with his father's help and understanding, to deal with the problem at its source.

I'm sure you are correct in stating that people of all ages sometimes question the meaning of life. It is true, however, that questions such as these become more compelling as one approaches the later years of one's productivity. Younger people, I believe, are much more caught up in preoccupations about "making it." By the time we are fifty or sixty, we face the reality of what we have achieved and what we are probably never going to achieve. It is a logical time to take stock of one's life and ponder what might have been. Thoughts about mortality and death occur at all ages but such thoughts tend to become more urgent as one experiences the regular occurrence of death among one's peers.

You are now a mature man yourself, Donald, and you have the perspective which would enable you to evaluate anything I might confide in you. I doubt though, that any person is so completely comfortable with everything that he or she has done, or thought or felt, that they could share it easily with another person—especially another person whose respect and approval are so important. Even you and I have secrets from each other, although I don't doubt that we are probably being more open with each other in these letters than fathers and sons usually are. It's hard to be completely open, even in the protected environment of the analyst's office, where every assurance is provided to alleviate anxieties about potential consequences of exposure.

What I'm saying is that even now, as adults who love and trust each other, we are limited in our openness and frankness. Wouldn't it, therefore, be even more unreasonable to expect that a child would be able to understand a father's self-doubt? Would a father be justified in opening up and sharing with his immature son, thoughts and feelings about which he feels shame or guilt?

I don't believe that I was especially secretive about myself or that I was uncomfortable about discussing sex with you when you were young. But that certainly is not to suggest that there were not many things I would not have felt free to tell you. Without thinking of anything specific, I'm sure there are things I would hesitate to share even now. Surely there were even more things I would have hesitated to share with you when you were a youngster. Nevertheless, I agree that it would have made me more human to you if I had shared more than I did.

You ask me what I would do differently if confronted by the pot party today. For one thing, marijuana is no longer the frightening evil it once seemed to be. My over-reaction was a consequence of the fear I had that you would become involved with dangerous drugs. Obviously, my fears were unfounded. Beyond that, it is always easy to say, with the wisdom of hindsight, that I would now react more calmly and intelligently to the whole incident, and I'm sure I would. But what if I were confronted with my teenager's defiant involvement in something truly dangerous to his future well being? How calmly and intelligently would I respond? I know what I'd like to say but I'm not sure that I wouldn't react as emotionally as I did on that occasion.

One of the most crucial aspects of emotional health is the capacity to learn from experience. Emotional growth and maturation presupposes the ability to evaluate experience with sufficient objectivity to emerge from the experience with a better understanding of what happened. The ability to do this is impaired by the very human tendency to try to justify and vindicate the self. Thus, if something goes wrong it was either the other guy's fault or bad luck. We feel clever when a choice we make turns out well and we feel successful. How often do we acknowledge that a choice we made was foolish and that next time we'll know better? More often we try to justify the judgment we made, and if the results were disappointing, we blame it on bad luck. People naturally brag about their successes and minimize or rationalize their failures.

The other extreme is also common and equally destructive. We both see people who are guilt-ridden and inclined to judge themselves harshly at every opportunity. Whatever goes wrong is perceived as a personal failure, further proof of being a born loser. Unfortunately, such prejudices tend to become self-fulfilling prophecies.

How hard it is to find the middle ground of objectivity! It's easy to fall into the trap of making excuses for oneself, on the one hand, or lapsing into guilty and inappropriate self-reproach on the other. This has so clearly been the hardest thing for me to do in responding to your letters.

Finally, I want to comment on your belief that although I knew you fairly well while you were growing up and even now, there is a lot more to know. Of course this is true. What is truly enlightening for me, however, is the extent to which I was able to know things concerning you while you were growing up, without somehow fully understanding. What I knew was colored by my own point of vantage and my own frame of reference.

It is difficult to fully put oneself in the other person's skin and perceive the world through the other person's eyes. This is what we attempt to do professionally and we are able to do this with some success because we are able to be more or less objective. With our children, we are deeply involved emotionally, we can hardly escape the distortions imposed by the complicated axes we have to grind. We have to negotiate our own guilt, our own feelings of responsibility, and that can be difficult. It is easy to believe that the child, though seemingly angry with us because of a particular issue, must surely realize that we mean it for the child's own good. How wrong we often are in making this assumption.

The parent-child relationship is tremendously complicated and bewildering. The child serves many needs for the parent; the child is, after all, an extension of the parent's own self. The child's success or failure is so easily perceived by the parent as his or her own success or failure, and is thus subject to all of the distortions implicit in self-evaluation and self-appraisal. It's tough for the parent, but what an awesome responsibility and burden to impose on the child!

No wonder growing up is so hard.

Love,
Dad

The Searching Twenties

Leaving Home with the Baby Boomers

You would jump ahead of me and correct my mistakes before I could even make them.

We tend, after all, to emphasize those perceptions that support our prejudices, and neglect or ignore experiences which contradict them.

* * *

August, 1982
Dear Dad,

I remember the summer of 1969 as a time of great excitement. Woodstock, the biggest rock festival in history, was about to take place and Joan Baez was singing *We Shall Overcome*, while the rain was pouring down on me. The women's movement was on the rise. There was also the Stonewall Uprising, the rebellion of the LGBT community against a police raid. It was the year the Jets, Mets, and Knicks all won. Scott Muni was a DJ on WNEW FM radio. People were dancing at the Electric Circus in the East Village and lining up for concerts at the Fillmore East. Abbey Road was released in 1969. Let's not forget Apollo 11—Neil Armstrong walking on the moon. I was beginning to prepare myself for college and the anticipation of what it would be like was building up inside me. Although it wasn't an Ivy League school, I was indeed going to college even if it was in Athens, Ohio. How did you feel when you sent me off to school? I barely made it. Headline news, "Ted Kennedy Sinks a Car off Chappaquiddick."

During this time we all seemed to be going through a difficult transition, and I felt caught in the middle of it. It was like tumbling into the kaleidoscopic wonderland of American counter culture. Little did I know that these would become some of the most unusual years any college campus had ever experienced. The Vietnam War was creating a great deal of anxiety and people were protesting all over the country—people were getting behind a fighter who used to call himself Cassius Clay. The country endured a tumultuous election as well as sexual discriminations and the civil rights movements began. We were trying to recover from political assassinations. I can hear the lyrics to the song "Abraham, Martin, and John" reflecting the mood of our time. And then of course we had Watergate in 1972, full of Nixonian politics.

It was a difficult period for me because I was concerned about being drafted, but fortunately was spared by a 300 lottery number. We were all huddled around the radio during my summer job at my uncle's publishing house. Some people were burning their draft cards. Of course, I figured that you would find some way to keep me out of the war. My future roommate at college was afraid of being drafted and talked about fleeing to Canada. One night he disappeared from a Grateful Dead concert, tripping on acid never to be found. Sadly many of my contemporaries died over there. They sacrificed their lives. Like most students my age, I wanted to have my cake and eat it too. I was still dependent on you, but influenced by a generation that was committed to tearing down the same values that I relied on for my everyday survival. There was now more of an opportunity to question and try new things. I could even receive three credits in college for chanting Hare Krishna and reading the *Bhagavad Gita*, and then go next door and take Physics for Poets. The university campus was a place to have fun and "do your own thing."

It was the "Age of Aquarius." We had the movies *Easy Rider* and *Midnight Cowboy*, and of course *Mad Magazine*. Ironically, while many of us were promoting a mood of peace, one could see that many people were destroying themselves. There were students who never recovered from bad acid trips and became psychotic. Recently, I had my friends over to watch the movie *Woodstock* and they were surprised at how turned off they were. People were becoming disenchanted and more interested in themselves. Music, particularly acid rock, was certainly difficult to dance to; people at parties were absorbed in themselves. I preferred Van Morrison. It was a time for many changes and great music with a new sound. Although it was a period of people preaching peace and love, paradoxically there was Charles Manson murdering Sharon Tate in a Hollywood nightmare. There were also the riots during the concert at Altamont. This was clearly a time of disruption and frenzy.

When I arrived at school, it became apparent to me that being your son gave me instant status. There was a mystique about being the son of a psychiatrist. It made me different from my friends. I had something they didn't have and now being different was appealing. The shift had now been made. There was joy for me in what you did for a living and a burning desire to share with everyone around me that my father was a psychiatrist.

Being a psychotherapist had become quite fashionable in the late sixties and into the seventies. It was no longer embarrassing to admit to being in therapy. People were into understanding themselves and "getting into each others' heads." Maybe we could thank the Beatles for that. Encounter groups were starting up all around me. Finding out which spiritual guru one should follow was a major preoccupation. People were carrying around books by Alan S. Watts and teachings of Zen Buddhism, hoping to integrate what they read into the journey toward self-enlightenment. We were protesting in our tie-dye clothing preaching free love not war. Humanistic psychology was coming into vogue. I was reading *Love and Will* by Rollo May, and sofa-surfing from house to house, meaning always a new couch on which to crash.

All of this contributed to my feelings of insecurity. Everything appeared uncertain and I could not avoid being influenced by all the choices available. The pseudo-openness was almost too much to take. There was an underlying fear that my future had no predictability. I pretended to live in the here-and-now so I could fit in, but it was frightening to be in college during such a tumultuous time.

It seemed like everyone was majoring in psychology during my freshman year. I began to see you as a man ahead of his time. What was there left for me to accomplish? How could I top you? The idea of getting into psychology was becoming appealing, but I was determined to find my own way. There had to be more to psychology than studying rats with 300 students in Psychology 101. I wanted to study the unconscious and its symbolism. All I had to do was get away from you to become the "intellectual" son I felt you had always wanted me to be. Unfortunately I received a D in Introductory Psychology.

It was difficult getting used to the new image I had adopted. My physical appearance needed major adjustments. I had the whole look—bell-bottoms, with the boots, hat, vest, and beard. The Nehru jacket went into the closet. Getting attention and being different became increasingly important for my self-esteem. There was a desperate need to find something to believe in. You always seemed so comfortable in your beliefs and had a way of getting what you wanted. I now thought that could happen to me. I wanted to matter and make a difference in the world.

During that first year of school, you even managed to get me out of my claustrophobic freshman dorm into a house. All you had to do was write that note explaining to the people in authority that dorm life was not good for my mental health. I was impressed with the power of a psychiatrist's word, particularly when I could benefit from it. What a way to get your needs met and have your feeling of specialness be reinforced! I couldn't keep my mouth shut and had to brag all over the campus that my father was able to pull off the impossible. It was generally accepted that freshmen could never get their own apartments. Still, the more you bailed me out, the harder it was to separate from you. This certainly has become a familiar theme in these letters.

I had become a radical on campus and left my jock world behind. I remember one whole day dodging tear gas as it became a way of life. Protesting for the "cause" had a kind of carnival feeling at times, and it even became a place for new romances. In some way, it became the new fraternity pretending it was so different from the traditional one. If you had an interest in a traditional fraternity you were seen as an outcast. And heaven help you if you associated with anyone from ROTC, better known as the "ROTCIES."

There was a tremendous pressure to not conform. I remember spending one whole day in Buffalo running away from tear gas and going from house to house saying hello to friends. It became a communal event, almost replacing the typical adolescent hangouts of Jones Beach and the Fontainebleau Hotel in Florida, where Holy Joe could be found reading the bible next door at the 48th Street beach. We were indulging in our own sun reflections.

I was against the war and I liked being part of something with a group of people that made me feel important. If you weren't into the cause, you ran the risk of being alone. The attention I was getting for my strong opinions was nice. Once again, I could have an image that would allow me to fit in with other people.

Thinking you were different became the new conformity. I didn't like missing anything, so it was hard not to be involved. I believe that it also had to do with my need to find a way to discover my own identity apart from yours. It was easy to knock a world that you created for me.

There were serious and scary moments involved. What I had the most trouble understanding was why fellow students would choose to be violent, and get satisfaction from breaking windows. It seemed rather hypocritical to be chanting for peace and then taking part in hostile, meaningless, destructive acts. Although I had an investment in protesting the war, it was frightening to think I could go to jail just for being associated with these people. I wanted to belong, but not to that extent. What if you took my credit cards away? People felt unsettled about the reasons behind trying to justify the Vietnam War. There was a fear of communism spreading, labeled The Red Scare. That paranoia was being felt across the United States as new protest movements were on the rise. Many people were threatened by all this uprising which brought on ugly outcomes.

Despite the dark side of the revolution, I was still determined to be the prodigal son—standing up with the Chicago Seven, with Jerry Rubin, at political rallies spouting all kinds of rhetoric. It was a high that was equivalent to my basketball days in high school, scoring points in front of a large crowd on a Friday night. I always thrived on performing in front of large audiences because it made me feel important. Here I was trying to make a mark for myself. I felt determined to be a child prodigy. "Like father, Like son." After all, Mom always presented you that way. It might have been different if you had been perceived as a mere mortal. This was going to be the beginning of my quest for sainthood. Your world was all wrong and my generation was going to change everything. After all, my generation's Saturday morning line-up included *Andy's Gang* and *Sky King*.

I really began to believe that money was unimportant, but underlying this was a fear of never being able to have it once I was on my own. What would I have done without that checking account you gave me and which helped support my new library? I wrote my very first check at school and it sure did not take me long to learn to get used to it. And how many freshmen had a new car and could go to Europe for the summer? I even had my expensive designer revolutionary wardrobe from Bloomingdales for the trip partially funded by my job cleaning houses for Mr. Maven. During those days we attempted to follow the guide book for doing Europe on five dollars a day. What it came down to was that I became a socialist on daddy's credit cards. Being the nice Jewish boy from Long Island didn't quite make it with my new image. It just seemed too ordinary.

I never did ask you why you decided to name me Donald. What goes into naming someone can be important. I became concerned with how other people were going to perceive my name and where I came from. The stereotypes of my past were negative and I felt defensive about them.

This was certainly a stage of life when I was extremely impressionable. I was at a true crossroads and I could have gone in one of many directions. Fortunately, I never got to the point where my name became such a disgrace to me that I would opt for changing it. During this time, many people were apt to do that as a rejection of their whole past. I never really wanted the clean break. The thought of being on my own scared me. As long as I could continue to be Mr. Philosopher, and have my beard, long hair, and boring raps, I was content.

Wherever I would go, people would spend their nights contemplating their navels and solving all the questions of the universe while listening to Bob Dylan, Janis Joplin, and Jimi Hendrix. I was good at pointing out the problems but not so good at implementing the solutions. Mental masturbation was a way of reinforcing an inflated sense of my self-importance. There was something appealing about taking the easy way out. My major preoccupation was how I could get out of taking required courses and beat the system. These were unstructured and undisciplined times, tailor made for my personality. That kind of lack of structure worked for me. I took pleasure in getting away with things, rationalizing away all my fears of feeling inadequate, making it easier to hide behind my undiagnosed learning disability. Although ADD, at times, felt limiting, it also forced me to come up with other solutions. In my last two years of college, I created a special major for myself—Philosophy in Literature and its application to the community. There was an openness to not be forced to take required courses. Being a traditional philosophy major meant I would have been forced to take Statistics.

What I really relished about going away to school was that I did not have to worry about you looking over my shoulder. I was aware that my physical appearance disturbed you. You used to tell me that it would give people the wrong impression of me, but as I have said before you seemed to care more about that than I did. I was convinced that you did not understand who the real me was anyway. All I could see was that this was just your way to maintain control and authority over me.

As I was becoming more immersed in philosophy it became apparent to me that this was a subject to which you never seemed to gravitate. For me, it symbolized a world of new possibilities and experimentation. (Hello, Carlos Castaneda and Ken Kesey.) This was an exciting time for me and my confidence continued to grow. I began to feel that maybe I could have something of my own. My new male hero was a philosophy professor from Europe and he was going to give me new ideas that would even shake you up. There was something mysterious about him never taking his dark sunglasses off. The Lone Ranger rides again. He was a far cry from the Roy Rogers and Hopalong Cassidy of my cowboy days. I was looking for an adult male role model who could provide me with answers to all my disturbing questions about the world around me. He was going to teach me all about existentialism and contemporary European philosophy. There was a strong need for me to find new answers to my questions about death. When I hoped for a comforting solution to its mystery, I did not get it. I asked this professor what happens to you when you die, and his response was, "you die." That was hard to swallow. I was still trying to get over Vinnie Serraco dying in a car accident in high school. Things like that weren't supposed to happen. I remember all of us going to his wake. Young people were not supposed to die. Suddenly, I remember that boy drowning in Mexico. Life is so tenuous when you think that in one split second your life can change forever. I remember being upset when Emile Griffith knocked out Benny "The Kid" Paret and he never woke up after their championship fight. It's hard to accept that dreams don't always come true.

My living situation was very different now. Instead of you and Mom, I had to contend with a moody jazz musician and his girlfriend.

Our dinner talks about my future had now been replaced by getting drumsticks thrown at me for no apparent reason when I would come home from a day of classes. I must admit there were times when I felt as though being home would have been a more appealing alternative. There was no joy in doing my own laundry. I was used to the finer things in life. Those concerns about walking in on you and Mom having sex were no longer a preoccupation because my room was so close to my roommate's that I had the dubious pleasure of hearing all his orgasms every night. Unfortunately, it reinforced my own loneliness—I was your typical horny freshman. At times, it seemed all I had at night was my psychedelic black light posters and fantasies of sleeping with a girl in my own house. It didn't get any easier hitching rides back east, excited about surprising my girlfriend, Dee at Syracuse University, and upon arrival discovering that my potential orgasm was flying west to visit her grandmother.

During that first year of school, everything appeared so transient and I was falling in love every other day. It was exciting to start to act on some of my sexual fantasies. In high school a girl was a tramp if she was open. Now it was considered attractive to be a free spirit. What was it like for you that first time? I was nervous, but I was able to get over the hurdle.

Even though my roommate intimidated me with his temper, I was impressionable enough at the time to let him influence me in terms of what philosophy books I should read. He was a playwright and philosopher as well, and for the first time I was having intellectual conversations with another man. We had some good talks, and if he said read Martin Buber, that's what I would do.

Many hours of my freshman year were spent alone reading books in my room. I could hardly wait to come home on my vacation and impress you with my new knowledge. All I wanted to do was read psychology and philosophy books so I could make up for those lost years when my only interest was sports. How ironic for me to admit that, when you think back and rediscover how much I resented you for encouraging me all along to broaden myself.

It seemed like such a revelation to read Eric Fromm's *The Art of Loving* in which he said you had to love yourself before you could love others. This inspired me for a long time and convinced me that psychology made sense, even if I did not know how I would make a living at it. As you know, this was a major fear of mine. Little did I know how prophetic that line in *The Art of Loving* would be and how much it would pertain to our future relationship. Feeling good about myself would have such an influence on how I felt about you.

The final days of my freshman year were mixed with sadness and satisfaction. Most of the campuses around the country had closed down because of all the political unrest and those four students from Kent State who had been shot down. Forgotten in the background was the ill-fated Apollo 13. They too were on a mission to expand our horizons and, like the students at Kent State, had their dreams interrupted. This would be the story of my generation. Some people would find their way back, learning how to cope with adversity, while the others never made it back, literally or symbolically. The difference was that circumstances permitted the astronauts to find their way home yet the students never had that opportunity. We had finally landed on the moon and what would that mean when our own country was in turmoil? We lost JFK and the hopefulness of discovering a new world. We never recovered after that. There was a loss of innocence in America, despite the Miracle Mets.

But on the brighter side, my grades were quite good. I was able to transfer to almost any school, despite a urinary infection that had sent me home for several weeks. I had proved something to myself and, I hoped, to you as well. For the first time I felt good about being a student and I wanted you to be proud of me. I was beginning to feel more secure about the idea that maybe I was a "late bloomer." Being labeled as the classic underachiever becomes a burden after a while.

My life seemed to reach a turning point when I transferred to Buffalo University, close to Dee, often referred to as the Berkeley of the East. My Buffalo Springfield and Grateful Dead albums went *Truckin'* along with me. The need to be controversial and different was growing even more within me. I needed a new intellectual god to follow. Would you believe that it was a nuclear physicist who turned me onto Jungian psychology? In the early seventies more students were becoming interested in spiritual values and the occult. Reading Herman Hesse and R.D. Laing's *Politics of Experience* along with *Tolkien's Trilogy* was routine. Eastern religion, meditation, yoga, and incense burning were part of everyday existence. Having a spiritual guru, like Krishnamurti, was as important as eating your three meals—vegetarian, of course.

Carl Jung became my model psychiatrist as he seemed so different from all the others. He was very concerned with integrating a philosophical and spiritual perspective into his psychological view of the world. I was shocked by the fact that a psychiatrist could perceive the universe that way. It was as if Pandora's Box had just been opened. My life with you was about to radically change. I was finding a new father—what would happen between us?

Jung also just happened to be a student of the great Sigmund Freud and was commonly thought of as his favorite pupil. As we both know, later on in their relationship Jung chose to break from Freud and go his own way, much to Freud's chagrin. Many historians describe their relationship as having been similar to that between a father and son. How convenient for me, so much so that I began to identify with Jung and the various feelings he spoke about in his moving autobiography *Memories, Dreams, and Reflections.*

I think this was one of the many Jungian books thrown your way over the years. Perhaps this was the most meaningful one of all. I began to identify with his struggles growing up and now felt a sense of peace in the idea that I had found another man who thought the way I did. More important was the feeling that he could understand me. This was a very weighty realization, and I felt less alone for perhaps the first time in my life. Jung seemed to give me a purpose and meaning for going on with my life. The thought of integrating his psychology into a way of life and making a living at it seemed too good to be true. Maybe there could be a future for me.

Like all predictions along the way, there tend to be many alterations in the process. So much has been made of the Freud/Jung relationship, perhaps because it had so many classic father/son dynamics attached to it. There seemed to be many parallels in relation between the two of us. Freud appeared to have been threatened by Jung's following his own path, and I perceived you as having the same problem with me. It was as if you took my interest in Jung as a rejection of you personally, which in a sense it was. I was determined to not let you interfere with my new ambitions, even if you did want to have authority over my fate.

There was always a concern that you would stifle me and break my creative spirit. It seemed as if you wanted me to feel the same way about things that you did, and I just wanted no part of it. I felt a demand to believe in your dogma and it appeared that no amount of reasonable discussion could change the situation. Our conversations were just not profound enough for me and at times felt circular. You seemed to always have the last word. Why couldn't you value my point of view? This was extremely frustrating.

Every vacation I would come home enthusiastic about my increased scope of knowledge, but by the time I went back to school I felt it was stripped away. Somehow I was not secure enough to hold my own with you in intellectual dialogue. You had a way of overpowering me. I began to dread our debates, but never knew how to bow out of them gracefully. Converting each other was a lost cause and the conversations just seemed to get heavier each time we would see one another. I would get angry at myself for letting you get the better of me. Your arrogance and critical manner at times were almost intolerable. It seemed you were less interested in answering my questions about the nature of my philosophical beliefs than you were in maintaining authority.

I felt you were putting me down when you would comment that the books I read were too abstract—if you could not understand them, how could they be any good? I was drawn toward abstract, philosophical works that you had trouble understanding because this made me feel better than you. It was also a language that made sense to me.

During my insecure moments, of which there were still many, I would feel that if you did not understand these concepts, then how could I? So I would begin to feel foolish. Maybe there was something wrong with the article I was studying. I was disturbed when those self-doubts would creep into my psyche. I could be hard on myself; where was my self-respect? There were moments when I would be so effusive about an article, and my expectation would be that you would have the same reaction. When you didn't, I felt disappointed and would take it personally. It just confirmed how different we were. That was hard for me to accept. I used to feel you had a lot of nerve not liking what I felt was an important piece of work. All of this was made worse by the fact that amongst a group of people, all intellectual discussion seemed invariably to be directed toward you. I would feel lost and at times invisible. It appeared as if people could value only your opinion. This was not a time when I welcomed being in your shadow. You were and are such a dominant personality when it comes to personal interaction. At times it felt that everyone in the room was on the edge of his or her chair waiting for your words of wisdom. It does not do much for the self-esteem of those who grew up around you. This may all seem like an idealization of you, but somehow I just don't think so. It was just plain hard getting control of any conversation that included you without my feeling like an idiot.

I wanted to take books out of your library with the hope that maybe someday I could suck up your knowledge and demand similar respect from people. Unfortunately, as you know, many of these books remain on my bookshelf unread, to which you have so astutely made reference over the years. You always did have a knack for seeing through me but it had a way of making me feel extremely foolish and inferior at times. When I was young, *The Mickey Mantle Story* had to be tucked under the covers when I heard your footsteps; now it was Jung and philosophy books. Some things just never change. The fear of being intimidated by what I felt was your condescending attitude continued. The connection between these two stages of my life, and my need to always hide something from you, has never been made until now. Playing hide-and-seek as a kid was more fun. I was constantly looking for ways to avoid embarrassment and confrontation with you.

It felt like I was never good enough. There was such a strong need to come home during school vacations and have those heavy talks that I had wanted to have with you as a kid. I now wanted to prove to you how smart your son was and that we could finally share the same interests. If you only could have known how much I wanted to have that with you. Going back to school after vacation meant building up my self-confidence all over again. I really resented you for that. There was a feeling that no matter how much I would change, you and everyone from my past would see me only as the ignorant jock with no opinion of his own.

I wanted you to see me as the guy who woke up and embraced Shakespeare at eight in the morning during a blizzard. In addition to these feelings came the awareness that you were concerned that I would never be able to hold a job, particularly when I was fired from one during a summer vacation. Part of me believed I would never make it on my own. Then came the guilt as I became conscious of the fact that when I would lie in bed late in the morning and have fun during the summer, you were at work every day in a business suit. It seemed as if I would always need to ask you for money and maybe my independence at school was all a fake. I remember when I worked at Crown Book Publishing in the warehouse and they thought I was stoned. It was more boredom because I was aware I wasn't going to be the guy who would someday run the family business that my Uncle Nat founded, and Uncle Alan took over.

I was actually afraid to tell you that my interest in Jungian psychology was serious knowing full well that you had been trained as a Freudian analyst. It seemed as though my spiritual preoccupations were seen as merely a fad, which you did not take seriously. Maybe my developing interest in religion was compensating for the lack of it in our household during my childhood. As I said before, I needed desperately to believe in something. Remember what I shared with you in a previous letter: that religious school and my Bar Mitzvah felt like I was just going through the motions. It was simply what every thirteen-year-old Jewish boy did, along with the piano and tennis lessons. I felt that my interest in Jung was threatening to you. All you could say to me was that Jung was difficult for you to understand, that he just involved himself with the metaphysical aspects of life. Your attitude would lead me to feel that you perceived Jungian psychology as meaningless and insubstantial and was taken as a personal put-down. I felt you were undermining my newfound identity, and that we were almost re-enacting the Freud/Jung, father/son conflict that persisted between them for so long. I was searching to find my own meaning in life.

Your views about my interest in Jung were so intense that I was convinced you were in some way hurt because I was not interested in your Freud books. Your attitude about life seemed to me so critical and reductionist and mine so positive and idealistic. You were the "headshrinker" and I was going to be the "soul stretcher."

It was as if I perceived Jung as more a product of my times, while Freud's values belonged to your generation. He was a tradition, the father of psychoanalysis. I wasn't interested in tradition. I felt that nothing could hurt me and that life was intended to involve risks but

I would always feel safe and secure. I had that desire to see myself as immortal and hide from my fear of death. Let's face it, my generation did not have to worry about the same things yours did. Boundaries were looser and there were more possibilities available for a kid growing up in my day. Our generation was reckless and often didn't see the consequences to our actions. We had and have so many more choices than you did. I remember you once saying to me that you felt it was harder to grow up in today's civilization. The power struggle between us continued and I remember still resenting you if you forced me to wear my glasses and buckle my seatbelt. You were only looking out for me, but I just did not want to listen. This was symbolic of our relationship for years.

In our debates about love, you maintained that love was based on conditions, meaning a relationship has to be a two-way street. Ours certainly was not going in that direction and I remember arguing with you that I believed in unconditional love. Nothing like a diehard idealist. This was convenient, of course, because then you could give to me and I would not have to feel guilty if I did not reciprocate. This was an ideal reinforcement for my selfish attitude. I was going to be the socialist driving around town in the sporty Firebird you bought me for high school graduation, while you were the capitalist.

Of the two of us, you were always the more realistic. How I once despised that quality in you. Jung seemed to have been a man who lived out all his fantasies without a fear of being different. My perception of you was that you were a man who played it safe and did not live out his dreams. That's probably why I always wanted you to write your book, live in Africa, study animal behavior, and buy your dream house on the water. Sometimes I thought Mom might have held you back, that she was the one who really ruled the roost, although generally it did seem like you did. I was looking for God to be my father, and Jung was my new ideal. It was not that long before that I had wanted you to be sports-minded like all the other fathers. You just could not win because nothing would ever be good enough for me. I had absolutely no sensitivity about what all of this was doing to you at the time, but I am anxious to find out when you respond to all of this.

You really seemed upset when I told you I was going into Jungian analysis as opposed to Freudian analysis. How could your son do this to you? It was the ultimate insult. Why would I not come to you for a referral? You had many colleagues who would have been willing to comply, but I needed to pursue my own destiny. All you seemed interested in was: Did he have the "appropriate credentials"? That was a big concern of yours, and naturally I didn't want to know about it. At the time, you seemed so caught up in such superficial things. I just liked the idea that the man from whom I did obtain a referral gave me status among the Jungian analysts in New York City, which was exactly what I wanted.

I felt as if you put me in a position of having to justify my interest in Jungian psychology. There was a strong need for your support, but I felt you were putting me down and questioning my motives. Sometimes I felt as though you had me on your analyst's couch. There were moments when I would actually fall into that dynamic and let you pick apart my dreams. But usually I found your interpretations self-serving and too "Freudian." I wanted to stick with the Jungian interpretations because they helped me separate from your overpowering opinions of me. Interestingly, I had read that Freud was threatened by Jung's view of him. They had very different ways of viewing dreams and Jung felt that Freud interpreted his dreams from his own desire to keep control of their relationship. It was documented that Freud felt that Jung's dreams revealed he had a death wish for him.

Being defensive about my need for individuality became part of my way of life. There was a great conflict between wanting to destroy you and wanting to please you at the same time. Jungian psychology and the people connected to it became my crusade. This world had nothing to do with my past, no connection to you, and more importantly was something I knew more about than you did. For a change I had control. At least I thought I had control.

It was nice that my sister was interested in the same things. She even turned me onto the mystical side of Judaism, the *Qabalah*. During those years we would visit Weiser Bookstore in the West Village. It was known for occult literature. Ellen and I finally had something in common besides *Chiller Theatre*. Having her share my new ideas seemed like a major victory. The rebellion against you seemed to be a partnership, so the responsibility for hurting you was not all mine. It was easier to not have the focus exclusively on me. We seemed to alter the triangle of our earlier years.

Ellen always seemed more like you and it was hard being the

younger brother of the family with a desire to please both of you. You both were one step ahead of me and I could not compete. This put a damper on my feeling special. I felt that Mom was the only one who understood my inner thoughts as she seemed to value me and I appeared to be very important to her.

Now my sister and I had developed a mutual interest in philosophy, spiritual teachings, and Jungian psychology. This gave me credibility with her. For the first time we were aligned on something. Unfortunately for you, we were posed against you and your Freudian background.

I had myself convinced that you were like the classical Freudian analyst I worked with in my first hospital experience after college graduation. What an introduction! He truly lived out the stereotype, with the pipe in his mouth and his every interpretation of a patient's actions reduced to something sexual. It took many years to recognize that Freud never intended his psychology to be misused that way. Freudians are not Freud and Jungians are not Jung. Max Cohen is not Freud or Freudian.

There were very few material things I asked for, but I did want Jung's collected works. When you bought them for me, I felt I was the most fortunate guy around. It was better than flipping for a Mickey Mantle baseball card. Although, it was fun to recently take Jared to Mickey Mantle's restaurant and have him autograph his photo. Amazingly he was alone in his restaurant and we had one hour with him all to ourselves. We drove down to the city when I found out he was there, and they even watched my car at the Plaza Hotel. After our outing with the Mick, we went to a Rangers hockey game. What a day we had.

Unfortunately, the price I paid for my sister's common interest was that she got the books too. Being the first child seemed to make it easier for her to ask for what she wanted. It looked as though you had to even the score. As a result of this, I felt my sister and I became competitive about material possessions—who would get the better gift or be slighted. I wanted to be the golden child with the one gift no one else would have. It was disappointing when she got the books too, but I had to surrender to your need to be fair. I wanted my sister's support against you, but on my terms. Sharing the books took away the exclusive feeling that I wanted. Maybe I was expecting too much from you, but why couldn't you give me something without feeling that you had to do the same for Ellen?

At this point I felt like the spiritual son who had to rebel against tradition. Your world represented hypocrisy and old ideals. My life was going to be more meaningful and more important than anyone else's in the family, particularly yours. I wanted no part of your life-style and values. Materialistic goals were secondary. Being the Prince from Long Island did not quite make it for me. As I said before, I was embarrassed and ashamed to admit that my background was ordinary since it did not fit in with my perceptions of my new extraordinary image. It was strange to watch Jewish kids deny their Judaism. I fortunately did not go that far. Some actually changed their last names, some temporarily, and others permanently.

This must have hurt you at the time. I remember your trying to find a way to deflate my ego and bring me back to earth. You almost succeeded with what I felt was going to be your ultimate weapon against Jung, a weapon that the Freudian community has used for years. You confronted me with the fact that Jung was anti-Semitic and did not help Freud escape the Nazis. This appalled me and seemed so inconsistent with his view of the world. I felt threatened enough to do some research on this controversial issue. To this day, there are many conflicting stories about this. Who cares right now anyway? What is important is for you and me to understand why this issue became so important in our relationship.

My understanding is that this was your final attempt to hold onto me as your son. Maybe this would turn me away from Jung and inspire an interest in your books. I had a loyalty to Jung and my emotional investment was too strong for this to end it. My identity was at stake. I found all kinds of rationalizations to pursue my interest in Jung, as if I was defending a different father against you.

To cap it off, my interest in religions other than Judaism continued. I was captivated by Eastern religion and philosophy. Naturally, Jung had had an enormous interest in the subject. I had to have a lot of courage to bring my best friend from school home to your country club wearing a turban on his head. You were a good sport about that one. After all, how often do you get a chance to meet a Jewish boy from Westchester who changes his name and thinks of himself as a guru? This was the same guy who used to get high and listen to Eric Clapton. Now the answers were in Kundalini Yoga and Yogi Bhajan.

Your sentimentality, especially when it came to family, was at times too much for me to handle. I remember how angry you were at me for not sending a card to your mother when she was very sick. There were always indirect ways of acting out my anger at you, because confronting you directly meant possible rejection. Of course now I would be furious if my kids were not thoughtful. I was certainly afraid of your anger.

In retrospect, I hurt you more, and I still feel badly about this, particularly when it comes to your mother. It was as if I had no control over what I was doing to you. I had trouble at this point behaving appropriately and playing the game of life. It always bothered me when you felt a need to remind me to buy a gift or card for special occasions and when to make the right call to someone. I felt infantilized, thinking why could you not believe in me enough to realize I could think for myself and take on my own responsibilities. You would jump ahead of me and correct mistakes before I could even make them. It was your way of pointing out the obvious. This made me so furious that at times I would be inattentive, to deliberately hurt you. Your mother must have been one of those unfortunate victims of circumstance. Enough self-justification, I must keep going here.

Actually, I admired how thoughtful you were and it had a tendency to make me feel selfish, when in fact I was the same way. It just seemed impossible to be as good a person as you. If you detect some sarcasm, there is, but I also am serious about this. The message from you was, "Don't make waves." But we all need to make our own waves and swim back to shore. You always seemed so self-assured, controlled, and able to protect yourself. I was always so vulnerable, and it was hard for me to hide feelings. My honesty tended to get me in trouble.

I never felt that you pushed me into psychology, but I do remember your advising me that getting an M.D. over a Ph.D. would be an easier and safer way to go. It was difficult not to be influenced by your opinions because they were so strong and convincing. I would look to you for guidance, but if you did not provide what I wanted I would be angry. There seemed to be an implied message that a Ph.D. in clinical psychology would not give me enough prestige. At the time there was probably some truth in this. There just was no feeling of encouragement coming from you, but then again you couldn't have had any way of knowing that I needed it at the time. I was always looking for you to have confidence in me but I just had trouble feeling it. There was a fear in me when you mentioned how difficult it would be to write a doctoral dissertation. I was intimidated and saw it as an impossible task to undertake. That line that you never thought I would graduate from high school is ringing in my ears again.

I never lost that feeling that you didn't understand the severity of my learning problems. Even after having completed college in only three years, I still felt as though I was looking for your approval and not getting it. The need to be acknowledged by you seemed so strong. Contrary to this, if it were not for your encouragement I never would have applied for Phi Beta Kappa. The credentials always appeared more important for you, but obviously I listened and went on to get it. The proof is hanging in my office now and I am not ashamed to say that I am proud of it. Of course, at the time I acted in my macho fashion as if it did not mean anything to me, but more importantly I knew it meant a great deal to you. Growing up, I suspected that my sister's accomplishments would give you more satisfaction. Remarkably many people did not attend their college graduations. It was seen as insignificant.

During this time, I was still preoccupied with not spending too much of your money and was satisfied that I saved you a year's tuition, as well as going to a state school at four hundred dollars a year. I could have never gotten into Buffalo after high school. My grades were that bad. You and I both knew that underneath this selfless gesture was a need to justify my ongoing dependency on you. Because of circumstances I was put in the position of having to ask you for something and this never came easily for me.

Let's face it, I had a good teacher, because you're certainly not comfortable asking people to do for you. When you did, it was a shock, and I felt unprepared to respond to your needs. More on this later. You were a generous father and I never felt money was held over my head, although you did have some control over what I should buy.

How many fathers take their sons to Israel for graduation from college? I was ambivalent about the trip and felt guilty about it. It seemed like a good idea until the reality of our being together for a long period of time began to set in. I never knew how you really felt about that trip to Israel. Unfortunately, I was very anxious about my future and would try to avoid being with you at all costs. The subject of what I was going to do with the rest of my life kept arising and I just did not want to talk about it—so much so that when you offered to take me to a basketball game when we came back from Israel, I couldn't wait to get away from you at half-time to join my friends.

We were better off during this period of my life having me watch a ball game in one room and you listen to opera in another. I was aware that my desire to watch sports did not quite fit in with the new image I was trying to portray. Ball games seemed to bore you, and I felt like the unappreciative son at the basketball game. It was hard for me to accept your reaching out to me. Why would you want my company when I was not even being nice to you? There was always a paranoia that you would question the seriousness of my interest in intellectual issues because I still followed professional sports. There were times when I would have the familiar embarrassment that you might be passing judgment on me for having my eyes glued to the TV. Now you would never respect my new image. I was the guy during my high school years who would hide out in the library on Monday morning reading the *New York Times Sports Section*. We all knew I was supposed to be doing my homework.

Sometimes you would walk in and I would pretend I was not interested in the game, so we would start to talk. I would become defensive and feel as if I had to justify why I was watching the game. I would quickly become bored and really want to go back to the game. But again, I held back the honesty because I didn't want to hurt you. You and I seemed to constantly walk on egg shells.

It was hard to avoid confronting my future. Everybody had to eventually face that terrifying moment of decision. When I got married there now was another person depending on me. I doubted that I would ever find a way to provide for anyone else. Did you think I was ready to get married? I had it easier than most kids my age and perhaps that made it even more frightening. How would I ever maintain the lifestyle I was accustomed to? It seemed easier to put it down and be critical of you. I could never live up to it.

My facade of being the good son was cracking, and it was becoming even harder to be around you. You became more of a threat to me now. I had it made with a father on the faculty of Columbia who was also a training analyst at the Psychoanalytic Center. This would have been every psychology major and pre-med student's dream at college. Everyone had the fantasy that if you had connections, life would be made easier for you. Part of me took comfort in that, but another side of me knew there was a danger in always counting on someone else to ease the struggle. Sometimes it seemed as if my whole path was laid out before me waiting for me to follow it. For years I watched you drive into the city at night for all those faculty meetings, just waiting for the day your son would join your world. How could I let you down?

A feeling of obligation would come over me almost forcing me to take advantage of such a good situation. Then there was something holding me back, a voice telling me that somehow I would never have the satisfaction of doing it on my own. I was concerned that other people would say that I never did it on my own. Maybe you were right when you said I cared too much what people thought of me. There I go apologizing for my actions. Guilt was easier than admitting to myself and accepting the responsibility that I felt a strong need to forge ahead without your help. Maybe I was cutting my nose to spite my face. Who knew at the time?

Being seen as Max Cohen's son was not enough for me anymore and maybe it never was. Even if my interest in Jung was just a stage, it did serve an important purpose in giving me a sense of my own identity, and it continues to do so. All of this was sitting on my head when we went to Israel. We were going to a place with so much past history in an attempt to understand the roots of the Jewish people and their future. Meanwhile, both of us were preoccupied about my future. It all seems rather ironic. There were moments when I believed this trip was designed to help me make a decision about my future. I was so mistrustful of you—constantly questioning your motives. Unfortunately, it got in the way of my being able to enjoy the trip and my heritage. At that time I wasn't interested in understanding the roots of my resistance to you or my heritage.

The timing was all off, but again how could I not appreciate what you were doing for me. How could I disappoint you this way, as I indulged in my guilt. The dissonance in my mind was like a headache requiring relief and resolution. I remember when you took me to

Mexico City when I was a young boy. You hired a guide and he took us to view the murals at the university done by Diego Rivera. Your intentions were to broaden my horizons and sadly I wouldn't let you.

During this trip I was torn between boredom, anger, guilt and my love for you. That about covers the spectrum of feelings one can have toward another person. There were times I just wanted to get away from you and was relieved when it would happen. This was similar to the feelings I had at the basketball game we attended together, but in Israel there weren't any friends to run to at half-time. I had nowhere to escape when we were sharing a room in Jerusalem, talking about my life. It was a strain on me because we had never spent so much time alone together and it seemed like we did not know what to say to each other. It was awkwardly forced and unnatural for both of us. I was just too anxious about my future to appreciate the special gesture you were making and I could not share your enthusiasm. Our time just had not come yet, and at times, I felt you were hurt and disappointed. There was the constant tension of wanting to be with you but needing to get away. I felt suffocated during our heavy talks. We just did not seem to know how to have fun and let loose with each other. We appeared to have nothing in common, and all I could feel was a pressure from you to live my life your way.

After this, I decided to make what I feel would be my last accommodation to you, and I became a pre-med student. On some level, I was never convinced that I could pull it off, but all that seemed to matter was that burning desire to see you proud of me.

Those pre-med courses were dreadful. The work didn't come naturally, but at least you were pleased with me. The students around me seemed comfortable with what they were doing and clearly wanted all this more than I did. They looked programmed, as if being a doctor was the end-all of life. It was as though their fathers decided for them at birth that they would be doctors and their lives were all planned out. Again there arose the feeling that I just did not fit in.

I was desperately trying to figure a way out of this mess and prove that there was another way for me. Could I back out gracefully? One of the most important decisions in my life came one day in Organic Chemistry class. I looked around the lab and realized I could not carry on this charade anymore. An awareness overtook me and I had to admit to myself that I was doing this for all the wrong reasons. So I packed my bags and never went back. I walked out of the lab for the last time, which probably made the other students glad since I was a hazard! They feared I may blow up the place with my klutzy hands.

How was I going to break the news to you that your son would never be a doctor? Worse, you had been my financial support and I felt guilty throwing out your hard-earned money. I wavered between feeling good about myself, and feeling like a useless loser who quit because the going got tough. You always seemed to have the capacity to stick things out no matter what the obstacle was before you. I admired your determination and patience with difficult situations—another source of intimidation. Would you now be disappointed and see me as a failure? To admit I couldn't go through with this meant I was failing as a person, since I had the belief I should be able to do anything. Now I was forced to be honest about my limitations.

My new problem was, now what? I just did not have the psychology courses and maybe being a philosophy major was indeed irrelevant. Again you were right. That really bothered me. But there was something challenging about doing things the unorthodox way and so I decided to apply to graduate schools to study psychology even without having the psychology requirements. Remember, I told you earlier that nothing could threaten me, or so I felt.

Thank God for my arrogance because it seemed to be a strong thrust behind my ambition. Maybe I caught my arrogance from you. I knew that I was putting myself on the line and in a position for possible rejection. Something in me seemed to get pleasure from this. I enjoyed living on the edge and taking risks. Once again, I was determined to prove to you, myself, and other people that I could beat the system. Could I defy the odds? Maybe I had finally met my match and there was no easy way out this time. My ego was inflated enough to believe I could pull it off because I thought I was different from everyone else. Still, part of me really did not believe that, so I threw in an application to the school of social work without your knowing about it. Could I ever ask you to pay for that now?

After spending six months living on my own in New York City and taking graduate courses in psychology at the New School for Social Research, I got married to Dee in springtime. That summer we moved into our first apartment and I took a job as a psychiatric aid at Long Island Jewish Hospital. That helped me build my self-confidence. As you know, I was rejected from the graduate schools in psychology but got into the master's program at the Columbia School of Social Work. Now what had I done? I was honestly scared and for the first time my arrogance was dissipating. Well, social work was where I was headed, and how I dreaded telling you this one. What a mess, and a humbling process. But not for long. That would have been too simple.

Your reaction, predictably, was that I would not be satisfied being in a profession that unfortunately was underpaid and historically attracted more women than men. I listened for a change and knew you might be right. Would I be able to support a family, and was my ego able to handle being in a profession that did not come close to carrying the prestige of yours? I thought, again, that I was disappointing and embarrassing you. After all, how could you tell anyone that your son was a social worker and explain why? There was still a double standard and you were a conventional man.

I compensated for all this by convincing myself, you, and everyone around me that the M.S.W. was a stepping stone to my eventually getting a Ph.D. in clinical psychology. Of course, I played that down around my social work teachers, particularly my faculty advisor. He was the god of social work and everyone looked up to him. His motto was, "The only way to learn is to forget everything you have read in all the books." I wanted to "kill him off" because he was trying to teach me humility. He came from the school that believed in making your students suffer because only then would they learn. His philosophy was similar to that of my track coach in high school. I couldn't tolerate criticism; it left no room for human error. Ironically, this advisor recently died and I felt very sad that another one of my gods had become mortal. In retrospect, he was a brilliant man who did teach me the value of getting off my high horse, as well as some group dynamics. Perhaps my goal in life was to have the ultimate conversation with God.

It was hard telling people at school what you did for a living because I had it in my head that they were all trying to figure out why I too did not become a psychiatrist. There were moments of feeling inferior, but somehow I liked to have people know what you did because it had a peculiar way of making me feel important at the same time. People seemed to treat me with a little more respect because I had been around the profession my whole life. Little did they know that I spent many years taking no interest in it. I liked telling people that I was a Jungian and you a Freudian; there was something intriguing about it.

My way of rationalizing this period of my life was to create an air of mystery that would give people something to talk about. I decided to make my years at Columbia part of my rebellion. Going into social work at Columbia certainly was different than going to medical school. At least I was admitted on my own merits. We both really wanted the same thing for me and that was self-respect. But I needed to feel it for myself and you couldn't feel it for me.

I would tend to romanticize life until you would come along and dampen it with your realism. Could you have accepted having a son who was a social worker? But the real question was, could I bear it knowing the dynamics of our relationship? There was a time when even you saw Ph.D.'s as lacking the prestige to compete with an M.D. But you always appeared to be aware of the changing times, and I had a sense you eventually became more comfortable with the idea of my making it in the world with a Ph.D. It had become a socially accepted degree and was improving in status. If anything, the recent article in *The New York Times* suggests that psychiatry is losing its credibility. I felt prestige was more important to you, but in fact perhaps I was less honest and more pretentious about those things. Some people really do not care, but we both did. Too bad I could not admit that to you then, but at least I can now. I was still going into your field and would be doing similar things. You could always prescribe the medication. The gap in the hierarchy between M.D.'s and Ph.D.'s is closing but I still feel it has a long way to go.

Your increasing support for my getting a Ph.D. served as a motivator and a vote of confidence. Interestingly, I began to sense that you were developing some respect toward me, but maybe I was just feeling better about myself. Social work training had been a very positive experience for me and I felt you really took an interest in what I was doing. I was enjoying being married and living in my own apartment. We loved living over a pizzeria and having our five dollar dinners. It seemed this was the first time you and I began to have anything in common, and it was so good to be able to share with you. I could invite you to my place for dinner and we could talk about our respective work with patients. It was a new arena for us, but I had trouble coming to you for suggestions about how to work with certain people. That would have been a big step for me at the time. Maybe I was beginning to realize that we were not so different and that we wanted the same things out of life.

I always felt you thought Dee was a good influence on me because in some ways she is more like you than I am. There were moments when I felt you gave her the credit for my maturity. You two seemed to have such a good relationship which I feel helped bring us closer together. How many fathers-in-law take their daughters-in-law shopping for clothes and out for lunch in New York City? I found myself resenting your closeness to her and it felt like my sister all over again.

Another problem I had with your relationship was that sometimes I was concerned you might have been more generous to my wife than I was. There were also times when I felt she put you on a pedestal, like everyone else did, and respected your opinion over mine on personal and professional issues. I had trouble getting over that. Sometimes I would get angry with her for suggesting that I call you to ask for your advice, but maybe her influence helped me to swallow my pride and reach out to you more. Despite the competitive feelings I had around your relationship, I knew on some level it was unusual and special for a father and daughter-in-law to be so close.

Jungian psychology was still allowing me to keep my separateness from you. It was not only the theoretical side of Jung that attracted me, but that his psychology was symbolic of a different lifestyle and perspective. It was still my private world, like my little toy soldiers that you knew nothing about.

I always thought you and my analyst would get along, and I had hoped that you two would meet. I had really managed over the years to split the two of you into "Good Daddy" and "Bad Daddy," yet I thought you might have a great deal in common. Let's face it, Freud and you had a father and so did Jung and my analyst. Another applicable thought was that your relationship with your dad, and my analyst's relationship with his, had to have influenced your opposite theoretical orientations, as well as the way each of you treated me. I was an Oedipal son to you and my analyst, but you and he were both Oedipal fathers who were once Oedipal sons, with all kinds of reactions to me that stemmed from your respective relationships with your fathers. Oedipal fathers activate Oedipal sons. As you know, people in the field of psychology call this counter transference. What I am relating to you are my feelings about how I perceived who you were, the effect on me, and how I have reacted to it. We have both affected each other and the transferential nature of our projected expectations kept our myth going, similar to Freud and Jung.

I believe that psychotherapists have not opened up enough about their own personal feelings, or about how they affect patients as well as their families. The therapeutic alliance is often a reenactment of a parent/child relationship.

As much as you wanted me to believe in your ideas about psychotherapy, I had an equal investment in convincing you that Jungian therapy was the ultimate. We needed to constantly justify ourselves to each other.

I was accepted into a Ph.D. program in Clinical Psychology. Dee and I were headed to San Francisco. Your son was going to be able to put "Dr." in front of his name. I liked that too. You taught me that other people consider credentials to be an important determinant in how they judge you. At this point I was beginning to admit this to myself but not as yet to you. There was still a feeling I would perceive in you and other people that: who I was had credibility, but that I could never "be you." There seemed to be the assumption that any success I had, or would have, was and would be attributable to having a father in the profession. This really troubled me until I was able to see that I did it on my own, and I was determined to do that. My new mission was to prove that an M.S.W. and Ph.D. were equal, if not better, training and prestige than what you had. But being a student forced me to continue to rely on money from you. It seemed the only way I would feel like my own person was to physically move three thousand miles away from you.

There was a lot of guilt tied up with leaving and it was certainly not alleviated when I felt your difficulty with letting go of me. I became uncomfortable when I felt you were denying the reality of what was going on. It honestly felt as though you did not hear me when I said that I could end up living out there permanently. The only way to make the break was to move out there with Dee and maintain that attitude. Dee and I both needed to grow up into adulthood. I was anxious about being able to provide for my future family the way you did for me. Until men can resolve that problem, they have trouble committing to a relationship and even feel it as a burden. I do not think we could have grown up living close to you and Mom. We were at the point where we could not make a decision without you. Although I felt you were genuinely happy for me, and knew this was in my best interests, there was that other part of you which had trouble accepting it. I remember your suggestion that I should leave my furniture in New York and rent a furnished apartment. You seemed to see this move as a rerun of my departure for college. That made me angry.

Even psychiatrists can have trouble with separation. It makes you more human and I hope that exposure does not bother you. (There I go trying to take care of you again.) I feel that we should reveal the more human side of ourselves—let's tear down the blank screen. The fantasies will come anyway. Look at our relationship. We know some of each other's vulnerabilities, and it did not stop our fantasies about each other. As I am writing it is clear to me that I still have the need to reassure you that writing this book will be okay. There is a persistent fear in me that you will not go through with it.

Anyway, back to moving out West and starting a new life. It seemed essential for my growth, as you were later able to acknowledge. There was some irritation with your denial of my need to grow up and I wanted to say, "Dad, I am not in college anymore, let go." Freud had to let go of Jung.

Maybe part of me wanted to punish you when I said that I might never come back. But there was also a strong conviction that this was all part of my destiny. There was no doubt in my mind that it was a healthy move for my own development as a person. I had always wanted to live in California and see how the other side of the country lived. Didn't the Torah talk about Abraham needing to leave his father, that his mission was to go away to another world? California was my calling, and San Francisco was the Holy City. How exciting and scary to go off into a world where I knew no one! Now each of us seemed to see in the other the realization of our worst fears about the father/son relationship—my fear of remaining dependent, and your fear of displacement. I was off to Marin County, that suburban paradise with the rainbow tunnel to help reinforce my need to feel special.

Moving to California was overwhelming. It was as if a whole new world had opened up for me. I really felt like this was an ideal place for me to grow up and establish a new identity. I think every phase of my life has created a need to be someone different.

It bothered me that my long distance conversations always seemed to involve you in my decisions related to new material acquisitions. Although I really did want your opinion, you knew that if you did not give me the answer I was looking for, you would certainly suffer my wrath.

It also bothered me that you would encourage me to be my own person and then contradict yourself by interfering. As much as I thought you wanted me to have the same affinities and aversions you did, I in fact expected as much from you. It seemed too hard to keep you out of my life. I was angry at myself for not being able to trust my own judgment, and soon enough I realized it was not healthy to consult you on everything.

First, Dee and I bought a sports car—very impractical, but fun. After all, if you could have your frivolous pleasures driving a sports car, why couldn't I? Dee was freelancing as an artist and I worked part time. I enjoyed that commute over the Golden Gate Bridge. The difference was that I was still financially dependent on you. Then, we actually bought a house. What made it worse, in terms of dealing with you, was the fact that you were always rather conservative about decisions that really excited me. I felt you did not trust or respect my judgment. I felt that your negative opinions were best exemplified by your telling me that it was too risky to buy a house in California. You had a way of reinforcing my self-doubts. All I wanted was some encouragement and for you to share in my happiness.

During this time one of your closest friends moved out West and, true to form, I became dependent on him for fatherly approval. He seemed to be the new god in my life: a psychiatrist who had left the establishment, came out West, and bought a gorgeous home in California. He was even going to be a writer. He was all the things I thought I wanted you to be. I went from wanting you to be the best sports fan in America, to wanting you to be the most interesting and well-rounded psychiatrist.

Now I realize that these apparent opposites are the flip side of the same coin. At the time, your friend seemed so carefree and open-minded. I was projecting onto him all my fantasies about what I could be. He seemed to be supportive of everything I was doing. He was the perfect stereotype, the gypsy shrink moving west to shake up his life. His home, lifestyle, and art collection left my tongue hanging out. We had so much in common, even both our wives were artistic. I enjoyed hearing him share old stories about the two of you.

From a radical in college running away from tear gas and putting all your values down, I was transformed into a guy who wanted only to find the right couch and a painting to hang above it. *House Beautiful* was now sitting next to all my Jung texts—very ironic seeing that I always thought you were the more materialistic of the two of us. Diego Rivera murals didn't look so bad to me anymore.

Buying the house was a turning point for me in our relationship because I went against your wishes and made a major decision by myself. Of course, it worked out because the California real estate market boomed, as we knew. Sunday open houses were the thing to do. For a change I could fling an "I told you so" at you because you always felt that if ever I wanted to move back East it would be hard to sell the house.

Whenever my decisions turned out right, you seemed to then be able to jump on the bandwagon, as if the past judgments had never occurred. I had the attitude that buying a house did not automatically signify permanence, and I began to think that only easterners thought that way. Now, in retrospect, it might have had more to do with the changing times and the difference in our generations. But I felt my buying a house was threatening to you because it meant I would never come back East to live.

Making an adult decision without your approval and support gave me a sense of real freedom and power that I had never experienced before. But, of course, there was still guilt attached to it because you continued helping me out financially. Again, this made me feel as if I had to spend the money the way you wanted me to. Our lifestyles had become profoundly different, but in a direction that was hardly predictable during the college years. Here I was with the nice California contemporary home and making decorating plans. You liked to look at art in museums but I only wanted to buy it for my house. This was the beginning of my passion for collecting art.

It has never been clear to me how much you wanted nice things and an impressive home. Did Mom's not wanting to move hold you back? She was obviously comfortable staying in the modest house Ellen and I grew up in. I found myself wanting you to get your way. As I have said before, it was hard to tell who was the dominant one when it came to this kind of decision, but it seemed to be Mom. There were certain things you appeared to have final say on, and I was aware that I had a need not to see you subordinated by Mom or anyone else for that matter. I wanted a sensitive father who could also be strong. You had a lot to live up to. It was disappointing to me when you didn't buy the house in Glen Cove on the water. It would have been a real risk and you know I had an investment in seeing you shake things up. I knew you got restless in your forties.

Whenever I would make extravagant purchases, like my stereo, I would feel defensive. There was some disapproval from you, as though I should have settled for something less expensive, "Why live on the edge and put yourself in a hole?" That seemed to be your favorite line. My response would be, "because I wanted to." For this reason, I felt better living my own life, making independent decisions and not even sharing my excitement with you.

Your friend in California seemed to be the other extreme. He was enthusiastic about everything. I questioned his sincerity at times, as well as my own. My own supervisor in graduate school once accused me of being insincere when I told a student I would see him later. She said, "Why did you say that when you know it's not true?" How many times do people say things they don't pursue? At one time a buoyant kind of response from your friend was appealing and I needed that to help sustain the confidence I was building.

I became a real California chauvinist and was convinced that this lifestyle was the only way to go. The weather was ideal, similar to an East Coast fall. During this past week I have become very nostalgic about my life in San Francisco, which has helped me to write this part of the letter. In my mind, living in the East was inferior and the new rivalry was emerging between us. Freud vs. Jung became East vs. West. It was a matter of who was going to have the bragging rights to happiness regarding their respective coasts. Our long distance conversations seemed to be a contest of who could make whom feel he was missing out on more. We could not even admit it to each other if the weather was bad. We loved to tell you about our full course meal courtesy of Bill Graham, the Rock & Roll Maestro of the Filmore

East and West, and being part of the Rock & Roll subculture of San Francisco. We felt privileged.

This became another power struggle and I was determined to give you the impression that I did not need you. Of course I did, but you were not going to be let in on that. Here I was, thinking I was emotionally free, but really all I had was three thousand miles of physical distance from you.

I was even becoming jealous when I realized that you and my sister were spending more time together. I felt excluded again and thought I was losing control. What made it even worse was that the two of you were beginning to have more in common professionally, and she was taking more of an interest in your approach to things. You were going to be proud of her and not me. Now I really felt alone and the misfit in the family. Fortunately, I was good at repressing these feelings at the time.

When you would come out to visit, I felt pressured to entertain you and often experienced it as an interruption in my life. That's why our trips away from San Francisco were more relaxed. It was the most concentrated amount of time we had spent together since Israel. But these trips seemed to take on a different quality because Dee and Mom were with us, and happily, Mom got along with Dee as well as you did. The women in our lives seemed to be a quieting influence on our relationship so that we could enjoy each other without all the focus being just the two of us.

Traveling outside of San Francisco we were on neutral territory and no one had to defend their respective homes as the better place to live. San Francisco was my world and I did not want anything that had to do with my past to take it away from me. It was my new promised land. It sounds similar to the way I used to feel about playing with my little soldiers, Mickey Mantle books, and Jungian psychology. It seems as though I always needed some sort of device giving me boundaries and a sense of having my own self. I would find any means to feel powerful in order to defend against my feelings of insignificance.

When I literally left you standing alone at Fisherman's Wharf one day, it was because it was uncomfortable being around you, similar to the feeling at the basketball game in Madison Square Garden when the same thing happened. I felt compromised around you, and the threat of losing my so-called newly acquired power was unbearable.

I did not want the same thing to happen that occurred during college vacations. Those feelings have been expressed earlier in this letter.

You just seemed to have a way of making me feel like a foolish little boy who had to obey his father. When I was alone I felt like a man, but you had such an intimidating effect on me. The only way I knew how to handle this at the time was to walk away from you. I was too timid to tell you my feelings at the time because I never wanted to hurt you, but now it is important for me to be honest with you.

The best part of writing these letters to you now is the perspective adulthood brings. At times you seemed sensitive and vulnerable, so I had to be indirect about my feelings towards you. In the long run, I know I hurt you more by not being open with you. I don't know if you ever knew I had these feelings, but now I hope you can understand where I am coming from. It sounds like an apology, and maybe it is.

This whole time must have been difficult for you. At the time, I thought of these visits as your "vacations to hell." You put up with so much grief, and I remember you being so angry once that you threatened to never visit me again. That hurt me and I would never have been able to live with it. I was just not secure enough at the time to maintain my own boundaries with you. The feeling of being controlled was hard to escape.

When you asked me to drive you to the airport at the end of one of your visits, I actually had the nerve to refuse. You ended up taking a cab. It was hard for you to ask me to do things for you, and hard for you to be direct about it. I felt you expected me to feel an obligation towards you because you would have done the same for me. My only interest was to prove to you that I did not have to do something just because you would have. Remember, I was the romantic idealist who believed in unconditional love. Whatever happened to good old-fashioned remorse?

Our relationship was clearly unbalanced. You were the one who said relationships are a two way street. I was going to assert my independence and my rights as a human being. Although I knew this was hurting you, something in me could not resist acting this way. Having to re-examine this time in my life is upsetting to me and I continue to realize what I put you through. You needed a lot of patience to deal with me. My son will probably test me in the same or some similar way. Part of my problem with driving you to the airport was that I always perceived you as a man who would do for everyone else and never ask much from others. After all, psychiatrists don't have needs; they are always helping everyone else with their problems.

Your reluctance to burden people has rubbed off on me. But I was too selfish. Your public and personal image contributed to my holding back on you because I was not used to having you demand much from me. I guess you could say I was spoiled. There was no way I was prepared for this dynamic in our relationship and my only interest was in maintaining a self-centered, one-sided relationship between the two of us. I could justify this by romanticizing my philosophical stance on unconditional love. Maybe unconditional love could be seen as just selfish love, but how unromantic. False independence is often a substitute for the inability to feel self-reliant.

Toward my graduation and Dee's pregnancy I began to confront the realities of my future. I could not imagine having my children grow up without you knowing them. It really threatened me when you would remind me of this possibility. The thought of not having you to share my professional life and growth was also very disturbing. I always tried to leave the door open about moving back East as long as I could save face. I had my pride and "independence" at stake. Part of me was doing this for my own protection, but I was also protecting you from being hurt and disappointed. When I rented an office in Mill Valley, a town outside of San Francisco where I lived, something in me knew I would never see a patient there. This suspicion proved true and finally I had to confront the fact that staying out West would be running away from you and from my self-doubts. One day the psychiatrist who was sharing on office mentioned that he noticed I never saw a patient. I smiled somewhat embarrassed and admitted I was moving back to the East Coast.

When you would tell me that I would never move back once I started my practice, there was a great deal of denial on my part. In my heart I knew you were right. Somehow, Dee and I both were afraid of looking back and saying we never had the chance to know what it would have been like to be adults on the East Coast. We left as immature kids and now felt a need to see what it would be like as adults. Could we do it?

At this point I felt a bit apprehensive, but more relieved, about my decision to move back to "home territory." I was excited about the prospect of being close to you. When you came out for graduation and met one of my teachers who knew you from his training days in New York, I felt proud to have you as my father. I felt important now and it seemed as though a bridge had been built between East and West as you watched me get my doctorate. It was a fulfilling and meaningful moment for me. I felt you were proud of me at last and that we could stand together as equals—maybe even as friends.

It meant a great deal to me that you flew across the country for my graduation. Here we were, sharing a room together again, but the difference was that now I had a more predictable future. All my rebelliousness seemed trivial and well behind us. Emerging was a new closeness, sense of trust, and the beginning of a friendship.

I had all kinds of fantasies about my new life in the East. Your friend, my recent "idol," had lots of connections and I was going to get a prestigious post-doctoral fellowship. How convenient that your friend was coming back too, and helped bolster my enthusiasm. He had all the right answers to justify moving back, and he certainly was a romantic at heart. His word was God and I believed whatever he would say. I was even willing to spend a year in your professional territory learning all the psychoanalytical literature that I had always avoided and negated. Naturally I was going to bring with me all my Jungian expertise and convert everyone around me.

I finally was sure I was pleasing you when you threw me a surprise party to welcome me home. You had happiness spread all over your face. Was the tension between us dissolved? Unfortunately, this was wishful thinking. The relationship just continued to evolve in an unpredictable fashion. Your son was going to come around and have a conventional training experience.

When I decided to live in Connecticut, I felt it was still important for me to have my own life separate from yours. I knew your friend was moving to Connecticut. I thought he would take care of my professional needs and he felt moving there was a good idea. He believed physical distance was good for our relationship and vital if I were to make my own mark.

Even though I knew you wanted me to live on Long Island, you really were great about helping me find a house in Connecticut. I felt you were actually enthusiastic about the house. You even said you would not mind living in a house like that, and you liked to show it off to your friends because you appeared to be proud of it.

Your approval made me feel good, but I also felt uncomfortable with the knowledge that your son was living in a nicer and more expensive house than yours. Some of this was alleviated by the fact that I used my own money, because we sold our house in California for a profit. The fact that I could practice out of the house, made me keenly aware that you to wanted changes at this stage of your life. This was the source of some guilt, however not precipitated by you. I was becoming more sensitive to your needs, and I wanted to see your dreams fulfilled. It was clear to me that you were starting to take me seriously.

I would feel badly when you would bring up the possibility of our establishing a joint practice. At times, it seemed an appealing prospect, but I was more drawn to making it on my own. I had visions of you telling me what tie I should wear to the office. There was that familiar concern about disappointing you, so I was keeping the door open. You repeated what you once told me when I was living out West, that once I got started with my practice in Connecticut I would never move. This time I decided to risk it and see patients in my office at home. I knew once again that you were right. I was not sure I could make it on my own, and in the back of my mind I had the security of knowing we could always practice together. Although I knew this was possible, it was also obvious that you could not present me with a practice. You couldn't simply bring me into the business.

My fear of failure became the substitute for my earlier childhood fear of death. You were the old ace in the hole; it does wonders for you when you are feeling insecure. It was so nice to know you were alive and well. During this period I was compelled to disagree with your opinions about my never moving for two reasons: one, I wanted to protect myself from the possibility of not succeeding on my own, and two, I felt bad for you. How nice it would be to have your son come into practice with you! At least that is what I thought you always felt, but maybe I felt it would have been nice for me.

It meant a great deal to me when you said you would never want me to go into practice with you if it was caused by my failure to make it on my own. I would rather reject something from a position of strength; then it would be by choice. Your statement was so important to me and made me aware of how fortunate I was to have a supportive father. It is, and was, sad because you did want us to practice together, but you acknowledged the fact that I needed to prove myself professionally, and I did accomplish that. I would never leave my practice and move to Long Island to work with you. It was a real paradox.

Things really seemed to be improving. Now we managed to put only one hour of distance between us. Again, what was important to me was that Connecticut had no previous history for me to overcome. The need to compare coasts was now translated into Connecticut vs. Long Island. Living in the sticks of New England vs. what you considered civilization was about the only distinction between our two lives. What would it mean if there hadn't been at least some of the rivalry still remaining from the past? We were progressing, or so it seemed.

Love,
Donald

* * *

Dear Donald,

Your last letter affected me differently from the way your earlier letters did, dealing as it does with more recent events. Our contrasts of perception concerning those issues over which we came into conflict apparently remain relatively unchanged. Perhaps more time will have to pass before we can both view these issues with sufficient dispassion to reconcile our views.

For now, I can only recount them from my vantage point, and in some instances it may almost seem as if we are talking about different events. Of course, these are just different versions of the same events, viewed through the eyes of different participants. This is the same phenomenon so brilliantly dramatized in the Japanese film *Rashomon* in which a man's rape and murder of his wife is portrayed several times as experienced through the perception of several participants. Each perceived something quite different from the others, and none of them accurately perceived what actually happened, illustrating the fact that perception is profoundly influenced by the perceiver's emotional bias.

I wrote the paragraph above after a first reading of your last letter, and then put it aside for several days in order to digest what you had written while trying to reconstruct my own memories of the events you described. My initial reaction was that you had unfairly portrayed my behavior during those years, and I was moved to put the shoes back onto their appropriate feet. I was angered and my reaction was to put the record straight and vindicate myself.

Within a few days, my anger and defensiveness subsided and I read your letter again, a little confused because what you wrote hardly justified my reaction. There were still disparities between your recollections and mine, but they were much more understandable as I contemplated where you were coming from. I had made a transition from the defensive "all selfless" father to the more compassionate and empathic friend who wanted to understand how you felt when the incidents you described occurred. As the process unfolded, I realized that I was evaluating your words more and more analytically, much the way I do in my professional work.

As I write this, I am aware that I am not adequately expressing the intensity of the emotions I experienced. It was truly a significant emotional experience for me as I began to realize how deeply ingrained in me this response pattern is. I wonder whether this isn't, in fact, the underlying essence of much of what you describe.

We all wear many different hats as we shift in our lives from one role to another. The role of father who is an authoritarian, teacher, and disciplinarian; the role of father as devoted and empathic friend and confidante; and finally, in my case, the role of father who is drenched in the outlook and mindset of the analyst and is conditioned to examine behavior in terms of underlying meaning and motivation. If this is occurring now, it surely must characterize my responses to you during all the years you were growing up.

Perhaps this accounts in some measure for the apparent confusion and ambivalence you experienced in your feelings about me. I was, I now realize, several different people to you, as I shifted from one role to another. It is even further complicated by the fact that I shifted from one mood to another as human beings inevitably do. How complicated we human beings are and how difficult it must be for a kid to make coherent sense out of such complicated phenomena!

You ask how I felt when you went off to college. I was both hopeful and apprehensive. I was hopeful because I knew that it was very important for you to separate from us and to find your own identity away from the umbrella that Mom and I had diligently provided. I was apprehensive because you seemed to have had so much trouble in high school sorting out your priorities and addressing yourself intelligently to your responsibilities. I knew that you had the personal resources, but you never demonstrated an ability to persevere when the going got tough. I was also apprehensive because I was aware of the growing social storm as young people were increasingly rebelling against a war which made no sense to them but in which they were being asked to risk their lives. Your generation, unlike mine, had been brought up to ask questions and to demand rational explanations, rather than to blindly accept the infallible wisdom of authority, and your generation was now asking questions with a vengeance.

The war was obviously wrong and young people were justified in their refusal to fight a war which they couldn't understand. They hadn't been asked, but they were expected nevertheless to obediently comply. But the challenge to authority, order and tradition didn't stop there. Every tradition was being challenged, and by their nature, traditions often cannot be rationally justified. Things are done in certain ways because this is the way they have been done for millennia. To deny their validity is to deny the validity of cultural evolution, and the trial and error process that governs the transmission of learned values and behavior from one generation to another.

Traditions survive because they work, insofar as they satisfy human needs and allow an orderly transition of social institutions from one generation to another. When they no longer work because they have become anachronistic, they either evolve gradually into something more consistent with changing needs and perceptions, or they change violently as they tended to do during the 1960's.

But as is always true, it is one thing to tear down what exists and yet another quite different thing to replace it with something better. Your generation succeeded temporarily—exposing the many hypocrisies my generation, and the generations before mine, had so blindly accepted. But since you failed to replace it with something better, there remained only a choice between chaos, and a regression to even more conservative values than my generation espoused. We are now witnessing a return to militarism and appeals to blind chauvinism, as we are provided the specter of a "window of vulnerability" so soon after we jubilantly buried the "missile gap."

Along with all the other parents of that era, we were terrified by the violent chaos which overran the college campuses. Mass hysteria reached a climax with the massacre at Kent State, and I vividly remember how frightened you sounded when you telephoned us at that time. I was apprehensive when you left for college, but I hadn't even contemplated the massive upheaval that occurred so soon after you left. Concerns about whether you would manage your life responsibly gave way to genuine concerns for your physical safety.

Interestingly, I never worried about your succumbing to the "drug craze" so prevalent in colleges at the time. Although I knew that you were trying very hard to look the part, I somehow knew that you, like your sister, were a "phony" hippie. You played the part because you enjoyed the scene and wanted to belong to the "in crowd." I confidently believed that you would not be seduced by the promise of a quick fix, or instant insight, on a psychedelic trip.

One memory is firmly fixed in my mind. Mom and I eagerly anticipated our first and only visit to you after you had been at Ohio University for several months. We expected changes, but hardly the transformation we encountered when we found you in your dorm. You looked like a bizarre caricature of the fashionable rebel of that era. Your hair was long and disheveled, covered by a funny leather wide-brimmed hat. You had a long straggly beard, and a vest, shirt, and jeans which, though probably clean, looked as if they had never been laundered. Donald, you were a weird and shocking sight to my eyes, completely remodeled from the neatly groomed kid who had left home just a few months before. I'm sure you anticipated my shock and distress, but you were still visibly disturbed by it.

I do recall my futile efforts to persuade you that you were doing yourself a disservice by giving the impression in your appearance that you were into drugs. You meekly but persistently retorted that when people knew you they would realize that you weren't what you appeared to be. I countered that many people would be put off by your appearance and never get to know you.

Can you have forgotten the episode which occurred that weekend that so vividly dramatized that whole issue? We were at a luncheonette just off campus and the proprietor accused you of having, a few days earlier, left the restaurant without paying your check He was obviously enraged, insisting that he was sure it was you because of your outrageous appearance. You were embarrassed and dismayed but quickly responded that you hadn't even been there for several weeks.

I was certain that you were telling the truth because I just knew this was something you wouldn't have done. Although you might absentmindedly leave without paying, something I might even do, I had no doubt that you were being truthful about not having been there. I confidently defended you and you appeared very relieved that I sided with you. That was the closest rapport we achieved all weekend, but I could not resist using it to support my argument that your appearance was a detriment which needlessly evoked scorn and prejudice.

It's fascinating to me that you forgot this episode or at least overlooked it in your account of that year in your life. Do you remember it now? Is it possible that you simply overlooked it or avoided thinking about it as you were reconstructing the events of that year?

Maybe it was much more memorable for me because it tended to support my bias about the struggle between us. We tend, after all, to emphasize those perceptions that support our prejudices, and neglect or ignore experiences which contradict them. This is true of the bigot who sees only the failings and shortcomings of the Black or the Jew, ignoring anything which might be inconsistent with the perceiver's prejudice. It is equally true of the snob who sees only evidence of his superiority. I recall a man whom I saw professionally who was terrified of dogs, even small ones, and sought to justify his phobic reactions by bringing me clippings from the newspapers about incidents of dogs attacking humans. From his point of view, one might think the newspapers were full of such stories, but he managed to find them.

I have a problem relating my memory of our relationship with your portrayal of the intensity of competitiveness between us, and your perception that I seemed so intrusive and controlling in my attitude toward you. Surely I was aware that you had such feelings, but not nearly to the extent that you describe. Your behavior should have informed me that you were indeed struggling to assert your independence and get out from under me. It's undoubtedly a case of knowing and yet not wanting to believe or accept, a phenomenon that we so often see in our patients. How many times do patients, confronted with a seemingly new insight, comment on the fact that although they somehow always knew, they never fully understood or acknowledged it to themselves. It's like being stuck on the logic of an argument based on an initial premise which is assumed to be valid. But if the initial premise is misleading, the whole argument is invalid.

In the case of the parent, the initial premise is that the parent knows best what is in the child's best interest, and if the child sees it differently, it is because of the child's immaturity. After all, wasn't it reasonable for me to assume that my way and my values and what I wanted for you were really what was best for you? How could you so stubbornly resist the logic of my arguments?

I knew, and yet I refused to acknowledge even to myself, that you were coming from a different place, that the world looked different to you from that place, and that you were frantically searching to find your own niche in the different world that you perceived. It's still amazing to me that people who are so deeply involved with each other can nevertheless be unable to relate effectively to each other's differing points of view.

Of all the things you've written about so far, your description of our discussions about philosophy and Jung was the most difficult for me to swallow. On my first reading, I felt that you portrayed me as pompous, self-centered, condescending, and self-aggrandizing, as if I was trying to reinforce my own self-esteem at your expense. How unfair and unreasonable it seemed! Here I was the defensive father, so maligned and misunderstood.

After a few days, and re-reading your letter, I began to relate to what you must have felt when I didn't respond to your enthusiasm about a particular spiritual or metaphysical issue with appreciation, admiration, and enthusiasm of my own. I felt so badly about having "put you down." That surely was not my intention. Maybe you are right about my never having been comfortable with spiritual or occult ideas. I was experiencing what is a familiar pattern. Following an initial reaction of anger, I then feel guilty and compassionate.

My recollection of those conversations when you came home on school holidays is naturally different from yours. I should have been pleased that your interests had shifted to more intellectual issues, and I believe I genuinely was. This, however, did not prevent my chagrin that you embraced ideas and points of view that were largely alien or incomprehensible to me. More importantly, your passionate interest in and devotion to Carl Jung seemed motivated by rebellious feelings toward me. I read the materials you gave me conscientiously, and I thought that I tried to understand what you felt was valuable and enlightening.

You seemed to ignore the distinction between philosophy and psychology, between metapsychological speculation and theoretical speculation which can be tested by observational data. Finally, you seemed to fall into the trap of reifying the ideas you were expressing, treating speculation as if it is factual and material. As you know, Freudians have often fallen into the same trap, and critics have often failed to distinguish Freud's metaphysical speculations from the more clinically-rooted empirical observations and inferences pertaining to human motivations.

I don't doubt that I was angry at you for so enthusiastically adopting a frame of reference which seemed so inconsistent with my view of man's place in the world. Man in my view, is the product of millions of years of evolution, countless trials and errors, as natural forces sort out those attributes which contribute to successful adaptation and survival in an often hostile and competitive environment. Man is supreme on earth because his brain had evolved to the extent that his capacity for learning, comprehending, and inventing has ultimately enabled him to largely dominate, control, and manipulate his environment.

This evolutionary view of man doesn't, of course, preclude the operation of spiritual values or divine forces. It has always seemed to me that it is the height of human arrogance and blasphemy to attribute man's most despised characteristics to God. How could God be prideful and vengeful? Indeed, why would such human experiences even be relevant in governing the manifestations of divine influence? It seems to me more reasonable to assume that ethical, moral, and spiritual values and beliefs have evolved because they serve man's adaptational needs. That is to say they are useful insofar as they promote survival, social harmony, and order.

Although I diligently read and pondered the materials you asked me to read, you made it evident that you didn't, in those years, reciprocate the courtesy by reading anything I suggested to you. It was as if you were trying to convert me to your new religion, but you felt no need to even understand my pagan beliefs. I addressed the ideas you presented with all the open-mindedness I could muster, but obviously I was biased by my own deeply held convictions. When we discussed these issues, I remember trying to approach them logically and feeling frustrated because you seemed to want me to accept your beliefs on faith, as an acknowledgment of your new maturity and wisdom.

I realize now that all you wanted was for me to acknowledge that you were my equal and that there were meaningful and valuable things you could teach me. And you did teach me. I remember discussions with you about Jung's concept of the collective unconscious and its similarity to the concept of cultural evolution, and the transmission of tradition and knowledge from one generation to another. Still, you seemed impatient with my efforts to reconcile our differing views.

Perhaps I seemed patronizing or condescending, but I really don't believe that I wanted to be. I did want you to admire me and love me, but does that mean I wanted you to worship me or be inspired by me? Even worse, does it mean that I wanted to humble you so as to enhance my own god-like image? My inclination is to reject the notion that my motives and goals required that you be humbled. But I wonder!

Is admiring and loving someone an inevitably humbling experience? The idealization of a romantically loved person certainly involves a humbling of the self. Can one admire or look up to someone without putting oneself on a lower level? How else can one look up to another? I do remember clearly the fantasies I had before you were born, and while you were growing up, that involved your admiring and loving me. It never occurred to me that the fulfillment of those fantasies required that you be put down or humbled.

In the normal course of growing up, a boy might reasonably

be awed by his father's superior size, strength, and wisdom. These perceptions might be intimidating, but in the presence of love and encouragement, the child will hopefully be inspired to emulate his father's admired traits. In the course of further development, the boy grows to be as big or even bigger than his father. He may also discover that he is smarter than his father, or that his father is no longer even admirable. In fact, he might even discover that what he believed about his father when he was young and naive was not even true. What a painful disillusionment for the son. What a devastating humiliation for the father. This is the Oedipal tragedy.

Do you remember Willy Loman in Arthur Miller's *Death of a Salesman?* In all my years of going to the theatre, I have never been more powerfully moved than I was by that play. I remember feeling choked up and tearful as Willy fell from grace in his sons' eyes. I remember being obsessed with this theme in the play long after seeing it, and subsequently reading it, and trying to relate my reaction to my relationship with my own father. It didn't quite fit.

Of course, my perception of my father gradually changed as I grew up, but there was never the traumatic disillusionment suffered by Willy Loman's sons. My father remained, until his death, someone whose love and approval I valued greatly. What was more remarkable was the lingering and persistent doubt that he loved me. He didn't do anything to inspire my doubts that I can remember, so I assume it derived from my own guilt. But guilt about what? Did I fail him in some way, or did I fail to measure up to some expectation of me? If not failure, could I feel guilty about being more successful than he was?

It seems like a no-win situation I'm setting up. Conflicts that permeate the issue of success and failure are inevitable. We are constantly measuring ourselves against other people. We aspire to be like or achieve like the people we admire, and these are the people with whom we compete. When frustrated in our pursuits, we think about the people we don't admire and whom we surpass, and we try to reassure ourselves that we are not failures.

If the people with whom we compete are the people we would otherwise admire, doesn't this inevitably generate feelings of hostility? Is the desire to measure up to or even surpass someone possible without some implicit hostile feeling toward our rival? We handle this dilemma by compartmentalizing our lives. A rival on the tennis court becomes a buddy as soon as the game is over. Business rivals may think of each other as friendly enemies, as in a game. The coaches who manage professional athletes speak of a "killer instinct" in successful athletes for whom winning the game is an all-consuming passion.

Interestingly, I never think about any of this on the tennis court except during the occasional times you and I play. I am acutely aware of the conflicts I feel about the competition. My satisfaction at hitting a good shot which you can't return is consciously tempered by empathy for your inability to make the return. I want to win, but when I'm winning, I'm aware of the mixed feelings about it. I wonder whether you have similar feelings.

When you were applying to doctoral programs in psychology, if you recall, I was very encouraging and even enthusiastic about your going to California to study. If anything, I always assumed that my encouragement was an important motivating force in your decision to go. When you, and especially Dee, expressed misgivings about being so far from your families and lifelong ties, I vividly recall reassuring you both that the distance would prove to be an exciting and rewarding experience which would be invaluable for both of you at that point in your lives.

Of course, I felt my own misgivings and concerns and I did expect to miss you. You're right in that I didn't view this at the time as a permanent move. I did indeed assume that you were going to California to complete your studies, as if you were going away to college, and then when you had completed your doctoral program you would return to the East Coast to settle down permanently. You both seemed to have trepidations about even this temporary move, and I never doubted that you also regarded it as a temporary move. I do believe that you didn't seriously consider living in California permanently until after you had been out there for a while.

The comments you make in your last letter about my unwillingness to believe that you intended to remain in California permanently are partly true, but I don't think that you really believed it then either. I didn't believe it, that is, until the moment of decision when you were approaching the completion of your schooling. You say I felt threatened by it, but I think that "threatened" is not the right word. I was sad and unhappy about the distance that geography would impose between us, and that Mom and I would be unable to know your children the way I knew we would want to know them. I also felt that it would be a loss for them if they grew up so far removed from any family.

At various times you've asked me for advice, and I always advised you to the best of my ability. Sometimes my advice was good and sometimes events proved my advice unwise. Yet I always expressed my best judgment and did so with as much conviction as I felt at the time. Obviously, you didn't always agree with me, and by this time in your life you surely were making decisions based on your own judgments, whether I agreed or not.

You reproach me for not supporting you when you came to me for advice, but how could I have supported what I didn't believe was wise? Once you made your decision, I accepted it and supported it as best I could. When one asks for advice or for an opinion, one inevitably runs the risk of receiving an opinion which is unwelcome. Otherwise, you're looking for support to alleviate your own anxieties about a decision you've already made.

This obviously was the case when you asked me for an opinion about whether you should buy a house in Mill Valley. You would have been more honest with yourself and with me if you had simply stated that, for better or worse, you had decided to buy a house, and that you wanted my blessing. I'm sure you would have received it, as indeed I believe you did once you acknowledged that you had decided to take the step.

This touches on another dilemma of parenthood. A parent is accused of being judgmental, controlling and unwilling to let go if he or she sincerely believes that an adolescent or adult son or daughter is doing something unwise or self-destructive. If a parent approves and supports behavior which the parent believes to be unwise, isn't the parent abdicating responsibility in pursuit of being loved by the child? A parent who thus becomes a rubber stamp is hardly the ideal.

This is an ongoing problem for parents and I believe it always will be. I'm not talking about a father or mother who controls or manipulates to serve some personal end or need. An over-anxious mother who cripples her child in an effort to alleviate her own anxieties may rationalize that she is thus expressing love. But we know that the child's real well-being is being sacrificed to the mother's personal needs. Similarly, a father who dominates and humiliates his child for the purpose of aggrandizing himself is clearly not behaving in the best interests of the child.

Here I'm talking about the reasonably healthy, caring parent who sincerely wants what he or she believes is best for the child. Such a parent also has the frequent task of taking unwelcome positions vis-à-vis the child. Such is the nature of discipline when the child is younger. Such also is the nature of advice to a more mature child.

Unsolicited advice is never welcome, and even solicited advice is unwelcome if it expresses an opinion which differs from the opinion being sought. Inevitably, the giver of unwelcome advice is viewed with suspicion and hostility. So who said it's easy to be a parent!

Our visits to you in California were, as you suspected, very painful to me because I experienced your rejection of me very sharply. Mom and Dee spent a great deal of time together doing things of interest to both of them. For the most part, especially on our last trip during your final year there, I went my own way while you were busy at school or at the clinics in which you were working. I'd look forward to your return home at night so that we could spend some time together, but you were usually distant and removed; on occasion you were even rude or overtly hostile in circumstances that seemed out of the blue. During this period of your life, we should have had much more in common, since you were heavily and successfully immersed in subjects of immediate interest to me and which I had a great deal to say. You were obviously uncomfortable with me and antagonistic much of the time.

Certainly you knew that I approved of what you were doing, and I was open in expressing my pride and pleasure at the way you were handling your responsibilities. Perhaps I should have confronted you, but I was reluctant to create a problem which would be left unresolved when I left in a few days, because we saw each other so infrequently. I also was fearful that if I upset you it might interfere with your work, which seemed to be going so well. I guess I was concerned that your successful performance was so fragile because of my vivid recollection of your problems in high school. It is hard to live down images from the past.

As for the incident with the airport, I never did ask you to drive me. You intimated somehow that I was leaving too early in the morning and you wondered how I was planning to get to the airport. Since it was apparent that you weren't planning to drive me on that Sunday morning, I arranged for a taxi to pick me up. But I never said anything to you. I think I should have, but my foolish pride prevented it.

At one point while we were all together, Dee asked me whether I felt that you should drive me. I responded that I would appreciate feeling that it was something you wanted to do. You both then gave what for me were incomprehensible reasons for why you felt it inappropriate. I recall having breakfast with you in your kitchen and sensing that you felt very uneasy and remorseful when the taxi arrived to pick me up. We made our hasty good-byes, but nothing further was said.

On the plane going home I was very depressed about the whole thing. I knew you were trying to make a statement about your independence, but what a crude and hostile statement it was. I wasn't aware of anything I had done to provoke your anger during the visit, but I felt that you had been horrible to me. I had been out there for a week, and I had eagerly waited for an opportunity to spend some time with you. When we were finally alone together on the Friday afternoon we had planned all week, you suddenly recalled something you had to do. You apologetically left me on Fisherman's Wharf to run some urgent errand.

I remember trying very hard to recall whether I had inadvertently said or done something to rain on your parade, but I could recall nothing. I was just a poor, misunderstood father. I did conclude, however, that I'd think long and hard before going out to visit you again. In fact, it would be a long time before I'd give you a ride to or from an airport again. In retrospect, I realize that I was looking in the wrong place for an explanation of your hostility.

At the time of that visit, your third and final year in California, you were clearly struggling with your own fears about being able to live up to your aspirations for independence. I suspect that you had insecurities about your ability to sustain the self-reliance you were struggling to achieve. Perhaps you questioned the reality of your independence, and were afraid that it was mostly just a posture. It was easier to feel self-sufficient when you and Dee were out there functioning very effectively on your own. Perhaps my simple presence evoked unacceptable dependent feelings which threatened the image of self-reliance that you were struggling to build. Rejecting me would then serve to effectively deny such unwanted ghosts of childhood feelings.

The occasion you mention about Grandma being sick was different from the way you remember it, but its meaning doesn't change. You had been home from college on vacation, and you left to go back to school angered by something that had occurred which I can't now recall. You knew that Grandma had been critically ill and that at the time you left there was some question about whether she would live. But you were angry, and you didn't communicate with us for several weeks. I was angry because you were able to turn your back and not even inquire during that time about how she was.

It is misleading, I think, to overemphasize the issues raised in these letters which naturally depict the more dramatic events, which are after all, easier to remember and write about. There were many more good times, even close times, during those years which form a kind of background against which these events occurred. I think that's the most important reason I was upset on first reading your letter. It seemed to emphasize the traumatic incidents, which were relatively few, I think, and ignore the more mundane, but positive, aspects of our relationship and interaction.

This is particularly vivid in relation to our Israel trip. Although I was aware that you felt under stress, we talked about many relatively impersonal things in those days together. There was a lot of conversation about the history and religious traditions evoked by the things we saw. I had specifically requested a driver-guide who was close to your age, and whenever possible, I encouraged you to go off alone with him in the evening. You were very intrigued by the concentration of so much religious history in the old city of Jerusalem, and you were fascinated by the ongoing excavations near the Western Wall.

I wonder why your memory seems so dominated by the negative feelings you recall, to the point of crowding out memories of so many positive experiences. You and our guide had some intriguing discussions about his life and world view and how they contrasted with yours. In these discussions, I stayed in the background and was almost entirely a spectator.

Your relationship with my friend Aaron was interesting. As you know, he and I have been very close friends even during long periods when we neither saw nor communicated with each other. I knew that this was a turbulent time in his life, having broken up his marriage and disrupted his relationship with his own kids. He and I spoke on the phone several times during the period you were struggling with the decision about where you and Dee would settle.

You may be surprised to learn that I was not displeased by your idealization of Aaron. You may have felt that I would feel threatened by your admiration of him, but I wasn't. I knew how he felt about me, even when his lifestyle and apparent values seemed to be so different from mine. We had shared, and still do share, each other's confidence and loyalty, and I trusted that any influence he might exert would reflect his understanding of my feelings and wishes. In addition, I was also aware of his increasing dissatisfaction with his life in California, and his growing desire to return to the East Coast. It was he who suggested that you might consider taking a post-doctoral job in Connecticut, where he knew many people from his earlier days at Yale.

Mom and I felt a very strong emotional investment in your returning to live in the East. Despite the strains in our relationship, Donald, I deeply loved you and wanted you close enough so that I could continue to share in your life. I was not so hung up on your practicing with me, or even on your living on Long Island. I did understand and respect your need to feel separate from me and to make it on your own. Secretly, I was even proud of your desire to do so. But I did want very much for you to be within reasonable visiting distance. I didn't want you to feel that you had to remove yourself from me completely in order to feel independent.

In my efforts to persuade you to return East, I probably pulled out every stop. I don't now remember, but I'm sure I played on your conscience as best I could without betraying my own conscience. I recall making a conscious resolution to use only those arguments in which I truly believed and which I felt to be consistent with your best interests. I felt with my heart and soul that you would have a better chance for a full and rewarding life back here. Connecticut seemed a good compromise, and when you suggested it, I was relieved and thrilled.

Your return home was one of those special times in my life and I vividly recall the intense joy I felt when you came to the surprise welcome home party we gave for you. Mom and I looked at houses in Connecticut for you, and we were both thrilled when we found the house which you ultimately bought. I remember when Dee came back to New York without you in order to look at the houses we had seen. When she loved the one we had favored, and you decided to buy it in spite of the fact that we loved it also, I felt as if you and I had finally arrived.

It surprised me when you seemed to feel that it would be too much for me to attend your graduation ceremonies with you. You had already moved to Connecticut and had started your new fellowship, but you were returning to California for your graduation. I can't imagine anything other than illness that would have interfered with my being there. How would you not have known that? You said in your letter that it meant a great deal to you that I wanted to go. Even then, I couldn't understand how you could fail to know how much it meant to me. I know I communicate better than that. Maybe it had to do with your own feelings of guilt for having pushed me away for so long.

Am I mistaken in believing that we were not so continuously at odds with each other in those years as these letters suggest? It seems to me that if you were a patient, and I heard from you about all the incidents and occasions when we were in conflict, I would have a very distorted impression of your development and my involvement in it.

I deeply believe that these were incidents and occasions which punctuated an otherwise deep and caring attachment to each other. Moreover, they were incidents that reflected your desperate and inevitable need to establish your own individual identity, and my imperfect understanding of a process in which I was so deeply and personally involved.

How often do you suppose we are mislead by our patients' accounts of their significant relationships because of this tendency to remember and emphasize the dramatic and traumatic, and largely neglect the more taken-for-granted good times and feelings? If this is true, it seems to me a pity. I intend hereafter to be more alert to this possibility with my patients.

Love,
Dad

⊷⊨⊜⊜⊩⊶

I have finally learned that having to share with another person is a privilege not an insult.

I wanted you to think the way I did, with all the seemingly confident wisdom of experience, and I couldn't hear your plea of 'me too.'

⊷⊨⊜⊜⊩⊶

Dear Dad,

I breathed a sigh of relief in knowing that you survived my last letter. As you already know, it is hard for me to see you vulnerable. My last letter could have been the catalyst to put you over the edge. Maybe that's just the omnipotent son thinking he has the power to destroy his father. As you know, that would never be my intention. At this point I feel we can have the kind of honesty that enables the two of us to engage in this difficult process of self-disclosure. Your ability to analyze your responses adds to my great respect for you.

I have found that each time I write you a letter, part of me doesn't want to even consider what it might be doing to you. The thought of hurting you would be a difficult thing for me to endure. Some degree of dispassion is in order just to alleviate some of my anxiety. So perhaps in some way this has turned into an analytic process for me as well, and my response to your words becomes similar to what I might experience in a therapeutic relationship. This demands from me a transition from the defensive "all selfless, righteous" son, to the compassionate and empathetic friend who needs to be open to understanding your perceptions of the particular events that have occurred between us.

Interestingly, I don't feel defensive about the differences in our perceptions. If anything, it has offered me the opportunity to consider whether I have distorted some of my memories. One always needs to be open to the fact that one can indeed be blinded by the tendency to see things through a one-sided mirror.

As confusing as your many roles and moods were, I am sure you were equally as confused by my different personalities. I had a need for you to play all these different parts for me, but unfortunately my needs and yours did not always coincide. On one hand, I did not want to burden you, but at the same time I couldn't help it. Some-times you probably wanted to be left alone, but you would not want to disappoint me, so you would always be there despite your needs.

There is always ambivalence and double messages between two people who feel so deeply about each other. It is true that sometimes I lived on the edge, never knowing which one of your hats I would encounter. The boundaries are thin between our various personas and we can get caught in believing that one exists without all the oth-ers. We become too identified with one particular role.

Human beings are really complex. I find that my patients get caught in the same dynamics in therapy that come up in the parent/ child relationship. The roles and boundaries are constantly confused and need to be re-established. At times it seems appropriate to be the authority, and other moments, it is equally valuable to be the empa-thetic friend. It all comes down to timing and knowing when one is more appropriate than the other.

The label of the "phony hippie" is a little hard to accept, only from the standpoint that my changing image was an important part of my development as a man. I don't want to minimize that in any way. There is some truth to what you were saying in that my identity was confused at the time. I am not convinced that makes it "phony." Is anything? Don't we all need to experiment and try out new things? I call them dress rehearsals for life or searching for the Holy Grail.

It did occur to me after writing my last letter that I had forgotten to cover the incident that involved me being falsely accused of not paying a bill during my freshman year at college. I find it curious that I forgot to write about that event. Maybe it was hard for me to look back at this episode because it was one of those infamous parental, "I told you sos." Perhaps the reminder of this reality was not something that enhanced my cause in my initial recounting of this period of my life. I was aware of the fact that the incident would have to be addressed in a later letter. As usual though, you managed to remember these significant events that, of course, would reinforce your position. When you think about it, that seems perfectly natural. It appears that the Birkenstock sandals and my James Taylor albums are all that remain of that previous image.

I must say I was relieved that you defended me against the authorities in the restaurant. What it comes down to is that people do judge you by the way you look. One has to accept the consequences that come with a decision to look a little different. Being vulnerable to the kinds of accusations that I experienced are quite common. Woodstock was over and so was my concern of pretending to be the "natural man" who freaked out because he couldn't find toilet paper at the concert. Maybe I am a creature of habit.

Recently, an adolescent girl came into my office wearing two different colored sneakers. I explored with her why she felt a need to present herself that way. Her reply was, "I am trying to achieve a look that works for me." People are capable of finding all kinds of rationalizations to support their cause. Was it my place to judge her at that point? Is it the role of a parent or therapist to sit back and accept values we don't believe in? How can we?

I found myself wanting to say to her all the things you once said to me about how physical appearance affects other people. Would that be unsolicited advice? She did not seem to care whether it conformed to other people's expectations of her or not. Opinions and honesty have their place, but how they are communicated becomes the crucial issue.

We both seemed to have difficulty at times accepting that we were coming from different places. It is easy to fall victim to that human feeling that we know what is best for the ones to whom we feel closest. I was insensitive to how the changes within myself were affecting you, and I completely denied your attempts to share your life experience with me. How often do children take an interest in understanding where their parents are coming from, particularly when it appears so alien to them? How sad that people are so invested in protecting their own points of view. We miss out on so much that way. If I had really trusted my own decisions I would not have been so defensive with you.

Your familiar pattern of getting angry and then feeling guilty about it, is something I was always aware of. I used to say to Dee, "Here comes the guilt call." We are not so different that way, "The apple doesn't fall far from the tree." I would have been disappointed if the call didn't come.

This personality trait has its strong points because your reaction to my last letter is indicative of the kind of openness we do share with each other. If you and I did not have this similar response pattern, we would have a very narrow and one-sided perspective to give people about a father and son relationship. I have no investment in having the more commonly accepted hostile communication that goes on between a father and son.

How unfortunate that a writer as brilliant and widely read as Franz Kafka had to destroy his father in a letter, and was unable to share those feelings with his elder. In his situation perhaps it wasn't safe. This is so often the case. Some people never seem to work through their anger to get over to the other side where one can experience compassion and love. I always felt affected by the fact that Kafka never exchanged letters with his father and whether things might have been different for them if they had. What makes our relationship special is that we can both do that now.

Recently a patient shared with me how surprised he was when he got a letter from his father after the Christmas holidays. The letter was an apology for not being there for him during Christmas because he had had too much to drink. They have had a long history of problems between them. The son is going to write back and tell his father how much he missed him. This is a big breakthrough for the two of them. The patient said, "Maybe now my dad will give up drinking so we can be together." For the first time, he was feeling hopeful.

When we first discussed the value of writing a letter he said that there was, "something permanent and direct about a letter." When you speak to someone, you may not be heard and you may be misunderstood. In writing, you can really commit yourself to a feeling, and if it is subject to misinterpretation, you always have a record of what was written to rectify any confusion. There had to be some reason why ancient traditions were big on the written word. A patient's fiancé recently encouraged him to go back and read old letters from his late father, and in reading them now, he discovered that his father really loved him. Suddenly the anger was gone.

Another patient decided to write a letter to his father even though his father had died many years ago. He had a need to work through his anger and make his father more human. There had been a long history of not being able to demystify his father. It was his way of internalizing his father and by bringing out his positive feelings, he felt that his father had become alive and human for the first time. It was nice to see the change from a cold, distant man to a warm and loving person. In some ways, his father was more alive than ever before.

I feel it would be too simplistic to reduce my interest in Jung to just rebellious feelings toward you. Yes, in part I could attribute some of it to that, and to my desire to have an interest that was foreign to you. But one can't discount the fact that we are two different people. Look how our personalities are reflected in our different writing styles.

One of the things that has been so nice about these conversations is that I have a feeling that you like and respect the manner in which I have chosen to write these letters. I remember that as a kid I had to struggle with my papers for school, knowing full well you would end up correcting and writing them over for me. It feels good to know we have gone far beyond that point. There are still moments when I expect you to scrutinize my writing, but they are slowly subsiding. This has been good for my confidence and has freed up my writing. I want you to respect me not only as a person but as a writer as well. (That need for approval never goes away.)

Jungian psychology gave me an appreciation of myself and of psychology. I still feel that you were blocked by a need for me to be more interested in what you liked. Why wouldn't this be so? You're only human. Ironically, I always thought I was more of the philosopher, but your letters are turning out to be more philosophical than mine. Maybe the philosopher in you is coming out more as you get older, but it probably has more to do with the fact that I can recognize that this was always a part of who you were.

Theoretical speculation used to be more comfortable for me, but I still feel that there is a thin line between that and observational data. We see what we want to see, whether it be philosophical or scientific. One distinction I did make between philosophy and psychology was that it would be easier to make a living as a therapist. Kant and Plato just won't pay the bills.

At this point it is hard for me to read anything that is too abstract or scientific. I seem to be leaning toward experiential literature, mostly biographies and autobiographies. Children's books aren't bad either. How can you understand any psychological, scientific or philosophical theory if you don't have an insight into the personalities who are behind the theories?

The one book of yours that I liked reading was Ernest Jones's biography of Sigmund Freud because it gave me something personal to identify with. As you know, Jung's biography had the same effect on me. In retrospect, I realize that what I was trying to do was to get a better understanding of you and I am sure the reverse is true as well. We can leave Freud and Jung to the historians.

We tend to gravitate toward material that helps to reinforce our personalities, and clearly there was a time when Jung did that for me. In some ways he still does, but I am no longer a fanatic about it. The transference seems to have subsided and more positive identification with you has contributed to that. Who needs another father? Actually though, some people do. I certainly did at one time.

It's true that metapsychological speculation was comfortable for me because I did not have to commit myself to anything. This was in part a convenient way for me to avoid living in the everyday world. You know I had an inclination toward hiding out as a kid. It's safer to stay one step removed, abstract and impersonal. The mainstream was not a comfort zone for me. My learning difficulties seemed to influence so many pieces of my life. It was my deepest secret.

Whether it be Jung or Freud, or anyone else, I agree with you that I can only now relate to more practical concerns of everyday living. Ideas are intellectually stimulating but they need to be applied. That does not eliminate philosophy for me, but nothing can replace human experience. It's more satisfying to live out what I used to read about and then go back to it to gain a deeper appreciation of whatever I was reading. Then it becomes a more meaningful and well-rounded experience. The laboratory has expanded beyond Organic Chemistry.

I have always been interested in theories that related to father and son relationships but I find the theories will make more sense within the context of a personal understanding of what really goes on between us. In my research, I have discovered how the theories fit in very well with what we are writing about, but the impact is much more profound as a result of our living out many of the classic dynamics between a father and son. It is nice to read books with the intention of evoking hidden emotions locked up inside. It is certainly different from research for a thesis in which you have to constantly worry about citing the correct references. Any time you have an original feeling or idea it is eliminated because you are not considered an expert on the subject. So much for academia. I had to finish my doctoral dissertation six months before everyone else, fearful, it would never get done. I still have a recurring nightmare that they called back my dissertation because it had insufficient results. How often we feel like an imposter.

I think Freud and Jung were after the answers, just like you and I. Every man is a son. We all have different ways of getting there. It would seem logical that anyone going into our field, regardless of his or her school of thought, would have a desire to gain a better understanding of human motivation.

I find it unfortunate that what are often debated are the theoretical differences between people; they often have such an investment in protecting their respective gods. It would seem more important to concentrate on the human qualities that help people be closer to each other, like learning how to be more empathetic, warm, and genuine. We seem to have gotten past our theoretical battles and we both agree that compassion for others is more important to human relationships than which god one should worship. There has got to be more than one key to the doors of ancient wisdom. Why not share the wealth rather than compete? Is it necessary for us as professionals to add to an already hostile and competitive world? In our profession we try to avoid the egocentric temptation to let people put us on pedestals. This requires us to have self confidence.

We would all be better off if we left God alone. He has nothing to do with what is directly related to our human imperfections. I have often felt that God gets bad press, and somehow it is easier to blame our problems on an abstraction and parents if they somehow do not live up to an expectation that we put on them. What a convenient scapegoat God has become. I no longer need to feel like the son of a god.

I used to confuse the ideal father with God. As I get older, I begin to realize that my expectation of you to be the perfect father would become confused by my need to think that God would make everything better. If He didn't, or I should say you didn't, I would be angry and disappointed. Where is my responsibility in this whole thing? How easy it is to pass the buck. It all now seems like a childhood illusion and I realize it's not fair to God to blame him for our human fallibilities. How unfair of me to compare you to Him. As far as I know, Dad, He (or She) never intended to be one of us, so why should we make Him that way?

Perhaps God is just a reflection of the imperfections that make us human, and a reminder that we have a long way to go before we will ever be perfect. If you look in the mirror, you will see that something is always a little bit off. In California, some people actually get tired of beauty. Why do some people enjoy the story of *Beauty and the Beast*? It's not so bad to be humbled once in a while. Job's test came with warts on his head. God may be inside and outside of us, but also somewhere present between us. I would like to see God defined, perhaps, as the "process" we use to attempt to connect with each other. I was inspired by the movie *Before Sunrise* which was about a friendship between a young man and woman trying to have a relationship. There was a passion building between the two of them as they were creating something meaningful together. One could say it feels god-like when you embrace a particular interest with passion. You just feel it inside you like a strong force that needs to be released.

Could I really tolerate you if indeed you *were* a perfect god? How would I ever be good enough to match that set-up for failure? Where is that middle ground between the idealist and the realist? In the end, someone has to be the recipient of all the displaced anger in the world. Who is it going to be? Is it too much to ask people to look within and own the dark side of their personalities? We just need to eliminate our false pride.

It's difficult to make a transition from where I just came. I don't think it is true about my not reading books that you would give me. At times that was true, but not always. I resented that assumption and felt condemned before I was ever given the chance. The old self-fulfilling prophecy never fails. You might have felt disappointed by my lack of enthusiasm about your suggestions just as I was with yours. I just had trouble understanding John Bowlby's work and research in ethology. How ironic since his theory in psychology was all about attachment.

It seemed interesting to study animal behavior, but I was having trouble relating it to human psychology. I just couldn't get turned on by it back then. Maybe it was hard for you to appreciate that at the time, and it hurt me that you felt I had no desire to understand your beliefs. It would be more accurate to say that I did not identify with them the same way you did during that time of my life. Should that really matter? Do we need people to feel as strongly about our interests as we do? I think it was also hard for me to understand it and often felt inadequate. It was difficult to admit that to you.

There is truth to your belief that I expected you to be converted when in return I was unable to do the same. How sad that we both seemed to miss the more important underlying motivation: you and I needing acknowledgment from one another. As much as I had trouble accepting your beliefs, I respected you enough to know that I must be missing some important points somewhere. I continued to carry your recommended books around with me probably because I did not want to hurt your feelings. There were times when I was self-conscious around you, when I felt you were critical of my reading anything but what you gave me to read. I did feel like I was letting you down. Over the last couple of years I find myself quoting Freud and Bowlby much more in my lectures at the university. Combine that with some Nietzsche and Kierkegaard and you have something special.

It's easy to confuse a perceived condescending attitude with the more mature understanding of your desire for me to admire you. I wish you could have been more direct with me about that.

When one is growing up, one's vulnerability tends to make him resist being humbled by those in authority. Who wants to admit to insecurity? It's hard enough just feeling insecurity and the effort to keep it a secret is exhausting. Why couldn't I admit my need to have you admire me? There must have been fear of rejection. Why wouldn't you want your son to be inspired by you? I certainly had a similar need.

At this point in my life I wanted desperately to humble others around me in order to support my own god-like image. We often tend to think that if we have that need so do others. Again, I wanted you to be like me and there I go with another assumption. I resented having to idealize you when I wanted to feel that way about myself. At that time it was hard to imagine that you had a father who must have evoked similar feelings in you. These are the types of realizations that might have made me see you as more human.

As the years progressed, I discovered that we are definitely both intelligent people. With that awareness comes an appreciation of you and respect for the differences in the way we put that across. An example of this is that, in the past, I would be concerned that your letters were better than mine. Now I can comfortably say they both have their value and their own merit even in their differences. My Oedipal tragedy seems behind me, leaving me to discover a new chapter in the story. I find your sharing with me helps reinforce and make a little more realistic the more positive perceptions that I had of you.

Your responses seem well thought out and deliberate while mine are more spontaneous and free associative. That, in itself, is a statement of our contrasting personalities. I seem to initially write to you as the child and end up responding later on, more as the adult. We now seem to be able to share a commonality of interests and can complement each other. You get my energy and I get your experience. We seem to be able to accept each other's weaknesses and draw on each other's strengths. Internalizing those strengths appears to have allowed me to be strong and independent. I can now like the parts of me that I like in you, and reject the similarities I dislike. Are we indeed creating a legacy for the next generation? "A wise son makes a glad father."

I have known so many people with fathers who let them down and they never come back. They could have been Willie Loman. You never took the complete fall because of your ability to come through for me as a father. As you said before, the negatives stand out more when they are compared against so many positive moments. It is easy to lose sight of that. I am also aware of how close you must have been with your own father, because without that you never could have given me what I am receiving from you now.

So often you see fathers doing the same things to their children that were done to them. In my practice I see fathers who come home from work and hide from their kids. A father will complain that his father behaved the same way with him. It was Shakespeare in *The Merchant of Venice* who said, "The sins of the father are to be laid upon the children." What is so frustrating is that intellectually these fathers know this is wrong, but they just don't change their patterns. As a result of this we often see child abuse. The unresolved anger at their own parents is put on their children. Often the mother carried the burden of having to take care of the kids while the father is out of the house, or home sitting in front of the TV. I found it very sad when one son said to me, "I have all this love to give, but my father is not around to receive it."

Certainly the situation arises where I see many men who are able to undo the past and become motivated not to fall into the same destructive patterns as their fathers. This is always a moving experience for me in the office. Many men do not have to go very far to surpass their fathers.

While I would complain that you were too involved in the details of my life, other men were feeling that their fathers should have been more involved. Many of their fathers were workaholics. Is there a happy medium? Is there some virtue in suffering and being made to work when you should be out having fun as a child? Does that build character? Sometimes a young man feels the pressure to work while his friends are out having a good time, because his father worked his way up. These men have a sense of immediacy about instilling their values. But you always made time to get to my basketball games.

An adolescent boy whom I was seeing had come to me because he was depressed. His father had been a poor man who later became a rags-to-riches success story. He had built up a business which he wanted his son to eventually have. The work ethic became his way of life. This kid had no time for a social life and it seemed as if he could never do enough to please his father. In the end, his father became disgusted with him and his siblings for what he felt was irresponsibility, so he decided to sell the business.

The boy was devastated, as he had always counted on going into the business. He ended up feeling guilty and responsible for the whole thing. So where is the justice in all this? Sure, the kid might have learned to work and be responsible, but at what price? He continues to look up to his father in the working world, but socially he is embarrassed to admit to anyone that he is this man's son.

I remember being around many people with backgrounds similar to the one just described, and feeling guilty for having it so good in comparison. Although I knew that I would not have a family business to go into, it never seemed to bother me. In some ways, I felt less pressure. You can only be a child once and who wants to be a slave to his master? I still managed to become a disciplined person despite being a kid.

When you have situations in which a father from the Old World dies while his son is an adolescent, the son has to completely Americanize himself and is left impoverished. What did his father know about life insurance? Often when sons lose their fathers at an early age, they have to teach themselves everything. The positive side is that they are forced to be self-reliant, but the negative side is that they miss all the love and complexities of a father and son relationship.

Sometimes a father gives his son the impression he will pay for his graduate school education, but the son ends up having to pay back the loans on his own. Does that build character? There are fathers who have the money but just want their sons to be financially accountable for their own education. The goal must be to instill responsibility.

When parents just don't have the money, it's a different story. I often admired men who worked their way through school and still managed to have a social life. They never seemed to take anything for granted. I worked, but I knew it wasn't absolutely necessary. Making your own money does massage the ego.

There was a time in the 1970's when many students at the university were getting food stamps even when they didn't need them. Finding ways to accumulate money without having to work for it became a game to beat the system. Being poor and surviving was a way of gaining credibility. This was something I found more prevalent among people from comfortable backgrounds.

Pop would have been proud of you because he wanted you to surpass him. I wish he could see you now and have the opportunity to enjoy not only how you turned out as his son but also as a father. Could you imagine you and your Dad having done something like this together? For the first time I can honestly say that if there were a way to go beyond your achievements my guilt would be minimal. But if I go that way I would like somehow to take you along with me. I think the reason for this change in me is two-fold: one, you have achieved so much; and two, you had a father who wanted you to go beyond him. As I said before, we often tend to do to others what was done to us. At this point, I feel like thanking Pop for giving you the kind of fathering that produced some healthy values.

I am beginning to accept the fact that sometimes you win in life and sometimes you lose. What's nice is that you can always make a comeback. There will always be people who are better than me at some things, and naturally the reverse is true. What it comes down to is that we are forced to compete and win in order to receive recognition in this society of ours.

Isn't the nature of gossip to put others down so we can build ourselves up? We somehow feel this will alleviate our feelings of failure. Are we so much better than anyone else? Maybe human beings are in part victims of their own circumstances. Some people will have advantages and opportunities which others are denied. The key is to do your best with what you are given and seize the moment.

I also realize that we are capable of losing control one minute and regaining it moments later if the circumstances work in our favor. To some degree we do have control over our destinies, but to what extent?

When we play tennis, we are forced to compete. It's always more difficult for me to beat someone close to me. I notice that when Emily and I play a game, it is easier for me to watch her beat me. How well is that preparing her for the realities of life? You may be giving your child the impression that he or she should always be the best. The conflicts you felt with me, I am now experiencing with my own children.

As much as I enjoyed winning, part of me tried to keep the other person happy. That protective tendency in me is slowly dissipating. Isn't it an insult not to try your hardest, because while trying to please others you run the risk of infantilizing them? Why not do it the honest way?

I do not like any friend of mine to tone down his tennis game for me to let me know what a good guy he is. Who needs this kind of heroics? Like I said, sometimes you win and sometimes you lose. If you don't play an honest game, how do you improve, or for that matter, even know if you have? I prefer a realistic game now because it prepares me for my next challenge. Conflict is good for the soul and even better if you try to work through it. The great coach from UCLA, John Wooden, used to say "You can't let praise or criticism get to you . . . it's a weakness to get caught up in either one."

You were very encouraging and supportive about my going to California. I had a strong need to hear you tell me that I would be missed. There could never be enough of that. It's true that Dee and I were anxious about the move out west, but I am unclear at this point if my perceptions are off regarding just when I decided to consider it a permanent move. It would probably be safe to say I left with an open mind and ambivalent feelings about that decision. I was probably scared to believe that part of me really considered it as a possibility before I left. I think I was more threatened about staying out there than you were and was denying my own feelings of sadness about what the implications of that decision would mean. The thought of your not knowing your grandchildren was upsetting to me.

I have found that having children is making me more family oriented. There is a need to be close to cousins now and achieve the feeling of some kind of extended family. I remember liking it as a kid. It hurts me to see how many people have not worked out their own family problems. I always felt fortunate that you, Dee, and Mom have such a good relationship. Dee has also become close to my sister over the last couple of years. And the children really reap benefits from this. It's quite simple: if the daughter-in-law gets along with the husband's parents, the grandchildren get that much more love. Children grow up so fast, and before you know it, they don't want anything to do with parents and grandparents. Remember those dreaded family Sundays when you wanted to be out with your friends? Watching you interact with my children has confirmed for me what a loss it would have been had I stayed in California. I am convinced we would never have resolved our relationship if I had not come back.

Of course, the reverse is true as well. Ideally, you want healthy backgrounds and a marriage that works, with in-laws who get along and have a good relationship with their kids.

Many men have unresolved issues with their fathers and have adopted their in-laws as substitute parents. There can be a tendency for the daughter-in-laws not to bridge the gap between the two families. I felt Dee did bridge the gap to the point that she sometimes felt freer to let you in on the details of our life than I did.

So many men lose out because although they adopt a new family, they abandon hope of ever being close with their own. They miss out on the opportunity to see a relationship form between their parents and their children. Many of them no longer have fathers because they have passed away when they were very young, or in some cases much later in life. But either way, it must be extremely difficult to deal with the void. People get hurt and for what reason? Should the children suffer for old wounds that people won't heal? Is revenge worth the price of less love for the ones most important to you?

It is troublesome to see a son-in-law alienate himself from his wife's parents, particularly the father, because he hasn't worked through his grief and anger about the loss of his own father. He has a father-in-law who probably wants to be the father he needs, but the son-in-law is busy rejecting the gesture. All he is doing is running away from a loss that still hurts. Unfortunately everyone will be victimized by his pain and anger, because the children get caught in the middle and are thus deprived of that special time they could be spending with their grandparents. The wife loses out as well because she is constantly caught between her husband and her parents. Tension in the marriage may be another reason for his rejection of her parents.

One also sees the reverse of what I have been describing. Sometimes the wife becomes closer to the husband's parents because of unresolved conflicts with her own parents. Sometimes it's just caused by unfortunate circumstances like physical geography when the wife's parents live far away. That's difficult for her parents because they are deprived of watching the stages of their grandchildren's development.

Somehow, the daughter-in-law quite often ends up being the one who gives her husband the father he lost or never had. This seems to be a disturbing reality among many people whom I have known in the past couple of years. What seems to go wrong between the son and his father that makes him leave home for good? Why can't the daughter-in-law encourage the closeness even if it's never going to be a match made in heaven? And then again, who says it can't be? What can be constructive about reminding a husband of what he never had, and not reinforcing what he did have? It has got to be better than nothing at all. Women often are put in an important position to help bridge the gap between fathers and sons. And what happens to the poor abandoned brothers or sisters who still are close with their father and no longer see their brother, or are caught between the two?

There are too many situations in which the daughter is caught between her father and brother. How do women arrive at this burdensome position? Isn't it time for men to fight their own battles? I never liked the idea of Mom speaking your voice. Men need to speak for themselves. It seems we are very good at digging for what we don't have rather than appreciating what we do. Things can always get a little better when we reflect, take responsibility, and risk.

There are other difficult kinds of situations like both parents not getting along with their respective families, and then the grandchildren have no contact with grandparents at all. It's so much better when parents don't let the past interfere with the relationship between grandparent and child. And it's also unfortunate when parents from both sides are deceased, leaving the children without grandparents. Where can the children go for that feeling of family roots? Grandparents are often so good at filling in all the historical gaps that parents forget to share with their children. It's not unusual for a child to learn all about a parent's past from grandparents.

I have seen a parent and child become closer when the child sees his parent being hurt by his grandparent. This often helps the child to understand how difficult it was for the parent growing up. In this case, the parent begins to open up about his past with his child.

With the high divorce rate and increasing occurrences of single parenting by choice or other circumstances, there is a stronger need now to reach out for other networks. It is my conviction that our family systems are becoming so fragmented that it is increasingly more important to offer a feeling of extended family and strong support systems. Are we going back to the old days?

Step-families have their own particular problems. In my practice I saw a boy whose mother married into a new family. It seems to have caused the boy to grow farther away from his natural father. Marital problems should never deter from a child's opportunity to be with both parents and both sets of grandparents. I feel we owe that to our parents and to our children. One's marital situation should never interfere with the love for one's children and what is in their best interests. In difficult marriages, grandparents can often fill the void at home with a great deal of love and emotional support.

Finally, when there is a strained relationship between a parent and a child, a grandparent's old wisdom can really help.

I am beginning to appreciate how hard it is to raise kids. If Dee and I need a break, it's nice to know you are around and have a relationship with them. This is my way of telling you that I am glad we moved back. My best friends in California were like family to me, but they wouldn't have made it as grandparents. Changing circumstances demand new support systems.

I now also really appreciate the fact that I have a sister, particularly as I have grown older and have children. I want my kids to have aunts and uncles.

My uncle was president of Crown Book Publishers and had two daughters. But he made the time to come to many of my basketball games. I am sorry we weren't closer when I was younger, but I do remember enjoying his company. He filled the empty space when you had no interest in watching football games. On Thanksgiving day he took me to the Polo Grounds to watch the old AFL New York Titans. It's easy to take an aunt or uncle for granted until you have your own children.

Sometimes the uncle becomes a substitute father, particularly the one who is capable of getting the Giants' football games on a special TV antenna. In the end you came through and gave me a special antenna for my birthday. Life takes strange twists. It was fun recently visiting a friend with you and watching a football game with Allie Sherman, the former head coach of the New York Giants. I will never forget my uncle arranging to get me in the Yankee dugout and meet Mantle and Maris. The M and M boys signed a baseball and the rest of the team did the same. In those days we didn't save the ball, we played with it. I certainly have regrets about that!

There were times when I had concerns that you and Mom would not be around and I still worry about that. It is comforting to know that I have a sister on whom I can rely for support. Recently we have become much closer. It was just like so many other things since we started this journey. Right after I wrote to you and mentioned that I wanted to be closer to Ellen, she called me. We both seemed to miss each other during the holidays while you were away. We were getting back to where we were when we were in our very early years. It is easy to once again forget all the positive times we used to spend together growing up. When you were both away this particular holiday, maybe we felt like the orphan children who finally needed each other. It is very important to me for my kids to be close to Ellen, and I am glad it is possible now.

Sometimes it takes a particular circumstance to help create the bond that was always waiting to be formed. Maybe this past holiday was what we needed. We seem to have both grown up in many ways. Our telephone conversation was timely because I was thinking of calling her right about then. It meant so much to hear her say she loved me.

I know that you and Mom have always wanted us to have a closer relationship. Over the years I was aware that perhaps you were uncomfortable talking about my relationship with my sister. I can understand why you would not have wanted to be in the middle of it now that I have a son and daughter. I can appreciate the pain you must have felt watching us not get along and wondering what you did wrong. Up to this point, I have noticed that you have completely avoided our relationship in your letters to me. I have not been able to understand that other than maybe it was uncomfortable territory. It is nice to inform you that it no longer is, and we became closer without you having to help. I know that over the years you have wanted to intervene but did not know how. In the past it would have been forced. It had to be the right moment.

I was really pleased when Ellen told me she wanted Dee and me to start going out with her and her friends. As a younger brother I would feel like an intruder in the kitchen after school when she and her friends sat around eating pizza. We had a stormy relationship growing up. I remember wanting you to protect me from her when I felt picked on. We often became competitive and hostile toward each other, particularly over material possessions. Who would get the rug from your trip to India? It was obnoxious. I used to enjoy when she would get in trouble because then I was the good son. In retrospect, I regret that I did not defend her more. There were times when I resented having attention taken away by her. I did not like taking a back seat when she had problems. One of the hardest things of all was having my joys compete with her bad moods and vice versa. It was as if my moods were being discounted. No wonder we never got along. I have finally learned that having to share with another person is a privilege, not an insult.

One of the positive things about having a sister growing up was that we would have each other to align with when you and Mom were both down on us. You were hard to split up and you always defended each other. That's when Ellen and I would become close. Whenever I battled with Mom and thought I was right, you would take her side. What more can a husband do when it comes to dealing with his children over a conflict with his wife? Can or should loyalties be divided? It must be hard to be in the middle of your spouse and your child. If you disagreed about how to deal with me, I never knew about it. Sometimes I needed you to take my side.

During my early years I wanted a big brother to protect me, and sometimes I wanted a little brother or sister to take care of. Even at an early age I was in conflict as to whether I wanted to be the son or the father. Now I can be both.

You were right when you said I would come to you for advice even when I had already made my decision. It was hard for me to trust my judgments and therefore I probably should have been more direct about my feelings. Perhaps I still had some guilt about the fact that you were still helping me out financially. I never came out and said, "Dad, can't you just be happy for me?" Those self doubts of mine gave you the opening to come on strong with your opinions. It's hard to trust your own gut feeling when for so long you didn't have to.

You always were honest and seemed secure about how you felt about things. I respected the fact that you were not wishy-washy, but it was difficult to contend with. You were far from a rubber stamp. I resented you because I needed you to make me feel good about my own decisions. Why couldn't I exist without your approval? My self esteem was on the line. Buying the house and sports car were to be my claims to independence. Of course, you had to be honest in your opinions, but it would have been easier for me if we had been on the same wavelength. However, that's not the way life works. I was forced to think for myself and accept the full responsibility, and possible consequences, of my decisions. In the end, you can't please everyone, including your own father.

I blamed you for trying to control my life, but maybe I was just afraid of taking control of it myself. Being three thousand miles from you left me very little choice in the matter.

There is an adolescent boy I see who always felt that he was being treated like a little boy by his family, and it didn't help that he was physically short. He resented it when anyone would pat him on the head. Then his circumstances changed and he got his driver's license. Suddenly, his younger brothers needed him to drive them places. This patient began to feel his power, and it was nice for him to be in control of his life. Other people become vulnerable to your agenda when they need you to drive them around.

I remember when I failed my road test; it felt like I would never be my own person. What I found out is, as I said before, there is always an opportunity to regain that feeling of mastery over your life, even when you feel as though you are losing it forever.

You were an unusual father when it came to being sensitive to my needs. I can't say I reciprocated in my treatment of you. My recollection regarding the incident about the airport is that I felt you expected me to drive you, and I would rather have thought of it on my own. Naturally, I also assumed that you were having trouble being direct about it. Neither one of us was very comfortable with putting the other in a position of obligation. You had every right to be hurt and angry at me. All you wanted was my company in the morning. It is hard to express your needs to someone to whom you feel close. I could have made it easier for you and more meaningful if I had been thoughtful enough to offer to drive you to the airport.

The unfortunate part of this incident is that a positive intention was turned into something negative. What's wrong with a father wanting his son to drive him to the airport to spend some extra time alone with him? My excuse about it being too early in the morning was ridiculous because I was already awake. I felt guilty and part of me knew it was a selfish act on my part. But who wants something done for them if it is not done willingly? No one with any dignity likes to beg for something. Again, we were looking for you to make the decision for us even when it came to doing something nice for you. Dad, I don't think I ever had the chance to say to you that I am sorry about this incident.

This event epitomized how three thousand miles does not guarantee independence. It was as if we still had no minds of our own. During this time we held Dee's parents in high esteem because they were less analytical and seemed more accepting. We would always feel encouragement from them after we got off the phone whereas the opposite was true when it came to you and Mom. This had all the makings of a classic in-law rivalry. What do you expect when you mix an analyst's family with a builder's family? It's hard to avoid these kinds of dynamics.

Fisherman's Wharf was another disaster for the two of us. I think your interpretation of what went on is accurate and it is interesting to reflect back to discover that I must have been terribly insecure. This was a period of my life which represented a kind of emancipation for me. The only problem was that I had worked it out in my head but not in my heart. I thought I trusted you but you did not trust me. Looking at it now, I would have to reverse that perception. You had every reason to become the rebellious parent, which, fortunately for me, never happened. That was true unconditional love.

Whenever I felt angry at you, I found it difficult to confront you directly. There was a fear that somehow I would be put in my place and that would be too devastating. It was easier to get my anger out indirectly, rather than confront the humiliation of feeling like the son who had no right to be angry with his father.

How easy it is to distort memories in the service of supporting one's belief systems. We see our patients do that all the time, only to discover that there are always at least two versions to a story with the truth lying somewhere in-between. Judy Collins, at one time a mere unknown, sang a song about it, "I look at both sides now."

It is amazing that I have found it so hard to remember our more positive moments during this time in our lives. Maybe you can help refresh my memory. Sometimes I feel I need that. I do remember going to a movie with you in Jerusalem and eating falafels on the sidewalk together. It bothers me that I have blocked out positive memories which you have been able to maintain. Why is it that a father (just like a therapist) can remember these things, and the son has so much trouble? Therapists tend to bring out the positive feelings because the patient has blocked them out.

One man I see has trouble remembering positive feelings about his grandfather because with that comes the sorrow that he is no longer around. Even thinking positive thoughts about him makes him sad over the loss. The man was only three years old when his grandfather died. How does a young child separate loss from rejection? It's a difficult task. There are many reasons for people to distort or negate certain memories. For this patient, it is a way to defend against the pain of having loss. He has trouble getting close to people because of his fear of abandonment. One of the ways he deals with that is to reject people before they can reject him, which is probably similar to what I did to you when we had our early separation in life.

I am fortunate enough to have my office at home which allows me to go in and out of the house during the day so the children see me. It's important for a child to achieve what we call object constancy, which means that the child learns how to internalize a love object to the point where he or she will know that if you physically leave you will come back. I have so much contact with Jared during the day that this might account for the fact that he was able to handle the separation when I went away. Although, I was recently told that he waited at our meeting place at the bottom of the stairs everyday looking for me at particular times. It seems as if my eye contact from the top of the stairs, just his being able to look up at me, made Jared very happy.

I purposely bring my children into the office periodically just to let them know that when I am home in that room I am not avoiding them. You have to build that basic trust. This is something I probably learned from you. When I was a young child, you occasionally put aside a few moments for me to visit your office. I remember that being very special. I liked seeing my pictures around your office. After we would visit, Mom would take me to Hamburger Express and I thought it was the coolest thing taking the hamburger off the train that circled around the counter. Franklin Avenue in Garden City, New York was memorable. Going to my orthodontist, who was in your same medical building, was always an opportunity to see your office.

The train reminds me of how you and I would build villages and create a diorama for my Lionel trains around the Christmas tree when I was a young boy. There is a story about a father working at home and the children never being told that he had an office in the house. As far as they were concerned, he just didn't want to be with them. The children began to wonder why Daddy was hiding from them.

A student whom I supervise, told me a story about a father who needed some space for himself. The only problem was that he forgot to tell his four-year-old son he was going out. As a result of the incident, the boy felt rejected. Honest communication is an essential ingredient to a healthy and positive parent/child relationship.

I find that watching you interact with my kids helps me to get back to some of those positive memories from the past. For instance, when you take Emily and Jared to Carvel, it reminds me of all the school nights you picked yourself up after a hard day at work just to take me for ice cream. (And in those days they didn't even have chocolate chocolate chip.)

To this day, you let me know that you are keeping up with the sports page just because you know I will be impressed. All of a sudden I remember you taking me to a dinner honoring Jackie Robinson when I was ten years old. Getting his autograph was one of the greatest moments of my childhood. Maybe Jared will be playing some sophisticated offshoot of Pac-Man and I will have to show my expertise at video games when it's obvious that I am no more into arcades than you are into the Super Bowl. What we will do for our children! Jared's early interest in Presidential memorabilia was a passion so far removed from me, yet I embraced all of it with him. He loved history and at age five was naming all the presidents backwards. Dee and I would take him to all these political memorabilia shows.

I find that many people tend to negate positive feelings and memories because of assumptions about how we perceive our relationships. There seems to be an expectation that if you are not completely satisfied with someone important to you, it automatically means your relationship is not good. Therefore, all the positive feelings are minimized. Couldn't one just say we have a very good relationship and it can get even better? Isn't that what personal growth is? One is always changing and striving for new goals. "How come I am still not completely satisfied?" If you are viewing this in a negative way, you are setting yourself up for failure. All the positives that one can build on, get washed away by all the negatives. Twenty minutes with a father is better than no time at all. When you are starving, you will appreciate a single crumb of bread.

In terms of you and me, Dad, these letters become another positive experience that will help us to expand on what I feel is an already solid foundation. We have unlimited potential. What could possibly be wrong with self-improvement? Why should we settle for mediocrity? Although it may never be enough, it surely gets better as time goes on. Being in a dynamic model is more appealing than remaining static. Why should it ever be enough as long as you appreciate what you have? It's also crucial to believe that who you are is enough.

When it comes to your friend Aaron, I have come to realize that it is easier to idealize someone you don't live with. It's like having an affair. You can have all kinds of fantasies about what this person might be able to do for you. There is an air of excitement about someone you don't really know. Aaron represented new energy for me. Ironically, one of the things I admired about him was his ability to take risks. Now I look at what you are doing and I have come to appreciate that my own father is pretty daring in his own way. How many people remodel a house they have lived in their whole life, start a new business, continue a full practice, write a book—all at the same time. And most importantly, still be there for his family. I feel excited for you right now. There can be many substitutes, but only one true father.

How often we refuse to see the real victim of the projections of our own unfulfilled dreams. How could any father have done more than you did? When I moved to Connecticut, I had an expectation of your dear friend Aaron based on some of our previous conversations. I thought having him close by would be very helpful for me professionally. In the end, Aaron had his own life and family. I could never come first, and why should I? I convinced myself that he would do all the things you would be doing for me had we lived nearer to each other. What I have discovered is that although you are an hour away, I call you, not Aaron, for support. You're the one with whom I play tennis and go out for dinner. The difference between you and Aaron is that if I need you, I know you will definitely be there for me. Isn't this the way it is supposed to be?

Being independent means allowing yourself to trust others who generally have your best interests at heart. I finally understand that when you involved yourself with my life and I perceived it as an intrusion, it had more to do with a concern for my well-being. It's so easy to be suspicious and assume the negative before even thinking about what the person's motivations really might be. By deciding I am being controlled and unaccepted, I deprive you of loving me and myself of feeling loved. And how can I love myself if I can't let you love me? In the end, it's letting someone love you that helps you love yourself. Instead of mistrusting you, why couldn't I just appreciate that you wanted to get closer to me?

I didn't really feel it would be too much for you to attend my

Ph.D. graduation ceremonies. I wanted you to realize how good I felt about your being there and how much it meant to me. That's all I was trying to say. There was never much of a doubt in my mind about your attending my graduation. It was your style to be present at all my special events. It was a meaningful day when I think back about how you were once concerned about my getting through high school. We have come a long way.

I remember being anxious for you to read my dissertation. Your reaction to it was hard to perceive. When I see it lying on your coffee table at home, I have often wondered what you really thought about it. Since I have graduated, it seems to have collected a great deal of dust in my office. I often wonder if anyone reads these things after graduation.

It was nice to get two recent requests—one from Italy and the other from an upstate college—for a copy of an article from my dissertation which I had published after graduation. It also pleased me to hear from one of my old dissertation committee members. I like the idea that people from my past keep coming back to remind me that they are still around. It lends a feeling of continuity to my life, just when it all starts to feel so transitory.

Last week a very peculiar thing occurred. As I was getting myself into the mindset of being back in graduate school, I received a letter from them saying they found an old copy of my dissertation lying around and wondered if I wanted it. I must say I paused for a second, not knowing if I really did. Then I began to once again be fascinated by these magnificent meaningful coincidences that keep arising during this process. This must be one of those "Celestine Moments" people are talking about. For some reason my dissertation is being rediscovered, but it seems so removed from the kind of writing I am doing now.

You may not be reading my thesis but I know you are reading my letters. I would say it's a little more personal.

I think we are often misled by our patients' perceptions of their significant relationships. That's why I have been doing more family therapy and making an effort to bring in the people who are an important part of my patients' lives. This experience has made me more aware of people's capacity to distort the truth and more careful about assuming that whatever I hear is the whole story. Not taking anything for granted allows me to be open to other possibilities, and gives the people in a patient's world more of an opportunity to be involved in the therapy. Interestingly, I find that quite often the patient does not object.

Dad, I feel that we are coming to the more positive part of our relationship, but I am afraid we have one more hurdle: the first year back in Connecticut and my fellowship. We need to get through that final obstacle and then wait to see what happens.

Love,
Donald

* * *

Dear Donald,

I enjoyed reading your last letter very much. It made me more aware than ever how difficult it really is to step out of the limits of one's own time warp, one's own vantage point, and point of view. Coincidentally, I've been reading Russell Baker's autobiography, *Growing Up*, and I came upon a particularly poignant and pertinent passage in which he writes about his psychotic senile mother:

> Sitting at her bedside, forever out of touch with her, I wondered about my own children, and their children, and children in general, and about disconnections between children and parents that prevent them from knowing each other. Children rarely want to know who their parents were before they were parents and when age finally stirs their curiosity, there is no parent left to tell them. If a parent does lift the curtain a bit, it is often only to stun the young with some exemplary tale of how much harder life was in the old days.

In another section, Russell Baker says of himself and his mother:

> When she was young, with life ahead of her, I had been her future and resented it. Instinctively, I wanted to break free, cease being a creature defined by her time, consign her future

to the past, and create my own. Well, I had finally done that, and then with my own children I had seen my exciting future become their boring past. We all come from the past, and children ought to know what it was that went into their making, to know. that life is a braided cord of humanity stretching up from time long gone, and that it cannot be defined by the span of a single journey from diaper to shroud.

Donald, I don't think I've told you before now how grateful I am for this experience you and I are sharing. What a marvelous gift for me that you and I can share so many of our thoughts and feelings about this period of time that we lived together. How few men have been blessed with a son who can teach his father so much about the free expression of feelings! What a rich and rewarding experience for me that I am now having another chance to better understand what went on inside you during the years we have shared, without feeling that we have a dispute to resolve, an argument to win, or an ax to grind. And what a rich and rewarding experience for me to learn, through your eyes and words, things about myself that I had long forgotten or never really knew!

In labeling you a "phony hippie," I didn't mean to derogate its significance and importance to you. I merely meant to suggest that it didn't really reflect the actual rejection of the values of your childhood. You were still the Yankee fan, secure in the knowledge that your tuition would be paid, your room and board provided for, and big safety net ready in the event you needed it. Most importantly, I knew you were cynical about and aware of the destructive aspects of the "drug craze" and that you were fundamentally committed to the preservation of critical traditional values. I used the word "phony" in the sense that you said that when people got to know you they would realize that you were not what you appeared to be.

I like your reference to, "a need to experiment and try out new things" in growing up. You also aptly refer to "dress rehearsals for life." Indeed, I had my own experiments and dress rehearsals in growing up but the times of my youth provided less colorful costumes. I do remember my high school years when all the "in" boys wore pegged pants with very wide knees. They were then considered sharp, and I sported my own sharp trousers as my entrance visa to the "in crowd."

There were the guys who were not only sharp-looking, they were also "cool" around the girls, and they sported a "hip" repartee of racy words and expressions which separated them from the "creeps." They hung around the neighborhood luncheonette and candy store where I grew up, often bragging about recent sexual exploits. It was to this exalted fraternity that I aspired to belong. I was able to effect all the superficial appearances, but behind the façade, I was no less timid with girls, no less fearful of my mother's angry tongue, and no less serious in my pursuit of academic achievement. The secret was to pretend that academic success was effortless, that I never studied, that I hardly ever even paid attention in class. As long as my friends believed this, they were willing to overlook or forgive my good grades. After all, I couldn't help it if I was so smart. Donald, was I any less "phony" than you were?

Almost in tandem with this period of my life, I became very intrigued by the preaching of the Marxist radicals of that era. I began to discover in my early teens that almost all the intellectually intense people I encountered were either communists, or at least Marxists. In those days, the distinction made between socialism and communism was one of evolutionary development versus violent revolution, but socialism was also viewed as a way station in the inevitable and inexorable path to communist utopia. To gain acceptance among these people, I had to effect a political sympathy for radical movements and organizations, and I do think that many of them thought I was one of them. However, though I was fascinated and persuaded by some of their arguments about the self-destructive evils of capitalist exploitation of the masses, I always distrusted and was frightened by the violent prescriptions they proposed or implied.

In those days, an organization called the American Student Union was actively proselytizing for members. I had one of my many crushes on a very pretty girl who was an active member and crusader. In more recent times, the ASU would have been, or actually was, classified as a communist front organization. I never joined because of skepticism and fear, but I sure nurtured the pretense that I was one of them for the benefit of this pretty blonde girl I coveted.

Don, these were my "dress rehearsals for life" and my version of the search for the Holy Grail. We are a gregarious species and we go to very great lengths to gain acceptance and status among our peers.

If we are strong, we won't compromise our crucial values in the process. Alas, we're not always that strong, especially while growing up.

During my last year of college, World War II was on. I was in naval uniform, and much of the Cornell campus had been taken over by the Army and Navy college training programs. This was a device for keeping people in college in anticipation of active military duty. There were large groups of students brought in from other colleges and we were all split up and assigned to various dormitories or fraternity houses.

There was one young man, a Cornell student whom I had never known before, who was the inevitable butt of teasing and persecution. If there was a bully in the neighborhood this young man would surely find him.

Well, he found them in abundance in our fraternity house. He was teased, verbally abused, even somewhat physically abused for endlessly listening to Baroque music, for being awkward, self-conscious, and strange. He was a sad fellow and I felt terrible for him. I befriended him, tried to advise him, but only timidly fought back in his defense. I was too afraid that these angry tormentors would turn on me if I defended him with the full force of my convictions. To this day, I'm ashamed of my timidity. I subsequently heard that my tormented friend had a schizophrenic breakdown.

This whole episode occupied many hours while I struggled with my feelings about it during my personal psychoanalysis. It seemed to epitomize for me all the compromises I had ever made with my values and my conscience. How much do we compromise ourselves, our integrity, our self-esteem, our basic values in the service of expedience, security, our perceived self-interest? We seem to admire the hero who martyrs himself for principle, but I believe that most of us secretly feel "better him than me."

There is only one exception that strongly moves me: that is to protect the weak and helpless against persecution and injustice from the strong. Other kinds of martyrdom often seem to be motivated by grand-standing exhibitionism and self-aggrandizement.

After each of your recent letters, I am amazed at the extent to which we got caught up in discussing and debating issues of real substance, but issues which touched only incidentally on the real conflict between us were ignored. I wanted you to think the way I did, with all the seemingly confident wisdom of experience, and I couldn't hear your plea of "me too." You wanted me to more clearly acknowledge your separate personhood, your independent claim to be your own respected adult person. Somehow I failed to give you that at the time and I deeply regret it. I think you knew I loved you and cared for you, but you wanted me to also admire and respect you. I could have done that if I had understood more fully; and if I had, I would have helped you in your "dress rehearsals for life" and your search for the "Holy Grail."

You're right on target when you comment about my discomfort in handling the competitive problems between you and your sister. You are also accurate in your observation that your mother and I had been very unhappy about it, but confused about what we could do to alleviate it.

I know that we are largely responsible for it, although the desire for exclusive possession of parents is a deeply ingrained feature of every child's psyche. Having always been aware of this, we thought we bent over backwards to avoid playing favorites. This was particularly true during your early life when we were acutely sensitive to the probability that your sister would resent your intrusion into what had been her exclusive domain.

I have long felt that in our eagerness to forestall Ellen's jealously of her newly arrived rival, we tried so hard to make her feel as if she had nothing to fear that we inadvertently gave credence to her feeling threatened. Perhaps we communicated our feelings of guilt about having complicated her Garden of Eden. She was two-and-a-half years old when you were born, and prior to your birth she had been the center of our universe. Now she would have to share that privileged central position with a newborn brother, and your mother and I were extremely sensitive to her anticipated reaction. We were so sensitive to it, in fact, that we must have conveyed our guilt and anxiety about it to the extent that maybe we enabled her to feel that she was indeed the victim of an injustice.

It's hard to know what happens in the minds of very young children so what we infer is largely a projection of our own thoughts and feelings. We didn't think these things at the time, except that we were mindful of the inevitable sibling rivalry. But I have no other way of understanding what happened to create the intense rivalry and the later relative alienation that occurred between you.

One inevitably tends to attribute the major role in this rivalry to the older sibling, but certainly the younger sibling picks up the cues very quickly. By the time parents realize what is happening, the situation has become so complex as to be a chicken and egg phenomenon, or "which twin has the Toni."

Over the years, our efforts to influence your relationship have proved futile. At times our efforts even seemed to backfire and make matters worse. Consequently, we resolved to stay out of your conflicts as much as possible in the hope that you would someday resolve your dispute between yourselves. I'm thrilled to hear from both of you that this seems to be happening now. Lord knows, it's nice to have someone to share the burden and responsibility of parenting. This will likely be even more true in the future as age takes its inevitable toll on your mother's and my competence and self-reliance.

You know how nice it was for me to have my brothers and my niece to share the responsibility for my mother's care during the last of her ninety-three years. Even before that, though, there is no one else who can share with you the way your sister can, the legacy of two parents who influenced your lives, and are likely to continue to be factors in your lives for some time to come.

As for your comment about metapsychological and theoretical speculation concerning human behavior, it is true that I have long felt that they often obscure and obfuscate our understanding rather than clarify it. We become fascinated and seduced by the beauty and cleverness of our metaphors, and we tend to lose sight of the fact that they are in fact metaphors and speculations. Simple and self-evident truths and observations often become obscured by high level abstractions, increasingly removed from the data of observation and experience. We examine a piece of behavior, apply a beautiful abstract theory, and delude ourselves into believing that we have understood or explained something about that behavior. You know from clinical experience that this doesn't help our patients and it doesn't even really enhance our insight into their behavior.

We are able to understand and help our patients when they trust us enough to allow us to get into their minds, so that we can better understand the dynamic interaction of their feelings, their thinking, and their actions. When they allow us to become a significant influence in their lives, to help them better understand how and why they react as they do, we can help them assume more rational control over their destinies.

It seems to me that this is a simple, perhaps overly simple rationale for what we do professionally. It has little to do with metapsychology or theoretical abstraction.

Before closing this letter, I want to reiterate my gratitude to you for giving me this opportunity to appreciate what a special son I have. You make reference to the fact that we are approaching a time in your life when our relationship became more positive. I want you to know that far from feeling put down at this point, I feel flattered and proud that we can communicate in this way. My affection for you is so clearly reciprocated, even in those sections of your letters in which you are seemingly at odds with me.

Love,
Dad

The Resolution

(EARLY ADULTHOOD)

The Transition

Now instead of being Freud and Jung, we could be father and son.

We, as parents, inevitably and hypocritically raise our children to believe in the existence of justice.

* * *

October, 1982
Dear Dad,

My feelings toward you during my first year back East were ambivalent. I was twenty-seven years old; the post-doctoral fellowship at Yale was loaded with expectations for me; my decision to move east was on the line; and I had such an investment in having good reasons to justify the choice. As you know, with high expectations comes disappointment. I have spent some time thinking about whether it would have been easier if you had been a failure in life.

That first year back was difficult. Dee and I moved into a new house in a new state, not knowing anyone around us. I was not used to working in a traditional teaching-hospital. It was different from all my previous experiences. But as I look back, that may have been true only on the surface. I was a Ph.D., right out of school, feeling overwhelmed by a system larger than I was. It felt like that big octopus that you protected me from when we went snorkeling together in Caneel Bay when I was a little boy. At the time it seemed larger than life.

The nicest part of coming back was that you and I could share professionally. While living out in California I had become quite envious of my closest friend's relationship with his father, who is also a psychoanalyst. They used to get together all the time. He had decided to follow in his father's footsteps and become an analyst like his dad. The two of us had a special relationship, maybe because we understood each other. There was a sense of brotherhood. In a peculiar way, being close to him helped take away the sting of you being so far away. I was aware of the fact, however, that while he was following his father's path, I was still involved with the Jungian community—until I moved.

I spent a great deal of that year struggling to make ends meet and making a life for myself and my family. At times I became overwhelmed by what I sometimes felt was an oppressive work environment. This all occurred during the time that Emily was born. That was also a new adjustment for me, but one I cherished. There were moments when the responsibilities of fatherhood evoked some anxiety in me. There were so many changes: having a baby, living in an unfamiliar community, and finding new friends. To make matters worse, our house was buried in the woods away from what I had always considered civilization. My moods went from periods of elation to moments of nostalgia for my life in the West.

I was having some difficulty being enthusiastic about the fellowship, sometimes wondering if I would have been better off had I taken a regular job. It upset me to think that maybe I was disappointing you. You seemed to have a great deal invested in my liking it. At last I was studying the psychoanalytic literature and having some intelligent discussions with you about it.

Whenever I would start to complain about the injustice of the system, you tried to defend my decision to take the fellowship. At times I had trouble seeing your point of view, and I had difficulty accepting your attempts to make me feel more positive about my decision to move back. It seemed like the only good thing coming out of this fellowship was that I made a close friend. In the end, that wasn't so bad, he was my colleague and companion during this tedious time.

During this time, there was still the possibility of my returning to California. I kept thinking life could be greener on the other side. Here I was, living out what I felt was your dream for me and I was resenting you for it. I know you wanted me to play the game with the people in authority and be the obedient student who does not challenge or make waves. But you know I was never too good at "kissing ass."

I remember having to go back to work two days after Emily was born and having a tough time getting motivated. It was hard to hear you confront me about my rebellious attitude when I felt I had some legitimate gripes about the way the trainees were being treated. There is always that thin line between the mature adult with his accurate perceptions and the immature adult who is constantly feeling victimized. I was angry when you labeled my behavior rebellious. Admittedly, there were times when maybe I could have avoided taking things so personally. This was a time when it was expected of me to pay my dues. I needed some acknowledgment from you condoning the way I was feeling. In your own way, I am sure you believe you did the best you could when it came to giving me the support I needed. Somehow it seems that people assume the ones in control have to be right.

My final fight for independence came when you bought me that Santa Claus outfit to wear for Emily on Christmas some years back. I was in no mood to take on your role. I felt pressured to wear a mask that didn't fit me. One gets into a conflict of pleasing others versus pleasing oneself. I actually had myself convinced that my behavior was justified, and that pleasing myself meant being assertive. I chose not to wear the costume. You were very angry at me and told me that I was being self-centered and bringing the family down. All I really wanted was to be left alone, but somehow I was having trouble being direct about it.

The transition from my fellowship, to hanging a shingle and beginning my private practice presented many challenges and much long-awaited excitement, as well as some trepidation. I knew you could not fill my practice with patients despite all your connections..

This was a time of uncertainty. My expectations of what other people could do for me were unrealistic and I was beginning to confront the reality that I had to create my own opportunities. What a revelation, both disturbing and enlightening. I often considered moving to Long Island and having you hand me a practice. That would have been the easy way out.

As time passed, my confidence grew, and simultaneously, all my idealized gods were falling from grace. This allowed me to feel closer to you. You always encouraged me to be my own boss and not work for someone else. I was beginning to appreciate that advice. You taught me that humility and heart are as essential as the head. It is important to go about your work without getting caught up in meaningless obligations, like impressing other people.

I always admired you for going off on your own and starting a private practice. Somehow you gave me the strength and courage to do the same thing. Neither one of us was cut out to work for someone else. We were two stubborn, independent personalities trying to prove our way was the right way. Now it all just seemed so trivial. The "right way" became irrelevant. What a relief not to battle you and your ideas anymore. You did not have to be someone who had to always assist me. It helped that I no longer needed your financial support. My practice was coming along.

As a result of what was happening to me, it was becoming less important whether I be a Jungian or a Freudian. I was no longer invested in participating in that rivalry, and my identity as a Jungian was passing. There was a growing realization that I could be myself, independent of anyone else, and I was beginning to feel closer to you and wanted to be your friend. The responsibility was on me now and I couldn't blame other people for my misfortunes. Ultimately, one had to be his own god and accept and trust oneself. There is no longer that need to conform to a standard for you or anyone else. Previously, I always had to look outside myself for something to hang onto, whether it be the image of the basketball star, the Jungian, or the bearded wonder.

Ira Benkow, a writer for the *New York Times*, commented in his "Sports Monday" column that while there may be some truth to the remark in *The Natural* by Bernard Malamud that, "Without heroes we are all plain people and don't know how far we can go." It is often the people around us, the Old Shoes, who truly make a difference in our lives.

If people want to have their own fantasies about who I am, so what, as long as I know what's real for me. I even had to release my interest in being a Jungian before we could get on with our relationship. Now instead of being Freud and Jung, we could be father and son. I don't feel a need to look for gods anymore because I'm secure with what I have and who I am. Finally, I can see he lives somewhere inside both of us. What I have been searching for is present at this very moment, not before or later. I think it's about trust and love. There was a concern that I was missing something or that I should have been more than what I was at the moment. Absolute truth is not somewhere else, and it is a bit frightening to realize this. Go see the movie *Altered States* about a man reaching for another level, only wanting to return to what he had.

Who said the world was just and fair? Although when I was a child, you sure made me feel this was true. Life is unfair and I never felt prepared for that. It would have been unfortunate to realize this too late when it would have been beyond the point of redemption for the two of us. Being special to you, and somewhat a piece of the image you wanted to see me in—seems okay now. I do not feel resentful about it anymore. We can take our masks off and shed our vanities. Your demand for respect and your ability to dominate a situation are now positive aspects whereas before they were threatening. You instilled in me an appreciation for my position in the world, an inheritance, recognition, and the privilege of being your son. I recall a memorable line from the movie *Shadowlands,* the story of C.S. Lewis's emerging manhood, "The pain then is part of the happiness now." It's our journey to manhood that takes us to our destination. I had to dig deep inside myself and we are taking the ride together. We must all confront the dark and light side of ourselves. It's our inside ride.

Listen to me! Whoever thought I would come to this! I can now appreciate that your strength gave me many advantages because you were there to help me reach this point. I am responsible to myself and other people to carry out a tradition that you and your father have laid out for me. Now that I have a son and daughter I want to pass on this tradition. When they fail, I hope I will help them to learn from their mistakes.

Having children seems to have forced me to grow up and be responsible for others. I like the fact that people depend on me, and the sense that I have earned your respect.

A major turning point in our relationship occurred when you finally approached me with one of your problems. Interestingly, I felt as though I had become the voice of practicality and reason for you. It meant so much to me to have you come to me with your inner pain; this is something I wanted from you for a long time. It felt so good helping you out. When you reached out to me, I got the inner you. How nice that a father could come to his son. You will always be my father but now you are also my friend. It feels so gratifying when you come to me for an opinion regarding your professional work. In the past I had trouble understanding why you did not want to burden me with your problems, but I know I am the same way.

There was a time I was jealous of my sister's boyfriend because you always seemed to seek his opinions about the world, particularly in the financial area. As I mentioned in an earlier letter, whenever it was the three of us, I would feel like the third wheel. He was the adult and I was the kid. It appeared as though you had more of an investment in pleasing him than me. I was extremely sensitive about this. My need to be valued was so strong.

Well, you're just not perfect, and if anything, I crave your fallibility now. At one point it would have been to gain control over you, but now the desire is just to be needed and treated like an adult. Somehow if you can make mistakes and not know all the answers, it gives me the same permission. There can be room for human error. At one time this would have scared the hell out of me and threatened my security.

The fault line is sealed and now it's just plain old taking responsibility for my own actions. The other way felt severe and created too many earthquakes between us. Sometimes you just make mistakes that come with being mortal. If we could live by this we could prevent future acts of hubris. "It's never good enough" is now translated into "I'm doing the best I can do," and that is good enough. In the end we are all flawed. The goal is to live authentically

I appreciate the fact that I have been exposed to your enthusiasm for work and your pride in it. You taught me something about the value of working for a living. In the past, I never wanted material things from you and would take them for granted. That was because you gave me so much. Being on my own gives me a deeper appreciation of the things I own. What I buy has more meaning because I spend my own money. It was a huge moment when we saved up to buy our first twenty-five inch colored TV. Do you know I actually read the business section of *The New York Times*, and I find myself saying to my kids why don't you ever pick up the paper? Having to control my financial situation has forced me to learn about the world of money, something I previously had no interest in, as you know.

As a man, I feel torn between my career, my roles as husband and father, and my private self. Haven't you felt that conflict about balancing your time? How do you do it right? Maybe I should not worry about that and just go with it. Now we can share these universal adult male concerns. Sometimes I feel a need to go to Emily's dance classes and play groups, but I have to be the responsible therapist as well.

Have you had moments of feeling taken for granted over the years? I have wondered if you needed more time to yourself when you would come home from work and everyone wanted something from you. I always admired your ability to cope with pressure. I like the feeling of familial and domestic comfort, but with it comes moments of alienation and loneliness. There are those times when there seem to be too many expectations, and I feel like I am drowning in them. External pressures and possessions become too important. Did you often feel like that? I feel more tuned into you and what you have been through. Now when you talk to me from work I can understand your time pressures and don't take it personally. You have to experience the same struggles before you can understand someone else's.

The struggles that marriage brings remind me of the fears and uncomfortable feelings that used to come upon me whenever you and Mom would argue. I could never understand who was driving whom crazy, and I still have trouble knowing. Maybe being in the situation now of trying to keep a family and marriage together gives me an appreciation of the fact that the sanity of both partners is often tested. It is hard to keep the passion alive. Sometimes it is difficult for me to discriminate the real issues. It takes two in any relationship.

It must have been hard for Mom to be in your shadow and compete with the rest of the world for your attention. In retrospect, I wish I had been more curious about her doing Braille for the blind. She never did seem to get the recognition she deserved as a mother, but she may finally be getting it as a grandmother. You never seemed to be one of those men threatened by women having careers. Although it seemed as though you were behind Dee and my sister having careers, I never really knew how you felt about Mom staying home. At times you appeared uncomfortable with it, but at other moments it was unclear. I had the feeling you thought Mom could have been success-ful at so many things and that you wished that she had pursued them. Incidentally, this is not so easy; I tried it for a day. You often would joke about it. Men should have that experience because it would help them understand what a mother and homemaker goes through. At least we get paid for working!

It must have been hard for you to know how to balance your priorities in life. You cannot be all things for people. There were moments when it appeared that you were the weak one in the relationship with Mom, but then you often seemed so strong. As you know, I had a need to see you as the dominant one, although at times, I felt you would take it a little too far. My mixed perceptions of your relationship would confuse me, but let's face it, you could be unreasonable and human like everyone else. Those moments always surprised me and took me off guard.

I always knew to get out of your way after you had met with your accountant and found out your tax bill. I felt sad that when I was younger you and I were not always there for each other. Of course, there were times when you had your own pressures and probably did not have the energy for me. l would feel like a pain in the ass talking to a wall. It would have helped me to know you needed some space, and your thoughts were somewhere else. Ironically, as my life is now becoming cluttered with responsibilities, I wish there was more time for you. I want to be with you now and there never seems to be enough opportunity. There are moments I regret not living closer to you so I could just spontaneously drop by with the kids or play a game of tennis. It would even be nice to practice together. I like watching you relate to my kids wondering if that is how you related to me.

The older I get the more I see myself doing things that were difficult for me to understand and accept about you. Now I enjoy being alone and run from the telephone. It is hard to believe I was once the kid who was afraid of his shadow. Life seems so different. Now I can appreciate things you did that at one time seemed so trivial. How often did you come home exhausted from work and get on the floor to play with me when you were really not in the mood? We make sacrifices as adults that are never appreciated when they are done for us as children.

It is nice to feel comfortable and be in a position to make my own decisions about life. Paradoxically, that freedom has allowed me to reach out to you more both professionally and personally. I enjoy our being in the same field. Being able to support myself and my family has given me a sense of power that I never understood before. When

I buy things for myself, there is no longer that need for justification, and if you have an opinion not compatible with mine I am not threatened. Loving myself has certainly helped me to love you. That first psychology book for me, *The Art of Loving* by Erich Fromm, has finally been integrated into my life.

I always liked it when you would share a compliment about me that someone else had given you. There were times when I felt you wanted to say positive things to me but had trouble getting the words out. It meant a lot to me when you would acknowledge that certain things came more naturally to me than they did to you. There was always a need through the years for me to be better than you at something. I find myself still wanting to pull the compliments out of you. It seems easier for you to express them now. Maybe we both have changed in the sense that you are more comfortable being demonstrative and I am more receptive to that kind of giving.

One of the most dramatic changes in our relationship stemmed from the fact that you were once the heavy intellectual and I was the lean athlete. That changed when you became Mr. Physical Fitness after your heart attack, and I was the guy with the huge body worried about being chosen last in a pick-up game with my friends. You always did have a way of motivating me. It would bother me when you would constantly tell me to stop eating and start doing some exercise. I knew you were right and had trouble dealing with it. That used to be reverse.

Losing to you in tennis was no thrill and I actually felt competitive with you on the court. There was a time when we were probably both reticent to compete against each other for fear of bruising one another's feelings. Somehow all that has changed and now it seems natural that we try to beat each other. That false macho-cool "I don't care" attitude is for the birds. Anyway it was just a cover-up for feeling inadequate and having a good excuse for losing. Why not play hard against each other? We don't need to protect each other anymore. It seems okay to beat each other now that we are friends and the boundaries of the relationship are clearer. There is excitement in the desire to win and be a good athlete again. It's even easier to accept losing now, as long as I do occasionally win.

As a result of your new body and athletic prowess, I am starting to regain that old competitive drive that I once had and later rebelled

against. I know this all stems from my basketball trauma. It is fun
wanting to win and physically improve myself again. It won't be long
before you get me on the golf course.

I used to need to demonstrate to myself that I had a mind that
worked like yours, and now I find myself needing to do the same
thing with my body. My past need to split mind and body would not
have agreed with my more recent interest in Eastern philosophy.

I always said I wanted you to be an athlete. So how could I dare
go the other way? At this stage of my life, when we play tennis, it
comes close to the fantasy and excitement I once envisioned for
myself as a kid playing for the New York Yankees and being a pro
basketball player. The only difference now is my ability to balance
fantasy with reality. Farewell to Walter Mitty. I am not going to leap
out of the broad jump pit and be Bob Beamon. There was a time
when if I could not be the best ball player around, there was no point
in playing. It was that familiar problem of never being good enough.
In the past, you didn't seem to have that quality, but now you appear
to be a driven man in sports, and I kind of like it. It's more honest.
Don't let me beat you. I can handle it. You always had the discipline
and persistence to be good at whatever you attempted or so it seemed.
You were the one with the thick skin.

As I am writing these letters I am aware that while recapturing
my youth and re-evaluating my life experiences with you, I feel like a
new person, lighter physically and emotionally. My physical identity
needed a change to go along with my emotional upheavals. It has
helped me to get back some old feelings as well as gain new ones. I
feel as if I have relived my life from a new perspective. I was in the
process of reinventing myself.

One could even say we are starting to resemble each other physically as we once did, a situation I changed when I grew a beard and
long hair. I like hearing that we look alike and have similar tempera-
ments now. We will never be twins, so it's okay.

Funny that I always thought you wanted your son to be an intellectual, and a while back you asked me to run two miles with you at
six-thirty in the morning. Well Dad, I'm not ready for that quite yet.
My baby steps used to beat the clock with plenty of time to spare, but
now as the stride refuses to widen, the pendulum of time still continues. At least now we can sit in a room and watch a ball game together

without feeling uneasy. One time we even compromised, turning the sound off the TV and putting on classical music in the background. At least we were together and now we could even sit and enjoy tennis or golf on a Sunday afternoon.

As my gods were dying, I became aware of the fact that it was time to put on that Santa Claus outfit you gave me. Perhaps it was symbolic that I was expected to take over that tradition in the family. I tried to convince myself to put it on and play out the role in my own house with my own family and friends. Life has a peculiar way of shifting its purpose, as I as I now must prepare myself for the day my son might want to tear off my white beard. Maybe shaving off my beard is my way of preparing for that day. My patients have commented on how much younger I look, and perhaps for some, it may have temporarily or permanently taken me off my pedestal. My need to project an image of godliness has subsided as well.

As my gods fall around me, my son is just beginning to discover his. I am aware of the fact that Jared will need to idealize me, and I must be careful not to take that away from him. My son's birth came at a time when my life had settled down and I could comfortably take responsibility for my power. You let me be a child and did not force me to grow up too fast. I really appreciated that. It is important for me to stay in touch with my own mortality but allow my son to accept me at his own pace. I never want to feel defensive for being imperfect but he may need to see me vulnerable. We know that will change.

You seemed so patient with me during my rebellion, and now I question how you were able to give me so much when often it appeared that you were being given so little in return. This book is my way of paying you back for the crap I gave you. Who knows what is ahead, but living with the unknown is part of the process. I hope there will be many occasions for me to share my life experiences with my children and be able to reach out to them the way you finally seem to be able to do with me.

These letters are a legacy I can pass on to my children. Even with our new friendship, I will always be a son to you and a father to my own son. Somehow these two parts of me, the child and the adult man, must learn to co-exist. This is a delicate balance. Freedom versus responsibility is a hard one for me. I never wanted to have a relationship in which I was in the role of being your father and you my son. For that I am grateful and the mutuality between us now does not have to negate that appreciation. Thank you for managing your life in a way which allows me to remain your son and simultaneously become a friend to you during this phase of our lives. You never lost your dignity. I know how important this was to you as the years progressed.

Remember when I would object to your comments about conditional love? When I was at the peak of my idealistic period, we used to argue about this subject. How naive of me to think that I or anyone else could be that way. You were right when you said relationships must be reciprocal: "You got smarter as I got older." How unequal our relationship has been and now it is my turn to give back to you. So do me a favor, Dad. Next time we go out for dinner, let me pay the bill for a change!

Indeed it feels as if I am experiencing my rite of passage into adulthood with you. Being my own person seems to have given me the freedom to let go of my illusion that you or anyone else can fulfill all my needs. In a curious way, it feels as if I am ripping off your white beard all over again, but the difference is that now I can accept it as a part of life. It sure is different looking at it through the eyes of an adult.

Job's struggle with God has always been one of my favorite stories in the Bible. Their relationship reminded me of a father and son struggling with the problem of disillusionment. Job had to pass a test of faith and patience, confronting the reality that his God couldn't make everything better for him. He had to follow that realization with a period of mourning the illusion, questioning it, and feeling a sense of relief and acceptance that somehow it was no longer there. Job had to accept his fate with God and himself. Both Carl Jung and William Blake had wonderful interpretations for the "Answer to Job."

You don't have to be anyone but yourself for me at this point in my life, and I want you to know that this gives me a sense of peace within myself. There can be so much freedom in the death of illusion. I want my own identity and to recognize that nothing is black and white. We can acknowledge that being a god to our sons and patients serves a purpose, but in time we must transform ourselves into ordinary people with mortal concerns. Despite all your friends in the field of psychiatry, I realized that I finally had to do it on my own and that even you were limited as to what you could do for me. The struggle was over and with that is new energy. I was no longer afraid to feel afraid.

In one of my earlier letters I expressed to you that going pre-med was my final accommodation to you. What nonsense, because there is no such thing. I will always feel obligated to you, and I am sure you will be to me. If we did not need each other, what would the relationship mean? Being obligated means pleasing a loved one who needs you. So what is wrong with that? It just took me a while to "get it." A recent sermon by the rabbi on Yom Kippur helped me realize this. It is nice to receive when you learn how to give. I don't feel like a taker anymore. How ironic that ultimately, I am the one going to temple and desiring to re-establish my connection to Judaism. I am finally ready for my Bar Mitzvah and the trip to Israel.

It is no accident that we chose a profession that requires people to need us. Being relied on gives me a sense of purpose that can easily be taken for granted. It is hard to believe that I can now see wanting to please you in a positive way. What makes it nice is that I feel you want to please me too, and we can now admit that to each other. At some point, the mental, physical, and spiritual rebellion must end. At least one strives for that.

I was sharing my restlessness about life, and I remember feeling envious when you said you finally accepted your life. You seemed so content and convincing when you stated that you could not see yourself having done anything so radically different, particularly regarding your career. It seemed as if your strongest concern was centered on the fact that a day will come when you won't be able to practice anymore. You were grateful for the fact that you can still work. It almost seemed like you were saying the search and dreams were over, and that living for now was something you could really accomplish. Of course, no sooner did you say these things to me than you embarked on several new projects. How reassuring to know that even at your stage of life it is hard to sit still. The struggle and search continues.

I realize that what mostly bonds us is our love for each other. There exists the mutual respect and honesty that is so necessary for a healthy relationship. Friends come and go, but not a true father. You are my best friend. No one could replace you at this point. It seems fitting to end this letter with a quote from the Talmud that inspired me (it was highlighted in *The Chosen*):

The King sent a message to his son to come to him.
The son went astray and the father let him go;
The King sent another message to say,
'Come back as far as you can, and I will meet you the rest of
the way.'

Love,
Donald

* * *

Dear Donald,

Since writing my last letter to you, I've thought a great deal about
the way I felt about my parents and the way you have apparently felt
about me. There are many more similarities then differences, though
the differences I believe are very real. But they are certainly not as
strong as I have tended to believe.

It surprises me, in a way, to discover how much you feel responsible for my happiness and well-being. I'm not talking about guilt feelings if you hurt or offend me. I'm talking about the concern I think
you express for me to be pleased and proud of you

One of the things that distinguishes your mother and me and
others of our generation from our parents' generation, is the extent
to which we endeavored to spare you and your generation from the
guilt and feelings of responsibility for the well-being of your parents
that we felt. You've heard and read a great deal about the long-suffer-
ing Jewish mother who agonized if her children didn't wear rubber
overshoes in the rain. This caricature had been exploited by many
humorists of our era.

She is an exaggerated version of what we all knew to be the pro-
totypical Jewish mother. In my case, however, it always seemed as
if she derived her power from the extraordinary need that we—my
brothers and I—felt to avoid my father's displeasure. All my life it felt
as if my every potential success or failure would govern my parents'
well-being. It was a very heavy burden.

Of course, we weren't going to do this to our children. We took
such pains, we thought, to avoid instilling similar guilt in our kids; our

kids would grow up unencumbered by the guilt and responsibility toward us that we felt toward our parents.

How ironic and pathetically naive we were! I realize now, as never before, that for all my pretentious wisdom and selflessness, I did very much the same to you and your sister. You're both very hard-working, conscientious replicas of your mother and me. You both are troubled by the awesome responsibility of pleasing us and making us proud of you.

The big difference, and I'm not at all sure it's better, is that you have been less aware of how vulnerable your mother and I really are. This clearly resulted from an attempted conspiracy on our part to conceal our vulnerability from you. Our attempt, however, was imperfect and only partially successful.

We obviously bled when you failed to live up to the standards we set for you, and you obviously knew it. There was, however, an element of ambiguity and uncertainty which encouraged you to test us, and test us you did.

By contrast, my parents made little effort to conceal either their weaknesses or their imperfections. By the time I was an adolescent, I had absolutely no illusions about my parents' omnipotence. I believe that you had trouble thinking about Mom and me as ordinary people who were subject to all the pitfalls and tragedies of life to which ordinary people are vulnerable.

Ten years ago, as you know, your mother had breast cancer for which she underwent surgery, radiotherapy, and chemotherapy. The whole process of treatment lasted two years. This was one of the most traumatic periods of our lives. I know full well how deeply affected you were, but isn't it remarkable that you never mention this period in your letters. I always understood your need to deny the seriousness of it as well as your need to deny the seriousness of my illness the following year. But the fact that you are able to effectively suppress the memory of these events in your account of this period of your life, it seems to me, attests to the trouble you have in accepting our mortality and our vulnerability.

We always tend to minimize to ourselves the crucial importance our feelings have on our children, and to underestimate the impact of our wishes and potential reactions on them. This is all the more remarkable in our case because we are so sensitized and tuned in to the impact our reactions or anticipated reactions have on our patients.

The failure on my part to fully understand how you felt, or how you were reacting to something I said, or some position I took, has been pointed up several times in the course of these letters. Your account of our interaction during your post-doctoral fellowship after you returned from California is a striking example.

I knew, of course, that you were unhappy and frustrated at times during your fellowship. I felt extremely badly for you and I knew that you were looking for me to support your struggle against the establishment. I didn't feel able to do this because I felt it would be self-defeating and self-destructive for you.

You felt successful and respected in California, but when you moved back to the East Coast you ran into a typical teaching hospital bureaucracy with all the competitive maneuvering that characterizes them. I understood all that and thought I tried to be empathetic.

As I told you then, I had spent many years working in such institutions and I knew what you were up against from personal experience. I don't believe I was suggesting that you "kiss ass," as you put it, but I was suggesting that you would make things harder for yourself if you needlessly antagonized the people in authority.

Since you thought of me as a member of the establishment, you seemed to automatically identify me with your superiors. You thought of me as defending them, giving my loyalty to them instead of you, my own son.

You didn't hear me when I said over and over again, "I'm not defending them. I'm sure that some of the people you disagree with are insecure and threatened by your questioning their assumptions and procedures."

In retrospect, I'm proud of you for sticking it out without sacrificing your independence and totally surrendering to what you perceived as an effort to stifle your assertiveness. I'm also glad that you tamed your aggressive defiance enough to avoid the consequences to you of an all out battle.

I recall telling you that justice is an illusion in the real world. We, as parents, inevitably and hypocritically raise our children to believe in the existence of justice. How else can we transmit a moral value system to them without clearly implying that virtue will be rewarded and evil will be punished? "The meek shall inherit the earth." But all around us, the growing child sees evidence of the fact that justice doesn't always triumph and the virtuous often go unrewarded.

This is a hypocrisy that has always been promulgated to the young in an effort to tame the aggressive and competitive impulses that can destroy the cohesion of the social fabric. Human beings have always lived in groups, bound together by the need for cooperative effort to deal with the hostile outside world.

"We versus them" is just one of the expressions of dualism that governs human existence. The child's tendency to simplistically view his world in terms of black and white, with no room for gray, the mythological dualism of "good vs. evil," all reflect the inherent dualism of the self as subject "I" and the self as object "me." What "I" can do to him as against what he can do to "me," is contrasted with what "I" can do for him as against what he can do for "me." This is the classic struggle between love and hate. This is the same struggle we all encounter in trying to balance our cooperative and altruistic impulses with our competitive and aggressive impulses. What I'm trying to say is that the situation during your fellowship was not as black and white as you perceived it to be, nor were you the noble warrior for the forces of good against the forces of evil as represented by the establishment. More meaningfully, I believe that during this period of your life, the forces of your own "I" were warring against the forces of your own "me." "I" the subject was asserting its right to be heard and respected; "me" the object felt put down and demeaned.

If I failed you during this year-long struggle, it was not because I didn't feel for you. It was, I believe, because I was concerned that your struggle might induce you to martyr yourself in futile fashion for a cause you couldn't win.

Maybe I have been more masochistic than you are, more willing to endure the indignity of being treated like an inferior citizen as a price to be paid for eventual acceptance into the privileged fraternity. This may not be as admirable as your reaction was, but I was raised in the tradition that it was okay to accept a certain amount of indignity in the service of being loved, cared for and accepted.

You are familiar, I know, with Harlow's work with Rhesus monkeys in which he experimentally induced neurotic behavior in monkeys who were then cruel and abusive to their young. Such baby monkeys, cruelly punished and rejected by their angry mothers, clung nevertheless with ferocious tenacity to their mothers, especially in the face of danger. Combine this predisposition with the common confusion that cruelty reflects strength and gentleness reflects weakness, and you have the typical clinical masochist. These are the women who are attracted only to men who are cruel or insensitive to their needs because these are the men who seem strong. These are the men who are attracted only to women who are relatively indifferent to them and give them a hard time because only such women seem strong and desirable.

Every relationship is in a sense a power struggle, a negotiation in which control and advantage goes to the person who seems less desperately needy. It's not very different from the dynamic process in any negotiation. If one person wants to sell a house and another person wants to buy it, advantage goes to the one who seems less eager.

It may seem that I've been carried away. What has this to do with your post-doctoral fellowship? I'm only trying to say that you were in a position of weakness, seeking entry and acceptance to a professional community. Your need for them was greater than their need for you, and this gave them a significant measure of control.

Is it any different from the hazing that represented the initiation rite into the college fraternity in my day? I realize that this is no longer the common practice and that this change paralleled the declining desirability of fraternity membership when you went to college. But in my day, if you wanted to belong you had to endure. Nobody seriously questioned the validity of the process as long as the hazing was kept within certain limits. "We went through it, so why shouldn't you go through it as well?" was all the justification that was ever offered. Or said another way, "To be humbled is good for the soul." Men who were once on the receiving end now claim the right to be on the giving end.

What a lousy system! But this is the system, and we can try to change it, but we're likely to be more effective as reformers if we first gain acceptance into it. Welcome to the system!

As for the Christmas episode, you never told me at the time why you were in such a foul mood. As far as I knew, things had been going well for you and I did not anticipate your mood or your reaction.

After all the trials and struggles, you seemed to have finally arrived. You were married, you had a beautiful child, you lived in a house you loved, and you were successfully building a professional identity for yourself in your new home.

Against this background, Mom and I thought that buying and giving you a Santa Claus outfit would be a meaningful gesture. It was my way of sharing with you the pleasure I had always had in playing Santa Claus for you. It felt as if I were passing on a tradition, that you would be pleased to be Santa Claus for Emily the way I had been Santa Claus for you. I was mistaken.

All I knew at the time was that you arrived at our house that day before Christmas and announced that you were in a rotten mood. I hoped your mood would pass and you would take pleasure in sharing the tradition of Santa Claus with me. But you didn't do it. I finally realized that you were trying to say "no" but somehow kept saying "maybe." I went ahead and played my old Santa Claus role as I always had.

You were bringing everybody down, and to this day I don't know why you behaved as you did. I finally exploded many hours later. I was merely giving expression to the accumulated resentment that had been building all Christmas day. How could I understand what you never made any real effort to explain? You were unhappy for reasons not given, and you weren't going to cover up your feelings for me or anybody else.

I believe it was the last quarrel we had. As I recall, Mom and I left for Florida the next day and I telephoned you soon after we arrived there. I remember the conversation clearly; "You know, Donald, how I can't stand it when you and I are angry with each other!" You acknowledged familiarity with my deeply-held secret and said, "I'm not really mad at you, Dad. Please, let's just forget it." I felt much better after we spoke, and was better able to enjoy our vacation.

For the past couple of Christmases, Mom and I conveniently arranged vacations so that we would avoid the Christmas scene. Jung would call it synchronicity, I think, but just as you and your sister were expressing sadness this past Christmas that a family tradition had been interrupted, Mom and I were saying that we would never again go away from the family over the Christmas holidays.

Hopefully, these conflicts are all behind us. We're resurrecting them now because we're reconstructing the history of our relationship, but they really seem much less important in the overall pattern of our connection than this correspondence between us seems to make them. This is a familiar theme in my letters to you and I believe it is an important one.

Realistically, of course, it is likely that we will come into conflict in the future over issues which cannot now be anticipated. We are, after all, two different people, and each of us has the right to assert a personal point of view. Perhaps we're both now sufficiently mature and enlightened to respect each other's differences and differences of opinion.

It does seem to me that for a long time you were as intolerant of my differences of view as I was of yours. Perhaps I had more reason to know better, given the advantage of years and experience that I had. The problem for the parent, however, is the need to augment responsibility with authority. You wouldn't expect a general to assume responsibility for the conduct of his army without giving him the authority to command that army. Yet, that is the situation of the parent who continues to have and feel responsibility for the well-being of the child over whom he no longer has any control.

For me, Donald, the power struggle is over. I no longer feel that I can reasonably exercise control over your destiny; nor do I feel I can reasonably assume responsibility for your destiny. Obviously, I will still rejoice with you in your triumphs and bleed with you in your defeats. This is in the very nature of intimate loving relationships. How else can it be? This is always the price we pay for caring, and how empty life would be without it! We both see sad and empty people who resist caring for others precisely because of their fear of being vulnerable. "*Vive la vulnerabilite!*"

There was a set of circumstances that I've never fully shared with you concerning my relationship with my father during the last three years of his life which I believe will be of interest to you.

In 1956 I was released from two years of active duty in the Air Force and returning to civilian life, when my oldest brother called me to tell me that there were some financial problems in the family for which he needed my help; not my financial help at that time, but my signature on some papers to forestall the threatened foreclosure on some property the family owned.

I discovered, to my great distress, that my brother had lost a very large sum of money gambling, and that in the process he had seriously jeopardized the family business and financial holdings. My brother engaged me in a conspiracy to conceal the facts of the situation from my father. Over the course of the next several months, I was torn apart by the accumulating evidence that the situation was much more desperate than I was originally led to believe, and I felt increasingly guilty about withholding this information from my father under the guise of "protecting" him. Finally, I resolved to tell him, which I did, in spite of my brother's pleading with me not to. In his effort to dissuade me from telling him, my brother portrayed my father as too old and feeble to handle the potential disgrace of losing all his money and property.

As it turned out, my father would have learned about the situation within a short time anyhow, because the situation was deteriorating at a rapid pace.

In time, I had contributed every dollar I had, augmented by borrowing on life insurance and refinancing our home in an effort to plug the leaks which were sinking the family ship.

During this time, I was surprised to discover how extensive the family holdings had actually been. My parents always lived conservatively, and I had no inkling that they had been relatively wealthy people. My brothers, of course, lived much more lavishly, but they were working, after all, and their earnings would justify a more expansive lifestyle. Though I never had to worry seriously about money as a young man because of my father's generosity, it became apparent that I had not shared in the family's wealth and accumulating equities the way my brothers had.

In the several years after I left the Air Force, my father was quite overwhelmed, as was my brother, by the cascading avalanche of financial problems that was engulfing them. I had to assume the role of leadership in the family because no one else was there to do it. Now I was a full partner in the family's economic affairs.

If you detect a note of sarcasm in what I have just written it is intended. I began to resent the position I was in.

My parents lived in Florida then, but my father would come to New York for several weeks every couple of months or so. In those days he was in New York almost continuously, and I met him for dinner almost every week. After struggling with my feelings of resentment for some time, I resolved to share my feelings with my father at one of these dinners with him. I told him essentially what I have outlined above, to wit: When the family was rich, I was a favored son who was largely excluded from sharing in the family's prosperity. Now that the family's fortunes have reversed, I'm the first one called upon for help! In effect, I was telling him that it wasn't fair! "When it came to sharing the rewards, I was at the bottom of the list. When it came to sharing the penalties, I was elevated to the top of the list."

Pop sat quietly for what seemed a long time, but in fact, was probably no more than a very few minutes. "Max," he said, "you're right, but I always knew that you would be able to take care of yourself, and I didn't have to worry about you. With your brothers, it was different. I wasn't fair to you."

We parted that night without saying anything further, and for several days thereafter I felt a combination of relief at having gotten it off my chest, and concern that I had upset him. After a few days had passed, my father called to say he wanted me to meet him but was evasive about what was on his mind. When we met, he presented me with some notarized papers which he had executed giving me title to what he said was the only holding he still had available to him that he could easily transfer. All he said was, "I want you to have this. I wish it could be more."

Several days later, my father returned to Florida. My affection for him was greater than it had ever been. A short time afterwards when he was in Florida, I received a phone call from a doctor in Miami who informed me that my father had suffered a myocardial infarction and was in the hospital. I excused myself from the patient who was in my office, and raced to the airport to catch the first plane I could, When I arrived at the hospital, he was resting comfortably in an oxygen tent, and I can still remember the smile on his face when he greeted me. His nurse told me that while she was fixing his pillow he had told her that he was so proud that I had come so quickly to his bedside after being informed of his illness.

After several days, his condition seemed to stabilize, and I returned home. Within hours after my return though, I received another call from his doctor informing me that he had taken a sudden turn for the worse. By the time I got there, he had already died.

I cannot honestly tell you, even now, whether I feel guilty about the last two meetings I had with him shortly before he died. I certainly don't regret having told him how I felt because otherwise he would probably have died with my resentment unresolved. As it was, it was important for me to feel that I had reconciled with someone I loved deeply after a period of alienation

But I did feel some remorse for having left his bedside and for having been absent when he died. How was I to know? How can anyone know?

At the risk of sounding briefly morbid, Donald, I hope you feel as much affection for me when I pass on as I did for my father. He died in 1958, but I still think of him often and almost invariably with warm feelings.

There is a close connection between the event I've just described and the event to which you refer which occurred last May while we were in Florida for your cousin Jared's Bar Mitzvah. I was troubled about some difficulty I had experienced in trying to get a letter of credit I required in connection with an investment I had made. Since I never borrow money, and therefore have no credit record with my bank, they were unwilling to issue the letter of credit without my putting up collateral. This I was reluctant to do, and I was thinking about asking my brother Irving to get it for me from his bank because his business requires that he have an ongoing line of credit.

I shared this with you and I also told you how difficult it was for me to ask him to do this for me. I had never asked him to do anything for me before and I could reasonably expect that he would welcome an opportunity to do me a favor. Still, I felt the gnawing fear that he would refuse me and I would never speak to him again.

At Jared's party, however, some incident occurred which made me angry with him, and he and I quarreled. I certainly was not going to give him the opportunity to turn me down now and I was furious.

You spoke to me for hours that night and you really helped me. It was as if our roles were reversed. You were able to see through all my defenses and reassuringly help me to see through them as well. You pointed out that I was behaving like the man and the car jack:

A salesman, dressed in suit and tie, has a flat tire on a lonely rural road. He gets out of the car, intending to change his spare tire, and discovers to his chagrin that he has no jack.

"On this damn farm road I'll wait a week before I see a passing car." Then, looking down the road, he spots a lonely farm house. "What a break, I'll just walk over and borrow a jack." As he walks toward the house he muses to himself, "I bet this farmer doesn't often get to see a city slicker, in suit and tie. Hey, what if he doesn't trust me. Country folk often think city people can't be trusted. No, he couldn't refuse to help another human being desperate in a situation like this. He'd have to be a real S.O.B. How can one person treat another person so cruelly, that no good son-of-a-bitch." At this point, he arrives at the farmer's door, and he is so pumped up by the anger he has generated with his own fantasy, he pushes the doorbell with an angry jab. When the farmer appears, he explodes, "You dirty louse, turning away a stranger in distress?" He punches the farmer in the face without even asking for the jack.

That story really hit home. I woke early the next morning and told my brother I wanted to talk to him. When I was finished with my story, recounting the thoughts and feelings I had been having, he embraced me and said, "How could you believe I would ever refuse you?"

This was the first occasion, Donald, as far as I can remember, that you had the opportunity to take care of and help your poor old dad. I'm sure it won't be the last and I know that I can count on you to be there for me if I ever need you. I'm also confident that if you're ever angry with me, or you feel I've been unfair to you, you'll come to me as I did to my father and give me the chance to make restitution as he did.

Love,
Dad

⤙◉⤚

Tactlessness often masquerades as honesty.

Yesterday's painful crisis is hardly remembered today, and will surely be forgotten by tomorrow.

⤙◉⤚

* * *

Dear Dad,

That last letter seems to be the point where you really decided to go public. At the beginning of our journey, you mentioned to me that you were going to "let it all hang out." You certainly have kept up your end of the bargain. It's now my turn to pick up the momentum.

As you know, I always felt that you had tried to protect me from the cruel realities of life, a natural thing for a parent to do. Just recently I had a dream about Emily swimming in a pool with the two of us. I was afraid that if I let go of her she would go under water and not come back up to the surface. It is so hard to give up control of your loved ones.

My reaction to Mom's breast cancer reflected the way I believe tragic situations were treated in our family. You and Mom tried so hard to conceal your vulnerabilities from Ellen and me, we had no other recourse but to conform to an attitude that encouraged denial. I felt that Mom was going to be fine and that you minimized your concern to me about the potential danger she might have been facing. Growing up I observed two packs of Marlboro cigarettes routinely on the breadboard in the kitchen. In those days we just didn't consider the danger of cigarettes. Only within the last week did you inform me that there was, at one time, a strong possibility that she could have died, because her condition was more severe than you had communicated. That threw me for a loop. Later on she developed lung cancer and I still was in denial. I never forgot how hard it was for Mom when she lost her best friend to cancer.

Interestingly, last week I began running a group with the oncology staff at a local hospital who spend every working day dealing with death and dying. Becoming my own person over the last several years has allowed me to feel more comfortable with my own mortality as well as the mortality of others.

In retrospect, maybe your approach with me made Mom's illness and yours easier to handle. Because you were not the type of parents to impose on your children, it probably alleviated some of my anxiety regarding what was going on, but it also prevented me from dealing with the growing pains that one must endure during critical phases of the life cycle. This only helped to perpetuate an immature understanding of how the universe treats it's pupils. My lessons seem to have been curtailed by your inability to see Ellen and me suffer any pain, even when it involved the possibility of losing both of you. This becomes understandable now that I am also a parent.

Occasionally, I consider the possibility that my time could be up even before you. I am thankful that you are such wonderful grandparents and would be there to take care of my children. I have said before that the loss of a grandparent deprives the grandchild of "an extra set of parents." Grandma used to refer to her grandchildren as her "dividends." I have a patient who mourns the loss of her grandfather more than the loss of her own father. How sad that a male patient was angry at his father, even at his funeral. How often I hear that!

It always impressed me that on one hand you were such a protective father, yet you sent me to camp where I would spend my summers sleeping in a tent with no electricity, where there was mandatory nude bathing in the lake every morning independent of the weather conditions, and a half-mile walk to the bathroom. Underpants were considered extra laundry, which meant wearing them was discouraged.

You were right when you said it was hard for me to knock you down from your pedestal. When it came to Mom's illness, I certainly felt spared from any responsibility that could come with a situation as severe as the one Mom had to go through. It became your burden, when in fact your children were there waiting to give you a helping hand if you needed us.

How can any child escape the desire to please his or her parents and make them proud? Parents feel the same need. As I have said before, I often felt your difficulties with expressing vulnerabilities reinforced an idealization of you. That made it more difficult to accept your mortality. One needs that dimension in a human relationship. Becoming aware of the fact that a parent can fall victim to life's unfairness makes a child only want to please his parents that much more. Someday the child has to confront the fact that his parents will no longer be around. I needed to know your struggles, particularly in your professional development, because this could only help to give me a more realistic expectation of what I would have to encounter along the way. Even now Mom is the one who tells me when you are stressed out.

My fellowship was a good example of this. I felt a need to know that you also had to pay your dues in order to join the society of adult men. It was important to know it did not come easily for you. Sometimes even the obvious needs to be verbalized. I never liked people to call me the "golden child" because everything always seemed to go my way. You and I both know that you have to create your own breaks and things just don't come handed to you on a silver platter.

All you can do is try your hardest and finish what you started. Each experience is a building block for the next one. You have to know when to move on. My generation was indeed more spoiled than yours and we were more encouraged to stand up for ourselves at all costs. There was a pervasive feeling of entitlement among my contemporaries. It's one thing to be spoiled and another to be a spoiled brat. Some of the people in my generation felt that working their way up in the system was an insult to their intelligence. Many of them looked for easier ways to make their fortunes. In the long run we didn't turn out to be any more virtuous than the generations before us.

We did come from different times. Nevertheless, Donald Cohen needed to do his job and make his father proud of him. That seemed to motivate me even more to pay my dues.

But there was also the concern that some of what Ken Kesey wrote about in his book *One Flew Over the Cuckoo's Nest* was occurring right before my eyes. You know as well as I do that institutions suffer the inevitable tendency to dehumanize their patients. It's built into the system and, of course, the patients usually enter the hospital with severely impaired life histories. Some situations within a bureaucracy can't be avoided.

I had become spoiled living in northern California, known for its avant-garde approaches to mental illness. I had been exposed to some very unusual treatment facilities. Of course, they also had their own problems. Coming back to the East and working in a more conservative environment was the equivalent of experiencing a degree of culture shock. California had historically been considered a looser and more relaxed environment. The East Coast has been generally accepted as more traditional and established.

With all the advantages of being exposed to the openness of the West behind me, I felt it was important to confront the conservatism of the East. I don't regret either experience in retrospect. They have a nice way of balancing each other out, similar to the way you and I do.

There was never really any doubt that I would stick out my commitment to the fellowship. I did not want a repeat of Organic Chemistry. It was only a matter of how much masochism I was willing to endure in order to earn the admiration one can derive from playing by the rules. There are moments when one is better off swallowing the pill. You had more tolerance for that than I did, and I attribute that to our being products of different generations. Yours was taught to be obedient and mine was encouraged to question. At times I wish I could have adopted a more unassuming style, á la Peter Falk, better known as TV detective *Columbo*. He was so good at diffusing a situation by being assertive but not aggressive.

When my dissertation was being dissected with criticism, I remember suffering the typical resentments, finally realizing I could write my masterpiece after I graduated. I needed to give up my grandiosity and finish my degree so I could get on with my life. Remember, the rock group The Rolling Stones said, "You can't always get what you want, but if you try sometime, you might find, you'll get what you need."

In the long run the price you pay for resisting the fraternity before you have been accepted isn't worth it. I had to go through the usual rite of passage and it would be difficult to change a long-standing tradition. Being self-righteous often becomes just another way of trying to prove your self-worth to others. I need to learn how to pick my battles without hurting myself in the process.

My intention was not to antagonize the people in authority, although at times I am sure I did. I was compelled to speak when I felt an injustice. This always had to be balanced by my expectations to learn from others who knew more than I did. I wanted to love the learning environment, as long as I could voice my opinions on matters that was important to me and my patients. I knew that I couldn't change a system that had outlived me many times over, but it was difficult to confront the limitations that one must face in trying to treat severely disturbed people. These patients were like infants, demanding unconditional love from an overworked staff. It was a built-in parasitic relationship. The trainee is caught somewhere between the child and his own emerging adulthood.

You hoped I would be provided with a worthwhile educational background in this environment, and perhaps I really could have been more tolerant and receptive to what they were trying to teach me. But because of my sensitivity and idealism, I complained to you about the unfairness of a system with which you had been dealing a lot longer than I had.

We like to think we will be different from the people before us. Somehow time is the true test of whether we will be any different from the people under whom we have worked. On occasion, I see myself taking an authoritative position with my patients and children.

Often it is assumed by authority that if they suffered so must the next generation. I can understand that psychology to a point, but somehow inflicting a tradition of masochism on people seems cruel. It certainly lacks virtue. Perhaps I am expecting too much of myself to think I am capable of avoiding that human fallibility. Are any of us so free of our darker sides? Is it possible for someone to work his way up the ladder and find new ways of bringing the next group of students through their initiation? The system tends to perpetuate itself even though we think a new god will come along and make it better. How seductive to consider that we could be the chosen ones who might alter a long-standing system of operations. What a burden this can become, and if we can't accomplish this, does it have to be seen as an issue of good or evil? Do we always have to be ruled by the hierarchies of right or wrong, more or less?

Throughout my life I recall my emotional involvement around my sister's three different boyfriends. Each one during his time represented a clan to which I wanted to belong. First it was the Varsity Club, then the poetic coffee house set a la Greenwich Village, and finally the fraternity in college, a cross between the first two. He was Joe College. It was as if I couldn't wait to become a part of this male society. The hazing that one had to go through to join seemed to be a small price to pay for that sense of belonging. Remember, it all starts back in that old tree house. Maybe that's why the movie *Diner* and the TV show *MASH* have been so popular. Men can identify with them just like I used to with Mugs and Satch and the rest of the *Bowery Boys*.

There is no doubt in my mind that in order to change the system you first have to gain admission. That in itself should provide some incentive for a degree of tactful obedience. In the end, it is like a parent/child relationship: the child gets more of what he or she wants when he or she is loved and accepted. The child's autonomy may depend on the extent to which he or she stays within the parents' boundaries during maturation. Parents don't forget, at least for some time, how they are being treated. Trust becomes a basic requirement. Maybe you were right when you said to me a long time ago, "We are all monkeys."

It never really was clear why I was in such a rotten mood that Christmas. It was difficult for me to completely understand what was going on with me that particular holiday. Sometimes we are just in conflict and depressed and we don't know why. It was hard to be in a bad mood in our family without everyone trying to figure out what was wrong. I let my feelings show and it affected everyone else. As a result, I brought too much attention to myself, which caused the situation to be blown way out of proportion. In retrospect, I wish I could have been more tactful about not inflicting my mood on others. As you once said, "Tactlessness often masquerades as honesty."

It was the last true battle of differences between us. We have said that before. As I embarrassingly remember and admit to childish pouting, I apologize to you. Perhaps I was not comfortable taking your place behind Santa's beard. We have certainly come a long way since then and I thought I was certainly ready to go happily "Ho Ho Ho" down the chimney. But it would never be the same again. It just didn't feel comfortable repeating the tradition. I would have been doing it to please you and it was hard to have you disappointed in me. Dee was uncomfortable celebrating Christmas. My loyalties were shifting. Although we celebrated with all our Jewish friends in the neighborhood growing up, Dee looked down upon us because she never believed or grew up in that way. I was torn between two worlds.

Something changed that holiday. I no longer felt a need to, or desire to, carry on the childhood tradition of Christmas the way we had always celebrated it. I wish I had been more comfortable and clearer about those feelings then. The philosopher Sartre once wrote, "Retrospection is introspection." There was some sadness knowing my kids would never grow up with the fond memories I had celebrating Christmas with you. I knew we never saw it as a betrayal of religion but more an opportunity for another celebration We always celebrated Hanukah as well.

My bad mood was the catalyst for our argument. I know I ruined the holiday for you and Mom, as my mood became yours. We had a huge fight, we hurt each other, but we have grown from it.

We should not assume that people are able to read our minds or expect them to know what is troubling us. The passive approach often prevents healthy communication between two people. It's always easier to put the blame somewhere else rather than assuming responsibility for our own actions. Being honest can prevent us from getting ourselves deeper into something than we originally intended.

I always had a general idea why you never wanted me to gamble over the years. But now I have a better understanding of why you were as adamant about it as you were. Maybe that's why you protected me when it came to dealing with issues of money. Over the course of my early development I never even knew what an investment was. I wouldn't be surprised if on some level you were afraid that if I knew a lot about investments, I might find a way to gamble the money away. Those limited partnerships can be destructive.

We often expect the ones closest to us to somehow know what is obvious to us. We forget that they have their own mirrors to look into, which gets in the way of being tuned into our needs. These are the limitations of the human condition. I can now appreciate why you have been conservative with your financial investments. I know you would never want to be in a position where you had to inflict pain on others. That was just not your style and I never thought that was your brother's intention either. I had become very fond of my uncle over the years and had felt that there was a deep love between the two of you. How hard all this must have been for you and the rest of the family!

In the end, I am glad you were honest with your father, because it brought you closer together before he passed away. Pop was right—

when push came to shove, you certainly did take care of yourself. I respect you for that.

If you had harbored your resentments, you would have always regretted not resolving that issue with Pop. You wrote the final script just the way you wanted to. I hope we can do the same. We are off to a good start. It's all about having conversations.

Your honesty with Pop exemplifies what this experience with you has been all about for me. I know as the years go on there will be new developments in our relationship, but for now I am satisfied with where things are. We do have some control over our destinies with our fathers as we evolve from the passive child into the active adult. The aggressive male energy is transformed into male assertiveness. Someone has to eat the last piece of cake. No one can make us feel guilty unless we let people do it to us. Pop must have been at peace knowing he could do something for you before he died. When you have been the responsible child, it doesn't feel good to be taken for granted and he realized that.

Your last letter to me obviously dealt with some highly-charged issues for both of us. I noticed that as a result of this some of the other points I had written to you about in my previous letters were not given much attention. Was there a reason? This often happens when we get involved in unresolved issues that are more pertinent at the time. Other feelings that I brought up in my last letter to you probably needed to take a back seat and seemed less important in contrast to the kinds of feelings that you chose to write to me about. I know this does not minimize my other points but perhaps these issues had to be addressed first.

The ghosts are gone for now and if there are any more in the future I think they will be easier to share as a result of this experience. I think we have both learned that if we wait around passively expecting people to read minds just because they are close to one another, there is the strong possibility that needs will never be met. That seemed to be the moral of the story between you and me, and you and your father.

I have also learned that one tends to perceive others with the limitations of one's own defenses. I have noticed many times that my own resentments and negative judgments of other people are ameliorated when I realize that the feelings are based upon a threat to some cherished self-perception.

Thanks Dad, for being there for me and responding so directly to my life and the letters that attempt to recapture the memories between us. It's hard to know how to end this letter but perhaps the only way is to just end it knowing there will be another time.

Curiously, as I write this last paragraph, I hear the Harry Chapin song "Cat's in the Cradle" on the radio, and suddenly realize that the words don't quite fit for us. You did have the time for me and now I want to have the time for you. I love you, Dad, even as a fraudulent god with clay feet.

Love,
Donald

* * *

Dear Donald,

It's hard to believe that with this letter I will be completing the project we embarked upon together several months ago. When you originally proposed the project to me I listened skeptically. It was hard to believe that we would really do it and it was even harder to imagine that, if we did, anyone else would be interested in reading it.

I knew that you and I would have little difficulty in being open and honest with each other. Our relationship by this time was so close and so secure that I felt there was nothing you and I would want to say to each other that would be too upsetting. But as for going public with meaningful revelations about our personal lives, that was something else. On this latter score I feel uneasy but much less skeptical.

Now that we're almost finished, I'm still uncertain about whether what we have written will be of interest to anyone else. But in a deeply-felt sense, that no longer seems to matter so much because this has been such an enormously valuable experience for me and I believe for you as well. In the course of living our busy lives, so many things go unsaid because we somehow assume that to say them would be superfluous. We tend to take for granted that what we think is already known anyhow, that our feelings are self-evident, that our concerns are obvious. Of course, they aren't superfluous, self-evident, or obvious to ourselves or others until we sit down and force ourselves to articulate our thoughts and feelings. In the course of doing so, I have discovered or re-discovered many things about my own life, many connections and nuances either long-forgotten or never known.

Beyond the self-knowledge gained, I'm stunned by the extent to which the depth and breadth of my understanding of your feelings has been expanded. We so much take for granted that we know and understand the people who are close to us. I'm more convinced than ever that no matter how perceptive and insightful we are, our knowledge of ourselves and even more so of others, is always incomplete and distorted by our own need to rationalize and our own need to vindicate ourselves. It really is so hard to be fully honest with ourselves. It is even harder to be honest about our feelings with someone whose opinion of us we care so much about. At another extreme, it would be impossible to be even minimally open to someone we care less about.

This, of course, points up the importance of certain fundamental conditions for the psychotherapeutic process. The crucial first order of business in psychotherapy is the establishment of trust and honesty in our relationship with our patient. Within the framework of such a relationship, the patient has to feel secure in the expectation that the trusted therapist will use the patient's revelations to help and never to hurt. As such, the therapist is viewed as a trusted, loyal and caring friend, even in the face of the patient's self-denigrating exposures. A therapist is only as good as his or her ability to respond constructively to these needs of the patient.

I am genuinely proud of the fact that I believe we have responded in this way to each other during this correspondence. I truly feel that I can be so open to you and that you will understand without being unduly critical. I believe you feel the same way with me, and I feel that in this sense, you pay me a very great honor. I respect and greatly value your opinion of me and of my thoughts and feelings, even when we don't fully agree. Interestingly, the instances of our disagreement seem fewer and fewer with the passage of time, but hopefully they will never disappear altogether. I say hopefully because I also value the fact that you are not my clone, that you are your own and separate person.

You mention in your last letter that there are comments you made to which I didn't respond. It usually reflected the fact that I am in agreement with what you said, and at least for the moment, felt I had nothing meaningful to add. Perhaps it is significant that I responded to those issues about which there has been some difference between us. These are the issues on which we tend to focus and that gives rise to the false impression of contention between us about which I have commented several times in previous letters.

It is true that in recent years we have increasingly moved in the direction of being equal friends, and we have been able to relate to each other as mutually loving and respecting adults. In earlier years, the parent and child aspects of the relationship make such equality and mutuality difficult if not impossible. It is in the nature of things that the child's relative helplessness and immaturity foster dependency and require that the parent assume the role of caretaker, disciplinarian, teacher, and role model. These circumstances inevitably inspire some struggle and contention which can only be fully resolved with maturity, when the parent and child can finally confront each other as equal adults. If the process is successful these adults can be close loving friends. I'm proud of the fact that this is where we are.

I do want to comment on your remarks about Ken Kesey's *One Flew Over the Cuckoo's Nest*. There is no question that being hospitalized in a psychiatric facility tends to be a dehumanizing experience, especially if the institution is insensitive to the dignity of the patients. This is especially and invariably true when the patient is involuntarily committed.

When patients are hospitalized because they are unable to cope with the demands of living on their own in society, and are thus deprived of the freedom and dignity of choosing for themselves what they are to do or not do, they suffer an insult to their self-esteem which is difficult and sometimes impossible to eradicate. We who have been privileged to live in a relatively "free" and "open" society tend to view the deprivation of such freedom in other societies with angry disdain because of their apparent disregard for the essential human requirements of freedom and dignity. Yet we are often insensitive to similar

THE INSIDE RIDE

instances of indignity which our own system sometimes imposes on individuals. There are critical social, political, and economic issues involved which go beyond the scope of these letters.

In the work we do, however, issues of human dignity are at the central core. The dehumanizing effects of involuntary confinement are self-evident, but subtler instances of such indignity to other human beings are less obvious. Any person who comes to us for help with a personal and painful problem is exposing a critical vulnerability. We assume a special responsibility to be sensitive and responsive to that person's vulnerability, and to protect that person's dignity in therapy in every way possible. The danger of dehumanizing patients, even in a freely voluntary and outpatient setting, is sometimes overlooked. If and when we permit this to happen, we commit an unforgivable atrocity. If we neglect to give the very highest priority to the dignity of our patients, we betray the most fundamental principles of our commitment to integrity.

Nothing angers me more than to hear a therapist talk disdainfully about a patient. It is abhorrent for a therapist to aggrandize himself or herself at the expense of a patient, to talk down to a patient, or behave in any way that denies the patient's implicit yearning to be regarded as a dignified and respected human being.

In these letters, the focus has been on our relationship, almost as if we are actors in a two-character play. This was deliberate because we decided at the outset that we would not unnecessarily impose our decision to expose ourselves on the other important people in our lives. Yet in a very real sense, this has imposed a misleading distortion in the account we have written. Obviously, the real story of our relationship involves much larger roles for the other people in the plot. In the beginning, this included mainly the other people in our nuclear family, Mom and your sister. With the passage of time, the cast of characters became larger and larger, and increasingly, our relationship was expanded and complicated by the participation of these other people—including, most importantly, your brother-in-law, your wife, and your children.

As you know, my relationship with Ellen and her husband has been very close and we have briefly commented on your feelings about this in earlier letters. For the reasons mentioned above, I am not going to further elaborate on these relationships. However, I do feel compelled to comment briefly about my feelings for your wife and, of course, your children.

Mom and I do indeed feel extremely close and loving to Dee as you comment in one of your letters. My relationship with her has grown progressively closer and warmer since you both returned from California, and at this point, it would be hard to imagine our relationship without her part in it. As a matter of fact, it feels almost as if she has always been an integral part of our family. We have sometimes disagreed and on a few occasions we have even been at odds, but never on my part at least, have I ever felt that our fundamental fondness and love for each other has been seriously threatened. Even when angry with our children, we know that the anger will subside and the underlying affection will soon be in the ascendancy again. This is the way I feel about Dee, and I confidently believe she feels the same way about me.

As for your children, I smile even as I write. Emily has become the central figure in the scenario in many ways as she has endeared herself to us during her short life. She is indeed special, as I have to concede grandchildren probably tend to be to their grandparents. Still, it is hard to imagine that anyone else has a granddaughter as lovely, charming, bright, loving, and altogether as appealing as our Emily is. Jared, although still too young to verbalize, will surely convince me in time that Emily's magic is not entirely unique.

Finally, but importantly, there is Mom, without whom obviously neither you nor this book would exist. Less obviously, without Mom, I wouldn't exist either, because without her input over most of my life I would be a different person. She and I have shared all the most important experiences of our lives for almost forty years. It is hard to even imagine my life without her intimate presence and involvement in every significant joy, frustration and disappointment in my life during these many years. The bond that evolves from having lived and shared together for so long all the important experiences of our lives, makes analysis of our relationship extremely difficult. In the process of accommodation that occurs between two people who influence each other so much over time in a successful marriage, it becomes extremely difficult to separate which influence came from whom.

You express confusion about who was the dominant one in the relationship between Mom and me. If two people accomplish a successful union of different personalities so that they become a reasonably effective team, one has to assume that a successful division of responsibility and authority has been achieved. I believe we have a successful marriage in which we are both strongly motivated to please each other within a framework which adequately gratifies both of us. I believe I'm saying that we deeply care for each other; indeed we love each other.

Without betraying each other, Mom and I both at times tried to buffer the conflicts that have occasionally arisen between one of us with one of our children. From my view, Mom was a wonderful mother, enormously devoted to the well-being of her children.

Observing Mom's relationship with Emily, I believe you see many of the qualities that governed her relationship with you and Ellen when you were young.

Patients sometimes express bewilderment at the fact that their parents manifest such loving attention to their grandchildren saying, "I don't remember their behaving that way with me when I was a child." In part, they are right. Since grandparents don't have the daily responsibilities of parenting, they are spared many of the stresses and conflicts which create tension in parent-child relationships. We come to play and have fun, and after awhile we return home with eager anticipation of the next visit. We have few of the conflicts that arise from trying to reconcile the discord between our own needs of the moment with the demands and expectations of the little ones.

You ask me in your last letter about how I balanced my own needs with my perception of my children's needs. I don't think I know the answer. All I can say is that only once will Emily and Jared be as they are now. There will never be another opportunity to experience them at this particular age, and obviously this is true for every age. Make the most of these opportunities as best you can, because you'll never have the chance again. Each age they go through is special, and each presents its special opportunities for joy and pleasures. If you do the best you can, I'm sure you won't regret it because the rewards are beyond measure. Pity the people who say, "I wish I had taken the time to enjoy my kids while they were growing up."

At this point, as we near the end of this project, I'm troubled by the fact that there isn't more humor in our letters. We seem to take ourselves so seriously and we tend to invest the many and varied incidents in our lives as if they are matters of grave importance.

We've revived a lot of old memories, mostly painful ones, and in so doing we've revived some of the feelings associated with those memories. With the perspective of time, they don't seem to warrant so much heavy feeling.

In the overall scheme of things, none of these incidents are really important. We ourselves are, in totality, important only to ourselves and to the handful of people who have been touched by us.

Yesterday's painful crisis is hardly remembered today and will surely be forgotten by tomorrow. But while we are going through it, each small experience is viewed as cosmic or at least of great importance. There is a silliness in all of this. Without the ability to live our lives with some sense of the folly of it, or at least some sense of our own folly, we run the risk of living out a life long soap opera.

Shakespeare said it best:

> "All the world's a stage,
> and all the men and women merely players,
> they have their exits and their entrances;
> and one man in his time plays many parts."

In closing, Donald, I would summarize everything that this wise old fool can teach you in just a few words. Try not to take yourself, or each day's passing trauma, too seriously, and when you can, remind yourself that "this too shall pass" and "tomorrow is another day." Platitudes they are, and probably impossible to live by. What bliss, if only we could?

Love,
Dad

Forty Something

(MIDDLE ADULTHOOD–LATE ADULTHOOD)

Settling Down

Sometimes I want to make it all better for you.

I look at you, and I look at your children; I see my immortality.

* * *

August, 1992

Dear Dad,

I finally made it to forty. Is one ever finished with what one has started? All of a sudden wherever you look there is a book or a discussion about male bonding. In the eighties it was how could you make the quick buck. Maybe we were ahead of our time, and I feel our experience in writing this book together is unique.

The world seems so different now. I am not the young kid on the block anymore. The eighties were so prosperous and hopeful, but now we are in a severe recession. The AIDS epidemic became a reality. Life seems so turbulent and unsettling at times. My needs are changing; I look for a more simple life in a time that is consumed by complexity. They talk about the sixties as a piece of history and the events of my life seem to come with higher stakes these days. I remember you telling me, "enjoy your life in between the rough edges that come along."

During these past ten years, I have been aware of how difficult times have been for you. Between Mom's lung cancer, and some physical problems of your own, you have been pretty overwhelmed. Your life once seemed simpler and more carefree. I thought it was supposed to get easier with age. Sometimes I feel badly that we have not had more time alone together, and as I get older my life is pulled in so many directions: marriage, career, parenthood, social life, and of course, those inevitable errands that come with ordinary living. I worry about having time for all of the above and of course, myself. Now I understand why you read *The New York Times* at midnight. How I long for that peace and silence in the late evening.

As Emily approaches her Bat Mitzvah, I become increasingly aware of how fast time is moving and the preciousness of life becomes more apparent. Over the years, I have enjoyed your enthusiasm with your grandchildren and wished there had been more opportunities. That makes me sad, and even frustrated. It was Emily who made Mom stop smoking. Mom would do anything for her.

The catalyst for this letter was my invitation to you for Jared's father/son weekend at camp. The last time we were alone together for any extended period of time was in Israel after I graduated from college. I was so confused then about my future and what I would do when I grew up. Well I am forty and still trying to figure it all out. Of course I don't feel as intimidated by you and your success anymore. In the end, after all my rebellion, I have been able to support my family and that has been good for my self esteem. I think a man needs that. During these years I sustained a private practice of my own, had a weekly talk radio and TV show, and my house in the suburbs. But there still is something that feels incomplete; I feel this driving force to do something that will be more meaningful than what I have already accomplished. Maybe it is immortality that I am seeking. What do you think?

As time passes by, I know that at some point you will not be here. It is hard watching my friends deal with their parents becoming sick and dying. I get frightened of the thought of life without you. Some of my contemporaries had no idea what was in their parents' wills and were not prepared to handle their estates. It's hard to talk about these issues. For so long I have wanted us to be close and do things together. The desire is there, but life's circumstances get in the way, and often it seems so hard to make that happen.

I was proud of you when you decided to branch out in a new direction and become a divorce mediator. It was great to see you take the risk, but I feared for your disappointment when it did not work out. I have realized how sensitive I am to your moods particularly when I feel you are unhappy and disappointed. Sometimes, I want to make it all better for you. When you talk about getting old, it makes me sad. I know you need a purpose too. When you tell me you are becoming more spiritual, I know times are changing. Our Freud/Jung debates might take on a new twist.

When I heard Jared was going to have a father/son weekend at his camp, I thought it would be nice if we could go together. Yes, little Jared goes to sleep away camp! It feels so grown up and surreal sometimes. I remember when you brought packages of candy to me on visiting day and it feels like it was just yesterday. Sometimes I long to go back there. This trip to camp was certainly different than the trip to Israel. How special and fortunate that three generations could be together on this occasion. As the time neared, I became more aware of what it meant to me. There was an anxious moment that came and went, taking the long drive together. We managed fine and even sitting in silence together felt comfortable, even if you do not like my music. Listening to some of my old radio shows and talking about the new one, is exciting. I appreciate how supportive you have been. It is nice that we can share that. Remember when I used to talk to myself behind closed doors. Now I do it publicly.

The strangest part of the weekend, not including two big guys like us sleeping in those bunk beds, had to be my giving up control with Jared in the sailboat, depending on my son to prevent me from capsizing at sea. There you were standing on the dock watching us sail into the wind. I must admit, I was relieved to get back, and part of me was shaken, but very proud. The other memorable moment was playing doubles in a tennis tournament with Jared, depending again on him to make the big shot and you smiling in the corner.

Of course the trip ended with us disagreeing about logistics. Did missing the exit on our predetermined route home cause us to have a longer drive? I guess there is that part of me that still depends on you to be perfect. If my son can take me sailing, I have to learn to let you show me a different part of Connecticut. So what if it takes a little more time?

It took forty years to put that together, but at least I got there. Thanks, Dad, for a great time and being part of my life. From one mortal man to another.

Love, Donald

* * *

Dear Donald,

I have been ruminating about your letter for two weeks as I processed the intense emotions and associated thoughts evoked by things you said.

You are quite correct in your observation that the past several years have been traumatic, dramatic, and disturbing on many levels, but particularity gratifying in other ways as well. Let me tackle the positive issues first since they are obviously easier to think and write about.

Watching you and your family grow, develop and flourish certainly ranks as one of the most gratifying experiences of recent years. I have been extremely proud of you and what you have been able to achieve; I glory in your evolving media career. Your mother and I feel that we have been very much happy and intimate participants in your family's life. We've grown closer to Dee with each passing year, and your children have both been a continuous joy. One of the true rewards of parenthood really is grand-parenthood.

The really profound impact of your letter, however was the reference to my current stage of life. Senior citizenship has been an emotional struggle for me. A crucial part of me still feels young, vigorous, and vital and is offended and painfully challenged by evidence of the aging process. In this latter regard, my own illnesses seem relatively unimportant in retrospect. I never believed my life was seriously threatened though it briefly was threatened when I suffered a gastro-intestinal hemorrhage and I recovered without any serious residual impairment.

Evidence of the aging process, however, is inescapable as I look around at my friends, some of whom have retired or talk of retirement. They all look so much older than I feel, and of course there is Mom. You know how sick she has been during the past several years. She has been better in recent weeks, but watching her suffer and struggle to hold on to her life through one illness after another makes it impossible to cling to any illusions about what is happening to us. This is the heavy part of what I have been experiencing, and this is the core of the feelings your letter so poignantly touched.

I've never thought of myself as a depression-prone person. I believe that although you certainly have seen me upset or troubled about one or another problem over the years, I don't think you remember ever seeing me depressed for any length of time. These last few years have been the toughest I can remember, and though it's been very difficult, I've somehow retained my essential optimism.

What I'm talking about is mortality. How do we come to terms with our mortality? This is a universal problem that afflicts us from childhood until we die. How can we possibly imagine what it is like to no longer exist? How do we conceive of the eons of time before we came into being? This is the essence of spiritualism and religiosity in every known culture.

You know that I've never been a religious person in the traditional sense. I find it impossible to believe in a humanized God to whom we assign even our most despised attributes. But I have become much more pre-occupied with spiritual issues in recent years, especially as I am forced to contemplate my mortality as something more proximate than the way we tend to deal with the issue when we are younger. As a younger person we tend to think, "sure we're going to die someday, but that's in the remote future and I can comfortably ignore it for now." This kind of denial no longer works very well for me.

The most comforting way for me to think about death is also the way I think about "being." We are each of us a part of a continuity; we are a dot on a continuum between an indeterminate past and an infinite future—part of eternity. I look at you and Ellen, and I look at your children; I see my immortality. When you study biology, you learn about the amoebae, a one-celled animal continuously reproducing by dividing in half. Therein is the potential for immortality.

Some months ago when you were excitedly telling me about your radio show, you asked me whether I felt competitive with you or envious of you. You were in the process of becoming, and perhaps I had already become whatever I am ever going to be. I remember responding with some surprise that I don't feel at all competitive with you. Quite the contrary I'm so intimately identified with you that I feel as proud of your success as I would be of my own. If you think about Jared and your feelings about him, I'm sure you will understand what I mean. What I suspect, though, is that you were attributing to me your feelings of competitiveness with me. Such projections of feeling, as you know, are common, and needless to say, sons feeling competitive with fathers is also common. Long live Oedipus!

Finally, I want to address myself to the angry tantrum you had when we missed a turn on the way home from camp. I didn't understand then, nor do I understand now, why you were so upset. I chose at the time to let it pass, because I refused to permit anything to spoil the wonderful and special weekend I had with you and Jared. I was very aware that I was the only grandfather there, and I was truly proud and overjoyed that you wanted me to share it with you. As for Jared, he is everything a grandfather could want of a grandson. He is bright, sensitive, creative, artistically talented, curious, and interested in everything. Most of all, he is warm and loving. Along with my other grandchildren, they are my ticket to immortality.

I am a lucky man. I must have done a few things right because I truly feel genuinely loved and admired by the people I care most deeply about—my wife, my children and my grandchildren. I say this with conviction and a deeply-felt appreciation that this is a proud achievement. Emily is about to celebrate her Bat Mitzvah. She is my first and still my special joy. I can hardly remember a time when we have been together that she hasn't made me feel loved and respected. Ali, who is adorable and is my youngest, rounds out the picture for now, but maybe not for long since she awaits the arrival of a brother or sister.

Having said all this, I still feel vigorous enough for new challenges, and most importantly, there is still plenty of room for improvement. I'm not sure what it is I aspire to, but I'm not finished with "becoming."

Love,
Dad

--=◎◎=--

All you wanted was to be close to me and do for me what I was now trying to do with my children, show me where I came from.

We can reasonably disagree about some issues without diluting that feeling of intimate connection, that feeling of accepting and being accepted.

--=◎◎=--

* * *

Dear Dad,

Twenty years later and the pilot says welcome to Israel. It gave me chills just to think about how much my life has changed since you took me to Israel after I graduated from college. Back then the only concern was what will I become when I grow up. Now I enter the country with my two children and wife. It was a proud moment. Suddenly I felt the history of the Jewish people, and I became emotional about our relationship. My history, and where I came from, seems more important to me now. You tried to show me that in 1972, but I was not ready. Now I will try to do the same for my kids. After all this time, I have a stronger need to know about the roots of my family history. I am ready now. Where did I come from?

There is an inner peace and desire to learn more about myself now. Those outside distractions of providing for my family and having to prove myself are less pressing. The battles of the past between us seem less important now, and I feel no desire to compete with you anymore. I need to put that to rest once and for all in this letter. It seems like it is hard for you to accept that I can be concerned about you and you can reach out to me for support without feeling like a burden. I remember how hard it was when you asked me if you should ask your brother for help several years ago, but you felt better when you did. Sadly, it was the last nice moment between the two of you. More of that later.

Just as our relationship has changed, so has Israel since you and I were here last. The country has survived wars and managed to achieve more independence. It sounds like I am also talking about our relationship. It dawned on me during this trip that in 1973, six months after our visit to Israel, the Yom Kippur War broke out. Israel was under siege. Here I was feeling overwhelmed about trying to achieve my own personal autonomy and the Israelis were struggling to fight off the Egyptians, Syrians, and the Jordanians.

This trip has made me more aware of who I am. It has given me a feeling of connection to my history and has enhanced my appreciation of having continuity in my life. When I recently went up to Masada, the place where the Jews tried to fight off the overwhelming power of the Romans, I remembered being there with you. I felt a sadness and desire to have you be part of what was happening for me up there. I wanted to tell you how much I appreciated you taking me away with you and how special that was for a father to do that with his son. At that moment, I became aware of what you were trying to do for me back then. All you wanted was to be close to me and do for me what I was now trying to do with my children, show me where I came from. We take so much for granted in life.

Amazingly, we approached the old temple at Masada and there was a friend of yours watching his grandson become a Bar Mitzvah. He and I were discussing how life goes full circle as he was remembering being at my Bar Mitzvah. I got very emotional and I began to think how nice it would be to have you come back with me to Israel in three years and come see Jared become a Bar Mitzvah at Masada. It gives me a warm feeling and puts a smile on my face.

There is one piece of unfinished business that still remains for me. This trip seems to have served as a catalyst for these feelings. I do feel a certain void losing my relationship to part of your family and I realize that my children do not even know the names of many of their cousins. One morning Jared and I witnessed a family of men dancing in a circle singing Jewish songs at a Bar Mitzvah. I felt very moved and I was not sure why. My mind wandered back to when the whole family gathered. It was nine years ago in Cincinnati, the last family Bar Mitzvah that we attended. I remember as a little boy always loving those occasions and being with everyone. It was a special part of my life. I do not know if you ever knew the depth of that feeling. It made me feel a part of something larger in my life, a connection. There was a peculiar security about it. I remember all of the uncles and their sons sitting around discussing our book and sharing family stories. Our book stimulated many emotions in the family. It was very

exciting for me. It was a wonderful moment for the males in our family and it was the last of that joy.

Money and family make a bad marriage. It was clearly the down-
fall of your relationship with your brother and my relationship with
that part of your family. To add salt to the wound, you were angry
because you felt Uncle Irving was putting down our profession. He
complained because he perceived that you did not help his daughter enough. She had been having emotional problems. Eventually,
my cousin escaped a psychiatric hospital and sadly was never found.
There were those expectations for you to be god-like again. It helped
me become aware of how complex and sensitive the relationship
between you and your brother was. I found it very disturbing and
uncomfortable. I had always loved him as my uncle, not someone
who created such misery for you. I always felt sheltered from that
reality until then, or maybe I just did not want to see it. It was upsetting to see you become so angry at him. My understanding of it is
that you had a quarrel over a shared investment. It has been so hard
for me to accept that two brothers could lose their relationship over
money. What a painful reality. It seemed to ultimately destroy what
was once a close relationship.

To me he was always Uncle Irving. My last memory was during
the time of this last family Bar Mitzvah, when he took my children
by the hand and went with them into a toy store and told them they
could have anything they wanted. Emily still remembers getting a
stuffed animal. The kids have always been confused by all of this. I
have recently tried to explain it to them and not protect them. You
have my permission to sit down and talk to them about it. How ironic
that Emily's memory of Uncle Irving was seeing him as a loving and
generous man. After that it was all downhill. He just became the uncle
who hurt my father. The family chain was broken. I have always felt
a sadness about that. He died and it was never completely resolved.
Money can certainly do destructive things to families. My kids now
have some understanding of that.

When Emily recently became a Bat Mitzvah, I did not even consider having my cousins with us. All connections with them had been
cut off after that last incident between you and your brother. The
division had been drawn, and everyone had to stay on their respective
sides. The family was now severed. I did not even consider inviting
them. It seems like too much time passed. Why do I write this now?

I think because my kids are getting older and so are we. Continuity feels more important to me now.

But, there is also the wound of you accusing me of being a disloyal son years ago when I expressed some feeling about having regrets about us all not being together as a family. This incident was triggered by the fact that several years ago there was yet another family Bar Mitzvah. It was your brother's other grandson. This time we were not invited. Who knows what I will do in three years when it will be Jared's turn. I have always felt badly about the fight between us. I felt misunderstood and guilty because I did not feel exactly as you did. I understood your hurt, but it also had its consequences for the family. I felt a loyalty to you, but I also felt like I had lost something. Maybe you never understood that they all meant a lot to me as a little boy. It was a place where I didn't feel like an outsider. When I was in Israel, that same feeling came back to me and it felt nice. In a strange way it felt like coming home again, back to something special and familiar. It surprised me, but those were my feelings then. Your rage with me has been a source of confusion for me. How do you feel about all of this? I do want you to know I empathize with the pain around what happened between you and your brother, but I want you also to know I have my own pain as well.

I am back from Israel now, and yes I do feel like I have come full circle with you. When you talked to your father before he died and shared that with me I understood your hurt over being the unappreciated and sometimes forgotten son. This is another reason why I can clearly understand the pain around your brother's betrayal. You have often asked me if I remembered the different things that you have done with me over the years. Now you might want to ask me if I remembered different incidents about our trip to Israel together and whether it has changed.

Dad, my answer is twofold. To answer the first question, what I remembered most about our trip to Israel is how much you loved me and how fortunate I was to have a Dad who wanted to share such a special place with me. The second question is answered similarly to the first. Israel is different now, it has matured and sees things more clearly for itself. It is more secure and knows where it belongs in the world. It has a sense and pride about its own history.

Love, Donald

* * *

Dear Don,

Strangely, your last letter affected me in two very different ways. Your description of your trip to Israel with your family and its emotional impact on you was profoundly moving to me, as were your reflections on our trip there twenty years ago. My reaction to your memory of events concerning my relationship with my brother, however, was very different. First of all, my recollection and perception of what happened is very different from yours. Secondly, it all seems very remote, even disconnected from anything relevant to me today.

These days I'm preoccupied with the warmth and closeness I feel to you and Dee, as well as Emily and Jared. I feel so comfortable with feeling accepted and accepting of you and Dee.

I feel comfortable even when I disagree with you, and I no longer feel a need for you to see everything, or feel about everything, the way I do. We are, after all, two different people, intimately connected but still quite different in some ways. We can reasonably disagree about some issues without diluting that feeling of intimate connection, that feeling of accepting and being accepted.

Parents generally feel that their children should reflect, in their view of themselves and their world, the same values that their parents have. I felt very keenly while you were growing up that it was my responsibility as a parent to inculcate my values in my children, that I help them to accept my views of what is important, and to accept my views of what is right and wrong. This does inject an inevitable tension in a parent's relationship with a child, especially with children of the same gender. I've come to believe that this is more important in creating and defining the issues of the Oedipal Complex than sexual feelings. Fathers want their sons either to be just like them or the way the fathers would like to be themselves. In other words, fathers want to fulfill their own ego ideal even when they themselves fall short. Not remarkably, sons often rebel against this imposition on their autonomy and individuality. Naturally, daughters experience comparable conflicts with their mothers.

Donald, all of this is past for us. I believe that we both recognize and accept the fact that we are different people. I believe we respect and accept these differences.

I do find your sadness about your distance from your cousins a little puzzling. It seems to me that if you feel such a need, the opportunity to re-establish your relationship exists. In fact, I'm under the impression that your cousin Andy took such an initiative and you blew him off. I've certainly expressed my comfort, and even desire, that you be closer to them and have even offered to arrange a meeting over dinner or otherwise. I encouraged you to invite your cousins to Emily's Bat Mitzvah, if you wished. You didn't and I assumed you had no desire to do so. I have to surmise that your desire to be more involved with extended family is an occasional sentimental and nostalgic mood, but when push comes to shove, it would require more effort than you're inclined to invest. Whatever your inclination, I accept it, and I have little inclination to change it. If you ever wish to join me when I see one or more of them, you and Dee are always welcome.

As far as Irving is concerned, we settled our financial differences long before he died, and we were on speaking terms. It is true that real friendship or intimacy was never re-established, but we were on good enough terms so that Mom and I traveled to Florida to attend his funeral when he died. I'm not aware that you felt any inclination to join us. In this, as with most other issues, we make our own choices. You speak about wanting it to be otherwise, but your behavior suggests that, on balance, you prefer it the way it is. And if you want to be more involved with your cousins, you certainly have my encouragement to do so.

As I said all of this seems relatively remote and unimportant to me now. Most of my current energies are enmeshed in the here and now and the future. I love my children and grandchildren and I feel loved by them. I find myself groping for a conclusion to this letter and decided that the concluding reference in your letter about how Israel has matured and changed since you first visited there with me many years ago, is most suitable. I would like to feel that I see things more clearly for myself, that I am more secure and know where I belong in the world, and that I have a sense and pride about my own history.

Love, Dad

Coming Home

You were secure enough in our mutual love for each other to allow me the time to find myself

Even the painful parts provided a contrasting backdrop for the infinitely greater joys in the moments of shared closeness.

The house of our childhood is an aging soul with wheezing pipes and trees so old they could fall on the roof. It hovers over its ancestral ground like a question: "Why do children have to leave?"
—Anne Raver, *Deep in the Green*

* * *

October, 1992

Dear Dad,

It was hard to give you that last letter and I was concerned about your response. I just could not get myself to mail it to you. The issue of your brother is like opening Pandora's Box. After all these years I was still afraid of your reaction and did not want to hurt your feelings. But true to form, your response was fine, reinforcing the fact that assumptions are useless without checking them out with the other person. As a matter of fact when I received your last letter, I was initially disappointed. It seemed anticlimactic. I thought to myself, is that all there is? Then I asked myself why I should feel that way? There were those expectations again. Now I am beginning to realize that we do not have to have the same feelings and what I need resolved is not necessarily the same for you. Accepting this has been difficult for me, but with ten more years behind me I am getting there. For so long I felt like you could provide me with all the answers, and life would fit into a neat package. That was one of the driving forces behind this book for me, but isn't it interesting that the actual writing is helping me to come to terms with the fact that everything does not have to be resolved with a particular answer. Sometimes it leaves more questions.

So when Jared or Emily ask me a question, I have found at times, I have to say I do not know the answer, although that is not always easy for me to do. People might call that growing up. I remember a lecture during which a well-known Jungian analyst didn't have an answer to a question from his audience. That moment stayed with me beyond anything else he talked about in his lecture. He was so comfortable saying he didn't know the answer.

One of the wonders of the human condition is how two people can live through the same experience and have completely different perceptions about what happened. This has been a recurrent theme in our letters. I do not have to dress you in a costume anymore, no masquerade, just a father and son being honest to the best of their abilities about who they are, appreciating the sameness as well as the differences. It is not an issue of right or wrong. We just choose to see it differently, agreeing to disagree. We can leave Freud and Jung to have their own debates in the history books. Our struggles in the past were often not over what was said, but how we would say it to each other. Communication is a crucial element in any healthy relationship.

There is a freedom and inner peace that comes with all these realizations, although it is sad for me at times. Part of this stage of life for me is learning how to mourn the loss of that innocence that comes with being a kid, and losing that feeling of invincibility that comes with it. In some ways, it is like saying good-bye to an old friend whom you have outgrown. Yesterday, I went back to my old camp for an alumni day and it was hard to hear those old voices. There are those moments that I yearn to bring it all back and embrace the memories.

As so many changes occur around me I always find comfort in remembering the eternal sound of Mel Allen's voice shouting from Yankee Stadium. On a summer afternoon I would hear his familiar "Hello there everybody." The dreams of my first girlfriend have faded, but they usually come up when a significant psychological separation occurs in my life. For many years you were a figment of other people's imaginations and I was a figment of my own imagination. Santa's was once a safe lap to sit on, but symbolically one has to leave the psychological home of one's childhood. Each stage of life tends to seem insurmountable, whether it is that first kiss with a girl, driving a car, or moving out and finally supporting yourself. You keep thinking that you have made the break only to discover that there is yet another level of this process waiting to be challenged right around the corner. Sometimes we cheat ourselves by writing the end of the novel before it is ready to be completed. It is human nature to project ahead, but the danger of that is we deprive ourselves of the experience and mystery of taking life one step at a time. We try to control what is around us rather than taking control of our own lives. You're freer to dream your own dreams if they are not connected with having to satisfy some infantile need that requires someone to make it all better for you, although I must admit at times it sure would be nice. I had another déjà vu, with a different ending, when we recently went away together to attend a workshop in Philadelphia. You asked me to listen to your music from the Broadway show *Passion* and I felt fine about it. I realized I could take control and help us get home instead of depending on you to always lead the way. It felt good and we got home without a problem, laughing. We have reinvented our relationship.

Hopefully, you get to a point in your life when you do not feel responsible for everyone else's happiness and what goes on in the world does not have to be your fault. Are any of us really that powerful or important anyway? I once felt you needed me to need you, but somehow knowing that is less true makes it easier for me to reach out to you now. That is true independence, where my rebellion before was more of a pseudo-independence, an unhealthy dependency, pretending I had found the so called path to enlightenment. How foolish, but necessary as a prerequisite for becoming my own person. I know now that you are there for me if necessary as you have come through so often for me in the past. Remember when I ruptured my Achilles tendon and you were by my side day and night? I hope the same is true in reverse because I know that has been difficult for you over the years. As you have said before, relationships are a two way street. I like when you ask me to respect your feelings.

You were secure enough in our mutual love for each other to allow me the time to find myself. Waiting for me and not rejecting me is true "unconditional love." Your values have clearly rubbed off on me. We are both hardworking and ambitious individuals. Family life comes first, and of course we are at times obsessed with wanting our kids to be happy, sometimes to a fault. As we both have learned, failure is a part of life. This indeed is one of the great lessons for learning how to deal with life's adversities, although when one of my kids is hurting it might as well be me. How I dread those restless nights of sleep worrying about my kids' happiness. I find myself telling Jared "its only a game." Before his games we used to sit in the car and listen to the song *Losing My Religion* by R.E.M. as a form of meditation. It relaxed him and served as inspiration.

I find myself, just like you, raising my kids in the same house they have known their whole childhood. That kind of stability is refreshing these days. Continuity is important to me, but I too have my conflicts about where to put my energy. We both like to follow our dreams and explore new possibilities particularly with our careers. It has been important to feel like good providers for our families, and I feel taking pride in that has been important to both of us.

I have become more appreciative of the fact that I do not have to practice away from home. You were there for us, whether it be school, social problems, or even plain old fun. It is easy to take all this for granted. How fortunate that I can be around for my kids and their activities. You gave us a neighborhood with sidewalks, street lights, the Good Humor Man, and plenty of stickball buddies, and I am grateful for that. Although we live in a more hectic world now, I tried to do the same for my kids. At times I find myself longing for the old neighborhood and safer times. There is my idealism again—drive-in movies, lemonade stands, *American Bandstand,* and *Lassie* episodes. Sometimes my two acres feel a bit isolating to me now, but it also has its beauty and privacy. My lifestyle has allowed me the opportunity to have an office at home and spend more time with my family.

I take pride in watching my children achieve and each become their own person. It is hard not to live somewhat vicariously through your own children as long as you keep it in perspective. Just yesterday I dropped Jared off at the airport as he was leaving for summer camp, two days after I had already said good-bye to Emily. The house will feel different without a ten and thirteen year old. I glanced over at another father, whom I barely knew, who was going through the same ritual, and we smiled at each other as if we were reading each other's minds. He said, "Now that they are gone what am I going to do?" and then we both laughed at ourselves. For that brief moment in time I felt like I was looking out into the window of my own mortality, where there is very little distinction between separation and loss, except now I was on the other side of it right next to you. Yet, isn't that the way it is supposed to be? My life is more settled now which is for me synonymous with security.

I still think those parents at the airport look like your friends, not my contemporaries, and in the background I hear an old voice chanting "Beat Brant Lake." How ironic that in the end that's where my son goes to camp. Separation and loss is often equated with death and stagnation, but for me it is now a summer to have some time alone with my wife. Is that so bad? That too was a difficult adjustment and challenge in my marriage. This was an early sign of the empty nest. That is when you and mom did your most interesting traveling. I have entered the decade of my forties, a time of reflection and looking back at some bad investments, passing friendships, a marriage that has survived while others around me have failed, my friends and yours getting sick and losing jobs, no more play groups, and wondering what is ahead. Oh, how I want to hold on to that *Big Chill* feeling. There are times when I feel mentally exhausted. These are the early signs of what I call male menopause. It was also the time I started writing poetry.

It is certainly satisfying to be less anxious about what I want to be when I grow up despite an unfriendly mortgage. The important thing is to keep growing. You have taught me that. In a *New York Times* article, George Burns once said about growing old, "Consider the alternative." Life experience goes a long way in building one's confidence and self esteem. Anna Quindlen wrote in that same article, "A Team Dream," which stated:

> Those guys won't be out there getting rich and famous; they're already rich and famous. Every lay-up, every rebound in Barcelona will be saying, 'Look at what we know.' Not youth, youth, youth, although some of them are very young. Experience. There's a moment when the ball arcs perfectly downward to the waiting web of the net—or when the words lie down just right on the page—that makes you feel as if you are going to live forever. The irony is that by the time you are old enough to appreciate the feeling, you're old enough to know that it's illusory. Experience. Experience. I never had a jump shot, and I'm no longer a kid. But experience I now have. Consider the alternative.

It is difficult when with little notice, Cousin Andy says, "let's meet for dinner in the city during the week" with very little notice. At this point in my life, it just doesn't seem convenient, particularly when so much time has passed. In response to your last letter, I did not blow him off. In fact, I remember inviting him to Connecticut, but he was coming to town on business so that did not work for him. I was glad to hear from my cousin. Thinking I blew him off is the kind of judgment and assumption that has gotten us in trouble with each other through the years. My kids were my priority, midweek dinners did not happen during this time of my life. It was just not the right moment for either one of us. My energy level is different these days and so are my priorities. Now I have ballgames and school meetings to go to. As you have said before, "Tomorrow is another day." But I am afraid there is so much hurt and anger over what has transpired through the years that sensitivities run high with the extended family. Who told you that I rejected Andy? Or is this just another *Rashamon* experience?

It is true that sometimes my behavior might seem to contradict my intentions when it comes to the cousins, but I do not like my feelings minimized or trivialized. Remember the momentum for us all being together was taken away years ago when my life, and everyone else's, seemed simpler and less complicated. At this point in my life, it is hard to jump right back into those old relationships with a family that has had some severe fractures. It is true and I appreciate your saying that I need to make my own choices. There was a time that I did not feel that way, and felt I would have incurred your wrath and disappointment in me as a person. That was not an appealing alternative at that point in my life. Now I want my decisions to be more on my terms.

Those superficial, but meaningful, family get togethers would be fine if they required little energy from me. Having some fun with the family and being part of a large group, is a fond memory, and it would be appealing now as well. I don't see it as a fleeting nostalgic sentimental thought. What if it is that I just value the continuity of meaningful parts of my past? Nostalgia is a sacred aspect of one's history. There were those deeper, more sensitive moments with the family as well. I remember helping Cousin Gary with his ambivalent feelings about marriage. The last time the family met, all the men sat around with their kids talking about our book, but we never got back together again to discuss the next chapter. It is not too late. I feel like we are reaching that point. Aren't these the values we want to pass down to our children?

Jared will have his own nostalgia as we have embraced the baseball and basketball Halls of Fame in Cooperstown and Springfield. Recently we were fortunate enough to attend the final regular season game of basketball ever to be played at Boston Garden. Of course it was against the Knicks. It was very exciting standing with Jared at halftime watching the old Celtics have one more fast break together, finishing it off with Bill Russell passing the ball to Larry Bird. Inevitably, the torch gets passed on in the various arenas of life. It doesn't get any better than that, but weeks later it doesn't get any worse than leaving the arena with eighteen seconds left during a game that the Knicks were winning to find out in the parking lot that they lost in those final moments. Reggie Miller just took over the game.

I would like to take you up on the offer and meet with my cousins in the city some time. My family would not be opposed to a reunion after we all take a few baby steps. This is not over for me. I have sensed your desire to have us get together again. There will be many more generations, and it would be nice for that fracture in the family to be repaired. My kids like the idea of having cousins. For so many years the extended family has been our close friends. Perhaps that is an inevitable reality of life.

I have had some good feelings toward many of my cousins, aunts, and uncles over the years. My uncle and aunt used to open their house to us in Florida when we would take the kids on vacation during those early years. They have fond memories of those experiences. It is hard to hold onto the positive times when negative experiences have clouded the way. In the end, I feel better remembering what was positive, but recognize the importance of remembering what went wrong as well. I do not need you to understand and see it my way anymore, although I have a feeling we both choose to see the glass half full rather than half empty. At times easier said than done.

Your mom and dad must have been ahead of their time when it came to real estate. Little did they know what it would mean to all of us. It has been the glue that has held the family together for more than a generation, for better or worse. With all the financial problems in the family unfortunately caused by your brother's gambling, I hope that the mythology of our family can turn around and change the storyline; hence the importance of not forgetting what happened. You felt betrayed by your brother and many people suffered, particularly you, your brother Carl, and your father. It must have been difficult for you to watch what your father went through, more so because they were in business together during the time that Uncle Irving lost all of his money. In many ways it would appear that his gambling hurt you the most because you were asked to bail him out financially at a time when you were just beginning to build a life with your family.

We have very rarely talked about this period in your life. Knowing you as I do it is amazing to me that you could even talk to him after that. Then years down the road you felt cheated in a joint investment. How often have we seen addictive behavior destroy people's families? I have certainly had my share of financial and emotional disappointments. Hopefully, we learn from our mistakes and try to involve ourselves in situations over which we have some control. So often in life you think that you are making all of the decisions that seem appropriate to make your life easier, only to discover that it does not always work out that way. Indeed a painful and expensive lesson. Many families have to learn the hard way and we were certainly one of them. The message is try to govern your own fate as much as possible and reduce the risk by depending on yourself.

Finally, about your brother's funeral. In retrospect, I should have gone. I accept full responsibility for that and to this day regret that decision. My mistake was letting my discomfort about everything that had come down in the family get in the way and perhaps by the time Jared's Bar Mitzvah comes around, things will be different. We'll have to wait and see. Time can be a great healer.

There is that part of me that wants more time alone now, another thing we finally share in common. My problem is that sometimes I bite off more than I can chew. I am still looking for the balance between the Idealist and the Realist, indulging in my *Sports Illustrated,* reading *Business Week,* and raising a family. Although it is getting easier. Yes, I do read *Business Week* religiously, while the Mickey Mantle story sits now in Jared's bedroom; but he actually follows the stock market, and, as you know, he has a serious interest in the political scene and collects its' memorabilia. I trained him early because as we discover in relationships, we tend to pass on to others what was shown to us. Sometimes the next generation just gets there a little earlier than the one before. In the end, we have to eventually come to our own conclusions about what is important to us. Everything in its own time.

So often you seem to have your priorities in the right place. You always wanted those family vacations, and if it could still work out logistically you would be organizing them now. Time with your family was more important than building your own monuments. You were often concerned about me not overextending myself. What I used to view as an intrusion, I am beginning to recognize is a father just interested in his son's happiness. It could really be as simple as that. Look at the alternative. Embracing victimhood is no longer a necessary requirement for life.

Despite that one hour of geographic distance and very busy schedules, we have found a way to be connected. There is the flea market that we are running on that property in New York that is part of the family legacy. Being in the same profession allows us to refer patients to one another and support each other's work. You have been able to call me on Monday nights from the kitchen I grew up in, calling the kids on my radio show, where I have teenagers discussing contemporary issues. And here we are still writing our book together. I hope you are aware of how much I appreciate all of this and how fortunate I feel. While life's moments can be so transitory, we have managed to sustain a certain degree of constancy. You are seventy years old and now I get to treat you to a boat ride around Manhattan.

Finally, my heart still wants and needs the history. I think it is more important to me than it is to you, based on discussions we have had. By the way, you never did trace our family roots in your last letter when I expressed a need for that. Was that just an oversight? You speak of the importance of the present and future. I agree, but what does any of that mean without a past? When the future feels uncertain familiarity brings me a sense of comfort. At another point in my life, familiarity might have been something I associated with being unsafe when I was rebelling. That is no longer true, and for that reason I am just glad you are still here to tell the story with me. Ironically, because of my learning problems growing up, in certain ways the unfamiliar terrified me. Life is full of contradictions.

Isn't it strange the way the novel gets written? You can never predict how the process of life will work out its magic, but that is part of its magnificence. Here we are running a flea market on the property passed down from your father. For most of your early years, your brothers were the businessmen, the princes of retail, involved with your dad. They were in retail and you were the doctor. My sense is that you felt somewhat on the periphery, more often accommodating your two brothers. You were the good son, the one people expected to be perfect. That line of Grandma Jenny calling me her "baby's baby" comes back to mind. She obviously adored you, and in your father's own way he must have too. But you were so different. In one of your last letters to me you indicated that you had felt taken for granted, and you shared that with your father. In the end, life has a tendency to go full circle, one long extended process. Your dad did indeed give you a large gift. Besides the extra piece of real estate he gave you as he was dying, he also left you the space, unforeseen at the time, to have your own business with your immediate family which is now the flea market. Just recently you shared a story with me about how Cousin Gary, being in retail his whole life, came down one Sunday to the market and got a chuckle when he said, "It's strange after all of these years seeing you now working on Sundays." You are now doing with your own family what Pop did with your two brothers and what they continued to do with their own children, in business together, "Like father, Like son." Although we did not go into practice together, we went into the same profession, and now we are in a business that gives us the chance to grow together in a new venture. We both know that's right up our alley. It keeps you vital. I am grateful and have the sense that this has been important to you. I feel your excitement about it. What is that all about for you? Whatever it is, it has a feeling that looms large. My sense is that it has to do with what I have already mentioned, a desire you have to give something special to your children. It gives you the opportunity to stay involved with us and your grandchildren. Last but not least, it keeps you connected to life. In a peculiar way, I feel Pop's presence when I am down there on Sundays. The Soho area on Broadway had become a second home for us. The whole area was transforming into a commercial area beyond what was once a street of textile fabric stores.

Who would have known that Pop's business, which originally operated in a building on this property in a relatively unknown area at that time, would burn down, and turn into a successful parking lot in a prime area of Manhattan? We have now created a flea market on Saturdays and Sundays run by you and your family. This is quite an evolution. Clearly a time to fill a gap in your story, because Pop is gone and now you are my kid's Poppy; the new godfather of retail. You can now share something that I sensed was not possible for you, with your dad and two brothers. Far fetched, maybe, but perhaps not. Once upon a time Pop was a peddler.

Another special element is that I feel this whole experience has brought you and Dee closer together. I always wanted you to be close to my wife and have you get to know who she is. You have established that, but this puts you in a different context with her and that makes me happy. I want you to see her as the multi-dimensional person which makes her so special. I am proud of her, and I enjoy seeing my best friends working so well together. Father, daughter-in law, and son-in-law make a good team. It is wonderful to see Dee have her own business because so many women get trapped in the suburban drudgery, staying in the shadow of their husband's success. Thank you for giving Dee the opportunity to exercise her talents. It has made her feel good about herself and she is so enthusiastic. I love her so much. She deserves it because she has been supportive of my work over the years. I would not be where I am today without her. My wish is that the flea market will open up new avenues for your relationship with each other. She is a person who brings a great deal to the party.

I want to share some final thoughts with you. Your generation moved to the suburbs; for you it was Long Island, the promised land, thirty minutes out of New York City. It was the American dream—Norman Rockwell comes to town. With all change comes consequences, and the roots of the extended family began to splinter as people became more mobile. Pop was from the Old World, the extended family. I have vague memories of your life in Seagate, but whenever I think of Coney Island and Steeplechase it gives me a warm feeling. I would love to visit with the kids sometime soon. Someday I will take you back to visit the old neighborhood.

Our generation came along, inheriting and rejecting the American dream in the 1960's, but reaped the material benefits through the eighties. Now it seems we are living in a time when the American dream is passing us by and it is frightening to me at times. Whatever happened to the visions of my generation? Steve Holden in the *New York Times Pop Review* responds "The answer that was 'blowin' in the wind' turned out to be something very different from the kinder, gentler, more tolerant world that seemed imaginable thirty-two years ago." The eighties was a time of self-indulgence, greed, and the beginning of fading opportunity. Here we are in the nineties, the baby boomers have turned forty raising families, and the country is full of political and economic uncertainty adapting to an electronic universe where consequences at times seem to have no rhyme or reason. We have beepers, the Internet, and sound-bites galore. *The Jetsons* futuristic 1962 color TV show was ahead of its time. It was on for one year because there were not enough color televisions available to keep it going. The country is in transition, the euphoria of the eighties are gone, and now people are frugal and scared. Our profession has turned to managed care. They changed the rules on us, Dad. But as I tend to say, there is a reason for why things have to happen. What comes up, must come down, for that is the way history works. It is all cyclical, traveling along a continuum. It helps to hold onto that idealism especially since I know that realism has the upper hand these days. I resist the momentum toward mediocrity. Being positive and trusting the process has gotten me this far. Life is linked to an endless chain of events that hopefully directs itself towards a meaningful purpose. I too have become more spiritual as I get older. It's getting to the next level that keeps me going, which allows me to make choices not governed by compulsion.

I have recently felt that the flea market is the emergence of a new order, and yet has a piece of the old way, the return of some of the Old World values for Emily and Jared's generation. Everyone likes a bargain, and there must be some reason why we have wall to wall people every weekend from all walks of life down at the flea market. I have even seen familiar faces from my past. Maybe this is our Coney Island. The flea market was also a place to add to my growing art collection. It was fun buying and hearing all the stories from the vendors. It was here where Jared began gathering Presidential buttons.

When I hear the kids refer to you as their Poppy, it is as if we are going back in time, full circle. The sight of Jared handing out flyers in front of the flea market, and you proudly walking around looking over his shoulders, while your daughter-in-law is talking to the vendors, touches in me a feeling of the warmer parts of the Old World. Three generations working together with a common purpose. Donald Kartiganer, a Faulkner scholar, referring to a Faulkner short story (believed to be his last published), states in his introduction to the piece, as "the supreme attempt to realize the paradoxical dream of maintaining a hold on the past while achieving a creative autonomy in the present."

Sometimes I worry about how my children will keep up with what they are used to having available to them in their life, similar to what I felt with you. Will they have the same opportunities we had? Who knows, maybe our children will be forced to look at a different lifestyle and remain closer to their roots. Of course, this is all speculation, but I wonder.

It is strange that I, the guy who had to move far away to separate and find myself would think this might not be so bad. Maybe it is not as strange as it seems. I am the one who wanted my two acres and now at times miss the old neighborhood. I hope my kids will be in the position to work this through for themselves as I did.

I find myself feeling that the final chapter of our family has not yet been written. "Experience. Experience."

Love,
Donald

* * *

Dear Donald,

You've been waiting for me to respond to your last letter, so I'll begin by trying to explain the delay. The most obvious reason is that it has been a very busy and hectic time. We've opened the market on Saturdays as well as Sundays, and as you are aware Mom has frequently felt ill. But by far the most important reason I have procrastinated has to do with the substance and tone of your letter which is so different in mood and content from your previous letters to me.

It is hard to believe that you are the same person with whom I exchanged those letters when we first started this journey together. Gone is the adversarial tone, the defensiveness, the reproachfulness.

More clearly than ever, I feel the affection and compassion from you that I believe I have always sought. For the first time in our correspondence, I felt as if we are truly and deeply friends and equals, every bit as much as father and son. You speak to me as an equal with intelligence, sensitivity and insight. This evokes very intense feelings of joy and closeness which choke me up. I literally became tearful when I read your letter.

That is the truest reason it has been so hard for me to respond. Such intense emotion is difficult for me, as irrational as I know this to be. It has to do with feeling in control of myself. Perhaps it even harkens back to my father's admonition to me that men don't kiss each other and men don't cry. I try to believe I've overcome this problem, but maybe I haven't yet completely succeeded. You have always been a model for me in this regard, and I'm proud to say that I'm learning from you to be more open and comfortable with my strong affectionate feelings for you. I love you, my son, and now I can say that I'm not only proud of you, I also admire you.

You make reference to the cyclical nature of life and experience, and how everything that goes around eventually comes around. You repeat with your kids what I experienced with my kids, what my father experienced before me and what his father probably experienced before him. This is the spiritual cycle which is even more literally expressed in Oriental religious philosophy. For the Hindu, the ultimate and desired goal of this endless travail is Nirvana, an escape from the endless cycle of material existence which is perceived as inevitably painful. There is hardly anything in our history together that I would have wanted to miss. Even the painful parts provided contrasting backdrop for the infinitely greater joys in the moments of shared closeness.

You ask about your ancestry. I haven't told you more before this because, regretfully, I know very little. I never knew my father's parents. His mother died when he was a small child and his father remarried. My impression is that he was never close to his stepmother, and his nurturing was left mainly to his oldest sister who, as you know, came to the U.S. when he was a child. His father saved and sacrificed to send him to America to join her a couple of years later. I knew this aunt when I was a young child as a kindly grandmother figure, but she died when I was a boy. I knew my mother's family and remember my grandmother as a loving and kindly old lady who always adored me. My grandfather, a clock and watchmaker by trade, seemed always grouchy and cold. I vividly remember my father quarreling with him at a Passover Seder in my grandparents' apartment. My grandfather was ranting and complaining because all the family were enjoying the opportunity to socialize and exchange news with each other. He was angry because they were disrupting the observances and the prayers. My father firmly protested that Passover was a festive celebration of the historic emancipation of the Jews from slavery, and that my grandfather was inappropriate, undermining the spirit of the occasion. I still remember feeling proud of my father and impressed by his good sense and wisdom.

Lastly, I want to talk about the flea market and what it means to me. For one thing it represents a new challenge for me at a time in my life when I seem to be expected to hang up my tools and retire to passive self-indulgence. Retirement feels to me now like the prisoner about to be executed being offered his final meal and last wish. That sounds morbid, I know, and some of my friends who are retired would be horrified by my metaphor. My enthusiasm about my professional role and psychiatric work fulfills the same function, but the flea market is something very new and very different from anything I've done before. And yes, you may be correct in speculating that it has something to do with completing a circle and reconnecting with my father. Equally important in all of this is the opportunity to work side by side with my children, and to be involved with Dee and Ron on a different level than would otherwise be possible. If you recall, it was very important to me when this whole business came up for us all to do it together. I believe this has been one of the more gratifying aspects of the entire enterprise. I love Dee and feel very close to her; and my relationship with Ron is growing deeper with each passing week.

Finally, I want to say that concluding this experience makes me sad. Of course the process never ends and I'm confident that our relationship will continue to evolve in a way that reflects some shift in our roles as you gradually assume more and more leadership. I hope to graciously accept my new family position of the proud elder, but I don't want to be an old patriarch. But, there is something sad about thinking this is our final exchange of letters; it has been such a rewarding and enriching experience for both of us. I keep thinking of the contrast with the earlier letters we wrote to each other, and how far we have come in our relationship, our understanding, and the affectionate closeness I believe we now share.

Donald, I love you!

Love,
Dad

Extra Innings:
The Last Two Years

LATER ADULTHOOD–MANHOOD

The Acceptance

Immortality lies in the memory we preserve for future generations.

I'm getting old and deteriorating and it seems like I was a relatively young man just yesterday.

It is the tragedy of generations that the youngest of us never see the oldest of us at their best.—Sports Illustrated, *Feb 26, 2018 "Carrying the Torch" by Tim Layden*

* * *

October 5, 2009
Dear Dad,

I just finished re-reading our earlier letters. What a different experience now, a page turning, quick read for me. And we did get you back home to Coney Island in 2007. At times I sat in awe amazed that we accomplished this together. I want you to read it again and be as proud as I am about what we achieved together. It dawned on me that I am now fifty-eight years old, the same age you were when we wrote the book. Recently, Emily's husband Jeff was stunned when he realized Emily is turning thirty-one, the age I was when I wrote my part of My Father, My Son. This is all reinforced by the fact that as I watch Jared and Emily defining their own identities, there is comfort in discovering that I exhibited similar behaviors towards you at their age. They are both busy building their careers, struggling to financially and emotionally make their own marks in the world. It is important that we all have our own initiation rites as we take the journey through life. One never stops having to redefine oneself; that is the nature of the human condition. So the book achieves one of our goals, to encourage an acceptance that people do what they need to do as we struggle to make our respective worlds feel meaningful. There seem to be predictable stages of development that we pass through from generation to generation. It is easy to forget where we once were, trying to build a secure foundation for ourselves and others. Life is challenging, and finding the balance of having so many responsibilities, particularly during a recession, is not easy. I am proud of my children, and my experience with you continues to provide more understanding and patience when I want more time with my children and they have less time for me.

With many years behind us and some distance, the letters between us offers a new perspective. Recently, I couldn't wait to share with you that Carl Jung finally went mainstream and made the cover of the New York Times Magazine. You came back after reading it and said he is only seen that way in Zurich, Switzerland. Somehow, that made me smile and brought home the reality that I had outgrown our personal Freud/Jung rivalry.

Dad, I just watched you experience both your granddaughters get married. What was that like for you? Watching my Emily get married was similar to an out of body experience for me. You are often quiet in public when the family gets together and I am curious what you were thinking about at those times. I feel some relief in knowing that my children have reached milestones successfully, and was able to provide for their well-being. Sometimes it feels surreal, as if it was just yesterday I was a struggling adolescent fearing for my future. Now, as I get older and feel my own mortality, I become more tuned into how hard it must be for you at this stage of your life. It's unsettling for me to see you not able to play golf anymore, and to be forced to experience the limitations of your body. In one of my poems I mention that our "bodies are for rent." When you recently resigned from your country club it made me sad. That was the end of an era, and suddenly I felt the loss, as I knew how much pleasure you and Mom had there. It was a central part of your life for many years. Despite all of this, I am so proud that you still work and drive three days a week to the office, even if I worry about your safety. When I suggested you see patients at home, you responded by saying, "I'm not set up for that at home." After that I had to back off, becoming aware that you're not ready for this change in life. I need to remember the man that does not want other people to make those kinds of decisions for him.

Some of our past letters struck a chord in me when you referred to your friends no longer being around in their fifties and sixties. I became aware, at age fifty-eight, that that is me now, with friends that are in their seventies. Another high school reunion is coming up, less people signing up. Some say it's the economy; perhaps it's easier to see it that way. Technology has taken over, and I realize there are bigger things going on with my friends now. We are way beyond broken arms and having our casts signed.

Jared recently mentioned to me how he will want to name his children after you. Apparently, you talked about the history of your name with him. If there is more to tell about your heritage, please share that with me. It is difficult to see our lives go by, and I no longer take it for granted. Not a day goes by when I don't miss Mom and wish she could have seen Emily get married. I got scared on Rosh Hashanah this year when you appeared to pass out at the end of dinner. I want to freeze time and not let us get old and vulnerable. What made your father change your name to Cohen, so close to a Jewish holy name? Where will our legacy go from here? How many special events will we both be around to witness? Unfortunately, you have also seen the country had fallen on hard economic times not experienced since the Great Depression. It was in this context that Bernie Madoff's multibillion dollar Ponzi scheme was exposed and accelerated the country's downward spiral.

I love you and cherish whatever time we have left together on this earth. I admire your courage and desire to continue finding ways to make life meaningful, and hope that when you wake up tomorrow you remember how many people love you.

Happy eighty-fifth birthday—as you say, "What's the alternative?"

Love,
Donald

‐‑⊨⊚⊜‑‐

Note to the reader: the following letters from my father were transcribed by me, as he had become physically unable to write on his own.

‐‑⊨⊚⊜‑‐

* * *

February 24, 2010
Dear Donald,

In response to your most recent letter, I was moved, and struck by how I am going through the same thing as you. I knew beforehand that I couldn't write back. It is difficult writing prescriptions, my body doesn't work anymore. I wanted more time to see if I could get better and didn't want to feel pressured. I was worried about being a disappointment, knowing how important our letters are to you. There was concern that you wouldn't believe me.

It was sentimentally intense watching my granddaughters get married. I thought about Mom missing the experience. At this stage of life, at the mere age of eighty-five, you think about dying. It's a funny stage knowing you are near the end. Sometimes I feel, "Enough already." But I think a lot about what Mom missed and what I will miss. When it comes right down to it, I won't know the difference, and in that sense it is a little more comforting. Your sister is more intense about my aging; your personality is different and you don't nag me. You have a right to advise me about how I live my life, but ultimately the decision is mine. I am getting old and deteriorating and it seems like I was a relatively young man just yesterday. I sometimes think I will outgrow it, but that's a nice fantasy. My whole existence is making doctor appointments. There's hardly any Wednesday or Friday that I don't have a doctor appointment. In contrast, you think you have doctor appointments also, but for you it's a more gradual process. For me, it seems to have happened overnight. I have mixed feelings about quitting the country club. It was a rewarding experience and yet sad that it was over.

I am impressed frequently by the progression of my aging friends and their disabilities. I have lived past my time, as if I am the sole relic of the Civil War. I frequently feel lonely and depressed, but don't like to articulate that. I feel more invested in portraying myself as independent, as far as I know I have always been that way. I am moved by the idea of Jared's wanting to name his children after me. This underscores the depth of his identification with me. I remember when he was a little boy he asked me to take a trip alone with him. Often I think that was the turning point of my relationship with him. It is interesting to me that he chose Washington, D.C. and now that is the central part of his whole life.

In your letter you asked me why your grandfather changed our name to Cohen. During that time the Russian government was controlled by the Czar and Cohen was a common name. He was afraid they would force him to come back after he joined his sister, who was already living in America. One could say it was kind of like hiding. Your grandfather moved to the Lower East Side, and became a pushcart peddler, then owned a textile store, and moved into wholesale.

I can deny my age by still working and we still have a couple of more weddings to attend. I am relieved that this experience together has worked out because I thought we might freeze up having me orally share my feelings with you. The letter writing has always been our way in the past. I was uneasy that we wouldn't successfully communicate, and I didn't want to disappoint you. It seems we still have a relationship that's in the process of becoming. We are still evolving. There is a reversal of roles that's expressed in your wanting to take me to the doctor; it implies dependency. Why should it? Just a thought.

Love,
Dad

* * *

March 15, 2010
Dear Dad,

I was impressed by how well it worked: sitting in your kitchen and family room with you responding to my letter in person. Having a letter writing experience transform into a live dialogue between us was inspiring. We have become very close through the years. We have had conversations of a lifetime.

Your resistance to my wanting to take you to the doctor was very revealing. There was no question in my mind about how deeply I feel about taking care of you and being by your side at this time. You took care of me my whole life, now it's my turn. It feels like the natural evolution of the life cycle. The fact that you need me now and have become vulnerable makes our relationship that much deeper and profound. I always felt that the word dependency would be better defined as people needing each other and being there, connected whenever necessary, rather than the negative connotation. As you said in a recent conversation with me, love comes with a feeling of attachment. I am grateful that after all these years we share.

It was a difficult visit to the doctor and it was hard for me to see you so vulnerable and confused. I am so used to seeing you in total control of your life. It was uncomfortable for me to see that you were having trouble driving, and it became clear that I have to be in charge and take better care of you. It was upsetting taking you to the hospital and seeing inhumanity in the world of medical care. I was surprised at how this reversal of roles was bringing me closer to you and making me more appreciative of the relationship that we have developed together over the years.

As your recent kidney issues have landed you in rehab, my goal is to get you on your feet and strong enough to go home. It has motivated me to help you figure out your life, as now it is obvious some changes are in order. I am extremely focused on you getting back to work. It feels like you are training for the Olympics, and the goal is for you to be back in the saddle working. I sense you have become more realistic about being an eighty-five year-old man and have become open to working at home. I have been surprised by the fact that your emotional vulnerability has been more difficult for me than watching you be physically less mobile. Perhaps that has to do with my deep love and connection to you. There is more of an awareness of how mortal we all are. I remember as a little boy, you seemed immortal. Through the years I was so used to depending on you and knowing you could always be there for me. I am aware now that your independence is something neither of us can assume. This realization has been very dramatic and life changing for me. It becomes obvious that the mantle of the family is shifting towards me.

I was touched yesterday while visiting you in rehab when you shared how you feel closer to me. I share the same feelings towards you, and was thinking of the same thing just at that moment you shared your thought with me. When I asked you what motivated you to share that at this time, you said it had to do with mortality. I asked you if you had the same closeness with my sister. Your answer was that it was different because of your identification with me. I assume that had to do with being father and son. You were clear that you were tired and wished to discuss more of this with me at our next visit. For now, it only means that I can look forward to our next get together, and I find myself curious about where that conversation will go. I thought, as I so often have, that our last letters have been written, but as soon as I came home I felt inspired to write another. Nothing else in my life feels as important as us right now. Perhaps that's how it should be when father and son love each other in the way we do. What could be more important or relevant at a time like this, when it was just last week that I confronted the fact that I could have lost you forever? That was once something unimaginable to me. We are attached and never want to take that for granted. What else could one ask for?

I cherish the opportunity to take care of you and have my actions speak louder than words. Suddenly I feel strongly about the responsibility of taking care of you. Not a bad lesson during the eye of the storm.

Love,
Donald

* * *

March 24, 2010
Dear Donald,

Upon reflection, I don't see a dividing line regarding my emotional and physical vulnerability. It was more difficult years ago to be emotionally vulnerable, but it is a gradual process over time. Things that were unacceptable are more acceptable now. You live with a different set of circumstances, and you have to adapt. I remember when Mom died and we went to the funeral parlor. Images recur to me frequently, reminding me of her tombstone, half of it is blank—and it is obvious who it is for. I don't know why that imagery is so powerful. *Mom, I am on my way.* Separated for almost ten years, there is a place reserved for me; I'm comforted by the fact that it brings me back home.

I think you feel closer to me because we are having a shared experience. You feel vulnerable when you feel threatened by losing me. I feel great about you taking care of me, grateful for the kind of relationship we have. It is implicit, maybe not valid, to believe women are more nurturing. Your relationship to me is more dramatic because with a son it is not as expected.

Work is a measure of my competence as a man. I am increasingly able to do more things. Your sister is going to give me a hard time about me wanting to drive. It was dehumanizing in the hospital. I felt demeaned and diminished. You are under the control of an authority, it's impersonal. There is a fear of dying, not wanting to miss anything.

The main thrust of your letter seems to have to do with the fact that I am more dependent than I have ever been before. There is an impulse to take care of me, implying unpleasant things. When you are independent, you are in charge and not in need of care. This does not suggest feelings are any less genuine. You are very genuine, but my vulnerability makes you feel strong. It reflects a competitive stream in your reaction to me. Perhaps it has to do with getting closer to being patriarch of the family. This might be something to think about.

Love,
Dad

* * *

April 3, 2010
Dear Dad,

I have given some serious thought to your comments about the competitive stream that gets evoked when a son is put in a position to assume the mantle. When I visited you today and watched you fall to the floor, you looked scared and vulnerable. That moment was frightening and sad. There is ambivalence about becoming the family patriarch. When I visit you, I never know what to expect. Sometimes you seem to be the father I always have known to depend on, and

I so much want to hold onto that, while at other moments you are the vulnerable aging parent. When that occurs, there is reversal, and I suddenly feel like the parent and you the child. Although it feels rewarding and empowering to be there to take control and take care of you, I find myself still wanting the father that's able to be the one taking care of me. There are some fears of being an orphan, and no longer having living parents, and confronting the fact that I am the next generation in line to be nurtured. In addition, there is the realization that I will be alone, no longer able to reach out to a mom and dad. I too must face my mortality. I like coming home from a vacation and being excited to share and hear your voice on the phone. You and Mom always waited for the call, anticipating our connection.

When you discussed the tombstone, I became aware that the burial plot is not for me and Ellen. I suddenly became uncomfortable about the final separation of parent and child. You seemed very comfortable and direct about the reality that my place was with my wife and kids. Remarkably, I had never thought about any of this before. I also realized that you need to be taken care of and receive whatever it costs to provide the safest environment for you right now. I know you worry about all of us, but we will all be fine. Money has always been an uncomfortable subject for the two of us. At this time, although difficult to bring up, I need you to be able to discuss financial issues with me and make sure your affairs are in order.

I found myself feeling the nostalgia of lost childhood when we took a walk down my childhood street. We used to ride the bicycle built for two together. I went back to my wonderful childhood: hearing the sound of the baseball and basketball games on the block; the old games of hide and seek; and Mom coming out whacking the baseball with my friends. It made me feel sad noticing that it no longer existed and that so many houses had been transformed into McMansions. It was comforting and somewhat strange to realize that the house I grew up in was unchanged but deteriorating. Once again a reminder of how nothing remains the same. It never occurred to me that one day you would be using a walker, and I would help you stand to avoid a fall. As I said before, why would anyone be ready for that? The concept of holding on and letting go is pulling hard at me right now. Just yesterday you shared your appreciation of how good it felt to have me take care of you. Having the thanks and respect are a rewarding experience, and that feeling beautifully illustrates what we have been talking about.

I finally understand why you kept Mom's clothes in the closet. You like visiting her, and every time Emily comes over she walks in and takes with her another memory of Mom. Recently she found her travel diaries.

Now that Passover is coming, it makes me happy that we celebrate with Mom's family. I wish she could be there and see how we have all come together. As you know, it took the death of Mom and Aunt Bobby to unite her family again. They didn't get along—a love/ hate relationship. It makes me sad that you are not connected to your extended family anymore. I know that that absence has been more important to me. Although you connected with Uncle Irving at the end of his life, it became too late for all of us. We lost so many critical years.

Lately our conversations have been enlightening and some of the most intimate we have ever had. I continue to find out things that I never had known. For example, I asked you if you ever thought I would be a creative person. This led to an interesting discussion about how you and Mom would stay up at night worried about my future. I was surprised when you told me that you and Mom were going to buy a summer camp for kids where I could become the director. Interestingly, that had always been one of my fantasies growing up.

I remember visiting Jared on parent's day in college and asked you in a private moment to read my poem about my ADD. Your reaction was, "But look how great your kids turned out." It was then I realized you were never going to see the ADD. I was disappointed. I just think you thought I was a screw up and couldn't hear my plea. I am convinced I have ADD. That condition doesn't go away, and you and Mom never understood what that meant. I was surprised that you never responded to my confessions around this issue in our previous letters. This was a subject that always seemed off limits. Somehow now it feels good to talk about it. I remember you taking me for some kind of testing, and then there was the tutor, but I never felt my problems were addressed. True confession: I was the one who messed up your TV in the kitchen recently but I didn't want to admit it. After all this time, I am still embarrassed. The good news is that I fixed it, and I imagine there was an element of surprise and satisfaction in your seeing me make that happen. Dad, you can feel OK about asking me to change a light bulb. That may have been part of the problem. Because I always felt it was assumed I couldn't do things, so I was never put in the position to succeed or fail. In the past, when I would bring up this subject you would become very quiet. Learned helplessness is not good for the confidence of a child and enabling never helps anyone.

Your tentativeness about going back to work concerned me, but I respect the fact that you didn't want to be vulnerable with your patients. As you can see we are both being vulnerable with each other about many subjects, and it seems to be bringing us closer together. This does not mean I am comfortable with completely reversing roles. If that was true, perhaps we would not be able to have these conversations. That reality may be one of my great fears. I wonder!

Love,
Donald

"My Heart Leaps Up When I Behold"

My heart leaps up when I behold
A rainbow in the sky
So it was when my life began;
So it is now I am a man;
So be it when I shall grow old,
Or let me die!
The Child is the father of the Man;
And I could wish my days to be
Bound each to each by a natural piety.

— William Wordsworth, 1802

* * *

April 17, 2010

Dear Donald,

Donald, your father feels like a broken fortress. Your letter is very impressive, you get the general sense that we are speaking as one adult to another. You are more comfortable in your current role than you used to be. It is reasonable and natural that one should grow up over the course of time. Being the patriarch is not so hot after all. The cost of being a patriarch is that you don't feel eligible for the kind of support required when you are becoming a vulnerable human being. You identify with both sides of me, and it is natural to feel that way. Your life has been about being my son. Now your patriarch is full of cracks and vulnerabilities. Is that what I aspire to? I experienced the same feelings when I became a patriarch, and as you are now experiencing, in thinking about becoming an orphan. All my life I thought it was a juicy role to play, and all of a sudden, it's not so juicy and attractive anymore.

It's not true about my being comfortable with not buying a bigger burial plot for the family. It was a big deal, but it meant digging up the grave. It bothered me that we would not all be together.

The cost of my care is a monster with several different heads. I don't like seeing myself as helpless and dependent. I see it as something to be resisted. That's a bigger part of it than seeing myself impoverished. It's not either/or. The money is an issue for me as well. You spend your life trying to accumulate a legacy and it goes up in smoke. I don't want to spend my money on self-indulgent nursing care. I feel bad about my investments and feel like a fool; a wise man wouldn't have done that. You get caught up in finger sucking, riskless investments, that give you a high yield. Knowing this does not require you to be a nuclear physicist, but one gets carried away by wishful greed. It was our money, and I wanted you to have the freedom to take vacations without worrying about paying for it. I want to preserve whatever I have left, balancing what's best for me and you. I have to think about you bringing up my having difficulty talking about money issues with you. It sounds like it has a kernel of truth.

I have a deep appreciation for you and Ellen right now. Over the years, I have witnessed many relationships, and a patriarch like me is fortunate to see the specialness of your devotion and affection towards me. It's strange to think that just a month ago in the hospital I was accusing you of being in a conspiracy against me with the hospital. Now I think it is funny, and you were being so nice to me during that difficult time.

For a long time I was embarrassed by the fact that Mom's clothes were never thrown out. That has evolved into a state of affairs seeming to be natural. Emily comes and finds something of Mom's to take away with her, and that's an opportunity she never would have had. I still think it's kind of flaky. This reminds me of your aunt Sofie who collected dolls and displayed them all over her house. Maybe I have come out of the box and am more like her now. I remember when people made fun of it, but I can see it has a place now.

When you wrote about Passover, I agree with you about wishing Mom could have a chance to visit and see her family come together. That was a very poignant thing to say. Money does filter into my feelings about my extended family. There has been a degree of selfishness and lack of gratitude, regarding my management of the family properties over the years. I felt bad for your cousin Detra when she was shut out of a share of the inheritance. If all the cousins had agreed to compensate her, I would have done it. It wasn't my place to step in alone. I give Detra a free pass when it comes to me because I felt fatherly towards her. I am not sure she knows that I talked to Grandma about making sure her part of 470 Broadway was preserved in her will. There are times when I feel sad about not hearing from her anymore, but I don't hold it against her.

I don't have much to say about your learning problems, but do you still feel that way? Mom and I used to worry that you had so much trouble tying your shoe laces, but it all worked out in the end. It is true that we didn't think you would go to college and that you were not a promising student. I knew you could not make a career of reading the Mickey Mantle story.

Going back to work has been good for me and I didn't feel vulnerable with my patients. It was important to be productive.

Regarding the issue of reversal of roles, you want to be a parent, yet are gratified by a change in roles and that was true with my father when he got older. I was a doctor treating patients; my father was relatively uneducated in a formal sense and the opportunity to act in a paternal role came with mixed feelings. What I mean is not wanting the responsibility, but liking the feeling of being strong and powerful—and at the same time, not wanting to achieve that feeling at my father's expense. It is gratifying for you and Ellen to care about me, but it undermines my confidence in myself. If you tell me I can't drive, I begin to believe it.

This experience has brought us closer together as I think about my mortality nearing the end of my life. I don't know how much time is left. What I do know is I respond to you and that is determined by how you respond to me. When you were young you pushed me away. I had to respect that and I had no control. It's the opposite now, instead of pushing me away you are pulling me closer, which makes me respond to you affectionately. That's a natural thing between two people.

As I said earlier in my letter, money is a concern that has a considerable effect on my accepting help in the house. I feel like I am spending our money and we may not have anything left.

I am not thrilled with the prospect of having to work at home. Yvonne, my nurse, does help me get dressed and it takes half the time with her help. This takes some pressure off of me in the morning. I feel depressed not being able to be physically capable anymore. Until I got sick, I never thought about being eighty-five years old, and that has made me feel depressed. It's difficult not knowing what is coming . . . I don't want to talk about this anymore.

Love,
Dad

* * *

May 24, 2010
Dear Dad,

I felt really good about your decision to move your office to the house. It made me sad when you said it made you feel like it was the last chapter of your life. I understood what you felt and recognized the importance of letting you work through those feelings. You did just that and that made me proud and relieved. I saw the moment as an opportunity to point out the positives. You will be safer and find working at home more convenient. In addition, I do not see this as a surrender to your mortality. If anything, I believe that it will prolong your life and give you a feeling of a new chapter. And we can make it festive. Celebration and ritual are an important part of the journey of life.

I will visit your existing office and take you out for lunch. As I have said before, I remember visiting often when I was a little boy, and it was always a special treat. Visiting you now will be an opportunity to have a good time, combined with a trip down memory lane. Dad, I have been impressed with observing a more realistic and accepting attitude about your mortality and physical limitations. I noticed that you are using the cane when you walk. I know it is emotionally difficult for you. I respect what a warrior you are and what a great role model you are for me. It's a fine line knowing when to ask for help and deciding when you're making the right choice to do it for yourself.

Hearing about Joanne's death has had a profound impact on me. Mom's two best friends are gone, and your saying to me, "Who's next," is enough to make me reflect on the fact that I will be fifty-nine next week. I see myself entering the third act of the play. As you recently said, "It seems like yesterday I was getting old and suddenly I am old." Dad, you keep going and working; enjoy the fact that the people that matter in your life love you. You're still here to enjoy many events and your patients value your company.

What's amazing is who would have thought that the men would outlast the women? I was glad you, Irwin and Larry went out for lunch together. It was never your thing to go out for lunch with the guys, but you're like the three amigos who need each other's company. I think it's a positive thing even though you find it a bit depressing. Joanne's funeral was a recognition of my history and struck a nostalgic chord in me, with thoughts of where does the time go. We need to live every day and be thankful that we have been given a gift. I can't believe, that next year I'll be sixty-years-old.

It recently hit me that I was born around Memorial Day. It is so fitting that I am a man who cherishes memories. How ironic that life could be viewed as a battlefield. It is the hero's journey with an inevitable ending; hence the importance of remembering those who have fought for freedom. All this takes me back to my childhood fantasy of being the cowboy riding his horse. Somehow I feel differently this year about this and feel more aware of how meaningful it is. I find myself more philosophical these days and becoming more like you, enjoying my alone time. With loss, there is the promise of something new and a hope that we still can have the freedom to grow and make a difference. Time moves on. When I watched your grandchildren speak so beautifully at Mom's funeral, it brought home the reality how powerful the cycle of life is. It dictates a sense of immortality that gives us something to celebrate and take hold of.

As you get older there is a relief in the fact that you have nothing to prove anymore and can bask in what you have accomplished. Is there brighter lighting ahead, or does life just become what we remember? How does it feel knowing you are about to become a great grandfather?

Love,
Donald

* * *

July 4, 2010
Dear Donald,

Your letter about my leaving the office and seeing this as a positive change in my life stirs up many feelings. This moment can be seen as a beginning or end; the two concepts are not mutually exclusive. There are contradictory feelings: I can see it as an accomplishment or an ultimate compromise. I don't think of it in terms of safety, but in terms of convenience. During this time in my life, there are many levels of feelings about getting old and dying. These feelings have been stated in previous letters. I think of this time in my life as an extra inning, I am going to be eighty-six years old, and it seems as if I am too old to be playing doctor. Leaving the office has to do with my perception of my role. Being home has always been associated with my family, not a place of work. I agree that I am more realistic about my situation in life.

I have been curious about how eager you have been to see my office again, but I feel less confused by it than I did before. It has something to do with a point of reference from your memory as a little boy. I don't have a picture of my father's office. Your interest in mine kind of expresses your fear of losing whatever the office has meant to you. It feels comfortable having you in my office. Your office has so much more going on. I am suggesting you reflect on my office and why you made your office the way you did. They are certainly very different.

My feelings about the life cycle being interesting was stimulated by my perception of my own shifting role as the family patriarch, as I see you looking after me.

There is one climactic dynamic ending. I am approaching the end of my life. I know I am going to die. Everything by comparison is seen in the context of this dramatic ending, as I am still deciding whether I am going to retire or not. It depends on my physical condition. My health is deteriorating. I feel I am closer to death than I was six months ago; my feelings about dying fluctuate. If I am physically in pain, dying does not seem so unattractive. When I feel better, I tend not to think about death.

I was depressed before I learned that Emily was pregnant. It was exciting to find out, but I felt kind of out of it, and not connected to what was happening. It was almost as if I couldn't be a full participant. I just feel like the party is over for me.

What to do about my practice is a big decision. This sits on my head now, knowing that it impacts a lot of people, patients as well as family. I feel like I am depressing you and that's enough for right now.

Love,
Dad

* * *
August 29, 2010
Dear Dad,

As we approach the end of summer I can't help but reflect back on its majesty. In early July I received a postcard inviting me to see a new off-Broadway play, *Freud's Last Session*. What a meaningful coincidence, the magic of synchronicity. This was a gift of grace. I was thinking how we can celebrate. I was thinking about how we can celebrate your eighty-sixth birthday, and there it was. I enjoyed the play, particularly watching you appearing mesmerized—sitting in the first row, viewing C.S. Lewis meeting Freud, debating their different ideas about life. I sat next to you, proudly smiling, only curious to know what you were feeling. My fantasy was that this was the closest I could come to sharing a meeting between myself, you, and Sigmund Freud. I never knew he died of throat cancer, and his demise on stage only reminded me of our inevitable mortality. The only one missing that night was Carl Jung.

You asked me to reflect on my need to see your office again after all these years. You were correct implying that part of my motivation was to connect with my past memories and find a way to transition myself to the next stage of the life cycle. I found it curious that I had not remembered your art collection and the stories behind it. It made me realize that you too had an interesting collection of memories and stories that, when I was young, seemed unimportant to me. I was the son who had no interest in Diego Rivera murals on our trip to Mexico. This realization reinforced to me my own transformation and how easy it is to take for granted the meaning of one's surroundings. Watching you sit behind your desk that day made me aware of how much this office defined your life, and how difficult it would be to leave these surroundings. For me, it made me think about my own journey and appreciate the importance of what it means to create a space that becomes such a meaningful place for collecting our own memories; they were memories that come as a result of taking part in so many people's stories through the years. It also made me reflect on how what we do in our work is so sacred to us. It clarifies much of who we are. In a brief moment in your office that day, I understood how full life was for you in your work sanctuary. More importantly it helped me capture who you are as a person.

We are both collectors and liked to be surrounded by beauty. My childhood bedroom of private imagination was no longer hidden inside my office or outside. I was born to be a collector and treasure the creative spirit of myself and others. My religion was my art and the appreciation and expression of beauty. This was reinforced by John Keat's poem "Ode to a Grecian Urn." "Beauty is truth and truth beauty. That's all we know on earth and all we need to know." Perhaps your office was an early inspiration for me. Maybe you exposing me to art during our childhood vacations planted the seed. All summer long I sensed an ambivalence and resistance to you moving your practice to the house. I got the feeling that the deeper meaning was moving the office to home meant retirement and the end of the road. It appeared like it was hard for you to view this transition as a positive step into the next stage of the journey. You seemed to know otherwise. I felt I was failing to help you see this as something to look forward to. What I have learned is that you need time to process this change, and perhaps it was just a vulnerable time packed with fears and unknowns, particularly when it came to your health. How difficult it must be to make a change after fifty years of traveling to the same workplace everyday, and then being forced against your own will to have to make this move. My goal was to help you move through this process and recognize the importance of your staying healthy and being able to continue seeing your patients. I know that work has been an important part of what defines your purpose in life. Any doubts you still have about it will hopefully be alleviated in the coming months. It must feel unsettling and anxiety provoking, both emotionally and logistically, imagining your patients still wanting to see you at home. What feels rewarding to me is that this possibility is now ready to be explored, despite your ambivalence about retirement.

Moving you out of your office was both rewarding and sad for me. I was proud to help you in this change, and sad knowing it wasn't what you wanted. I watched you sitting behind your desk as your office was being dismantled, and collected memories removed from walls. I could only imagine what was going through your mind. I appreciated some of the stories behind your collection, the specialness of your relationship with your patients, and knowing many pieces of art were created for you. I too was identifying with the fact that we were not so different, and someday this will be my reality. The Freud head, sculpted by your patient now sits on my office desk, the ultimate statement that bridges the differences of our ancient Freud/Jung debates. Ironically, the female patient's last name was Cohen. More synchronicity!!! Now your history sits with me in my office alongside the Carl Jung and Sigmund Freud action figures on my desk. At the same time my childhood bedroom has been converted into the secretarial space for your new office.

My office has now become a place for me to hold my memories with yours, and cherish the fact that my grandchildren can be inspired by my workplace similar to what your surroundings did for me. Someone needs to hold the stories and pass them on. We have gone full circle. Now your office has moved home, it has forced me to clean up all the boxes of memories that laid untouched for so many years in my room. Going through those boxes of pictures and documents forced me to revisit generations of our family. I discovered many old letters and pictures that evoked a feeling of appreciation of family history, and my travels from early childhood through the present time. I even found all of Mom's diaries from your travels all around the world. Before she died, she took me around and shared stories of her favorite pieces at home. It made me aware of the importance of my heritage, its continued evolution, and the responsibilities that come with it. We are the torch bearers of our legacies.

It was you who helped to inspire the memory man in me, and to know I was a collector with an imagination. In one summer, you moved out of your office; Jared took on a new job at Google and moved to New York with his girlfriend; and Emily is a lawyer about to have a son, which will make me a grandfather and you a great-grandfather. At times all of this feels surreal, yet at the same time, it gives me a deep appreciation for how profound life is, and the meaningfulness of embracing the life cycle as it unfolds before our very eyes. Growing up becomes inevitable, and with it comes an appreciation that seems to remind us that transformation is not meant for us to resist; and accepting one's fate upon reflection is a lesson to be learned. It is our later adulthood to manhood. Perhaps retirement is just a state of mind.

Love,
Donald

* * *

September 6, 2010
Dear Donald,

The night of the play I was more aware of being with the family than what was on the stage. I felt immensely grateful to be with all of you.

My office seemed bare and naked compared to yours. I was surprised you were interested in my art, not thinking my art was special. I do share the pride in the silk screen above the couch. Originally it was just a scarf before I designed the frame. The focus on my office has more to do with you having more interest in me now than when you were a kid. My surroundings take on more importance.

Regarding your comment about perceiving the move from my office as positive, I still feel otherwise. I am in extra innings. I never gave a lot of thought to the fact that my continuing work meant so much to you and Ellen and perceived the sadness you felt when I talked about retirement. As a result I was afraid to talk about it because of your feelings. The move was against my will, and I would have preferred not to. "I am what I do." What I have done for so many years constitutes the essence of who I am. I have trouble conceiving seeing patients at home—the physical setting is not what I am accustomed to because there is no waiting room. It was the best decision to come home, and surely required chutzpa that I didn't think I had. And a commitment at eighty-six years old to think that what I am doing could go on for another five years! I don't know another ninety-year-old psychiatrist. I feel uncomfortable about posturing that I could pull this off. Maybe it's a little masochistic, or perhaps it's good for my head—maybe both. There is an element of truth in work defining my purpose in life. If I end my career, it underscores my mortality and vulnerability. I am anxious about working at home, fearing it won't work. There was something unmistakably business-like in my old office. Any significant change in the structure of my work is unsettling. The dismantling of my office is only one part of the process. I took a passive role in the move, it has something to do with giving up the mantle and passing the baton. I was much more passive than what would have been my customary demeanor. This is my last season as a professional pitcher. When my office was new and fresh, I was proud of it.

It was impressive to me how moved and emotionally involved you were during this process. I also noticed the intensity of how involved Dee was. I never saw anybody work as hard as she did. I felt appreciative of her. She's wonderful. It surprised me that it didn't surprise me that her emotional investment was what it was. I was less surprised by your involvement because it was your childhood, your part of my DNA. There is a primitive identification for your children, but her long history gives her that feeling as if I am her immediate family. That makes me understand her involvement. Our personalities are different and through this process I was depressed and quiet. For many months you were more flamboyant about what you felt.

There is something that bothers me about my relationship with Emily. That is the fact that I wasn't more excited about the news of her pregnancy because I was depressed. It is implicit in the conflict. On the one hand, we see our children leave their childhood behind— embracing a new world. However this underscores the pretense in my continued striving for my own limited aspirations.

Patting me on the back is all part of the natural order of things. I am passing you the mantle.

Love, Dad

* * *

November 28, 2010
Dear Dad,

Many events have happened since our last letter. Your office moved home and now you see patients there; two granddaughters are pregnant; a grandson is speaking as the honored guest in front of a sold-out audience at Fairfield University; he is in a serious relationship with a woman; and, finally, home videos have been converted to DVD watching together as a family on Thanksgiving Day. The only difficult feeling is that Mom wasn't there to witness it all with us and that makes me sad. She always brought up the marble cake that she knew I loved. Life is full of milestones and none should be missed. So often I try to get inside your mind as these moments take place. Maybe it's harder for those loved ones left behind. But I, like you, want to stay around as long as I can. You are my inspiration, and your desire to prevail is impressive. I know you never want to burden us, but at the same time, it is harder for you to physically maneuver yourself independently. Sometimes your mortality gets mixed up with my own and I realize how important it is to take care of myself. I feel scared about losing you as well as I fear for my own finality. There are moments when the loss of Mom is unbearable. How can you live such a full life and then one day not be here anymore? What's the point to all of this? Mom missed so many moments, and I have to believe somewhere, somehow she is feeling these celebrations. I want to believe when that feather fell on me at the ballpark in Coney Island, she was there with us. Dad, I don't want to die and can't fathom life without either one of us.

I felt sad when you were told you needed dialysis, but remarkably as things turned out, it wasn't necessary. It seemed like just when I was being your cheerleader it was all changing. It's these moments when I feel the unfairness of life, but here you are still working and seeing patients. You are my hero: a warrior, and most importantly, not just my father, but my best friend. I was deeply touched when recently you told me that you will take on whatever is necessary as long as you can stick around. Suddenly it dawned on me how brave you are and how much you cherish life, particularly to be with those most important to you. Although I know you feel like you have become an old man overnight, I believe there are more lessons to be learned.

Keep going and never stop believing in tomorrow. "Memories are our futures now."

Love,
Donald

* * *

December 27, 2010
Dear Donald,

It feels sad not having Mom around, and after watching the video, I realized that I had forgotten how she used to look with dark hair. Something I think about since Mom died is that it reminds me how I felt when my dad died—aware of what he was missing. It doesn't really matter because they are not aware of what they are missing. Becoming a great grandfather is different, more monumental, because I feel like it is a reminder that I have lived a long time.

Approaching grand finality is an unwelcome thought. I feel fortunate to have lived long and want to stay around to see what happens to Jared. He has a noisy life, and his achievements make you feel like something important might happen. He has distinguished himself at an early age. In the past, people didn't live long enough to have great-grandchildren. It's like having a special encore. Mom would be in seventh heaven. When I think about what made Jared's performance at Fairfield University so impressive, it was how he kept his dignity and stature without being condescending. As a kid, not even that long ago, he thought it was amusing to brag—not a good way to impress others. The best tact is to be modest and it seems now he is making a conscious effort to do it. I am glad Jared finished reading our book and is looking forward to us having dinner and talking about it. I enjoyed watching the family video, and it made me feel nostalgic.

A lot of things influence you when you're ill or in pain; being isolated is not appealing. I have been a good role model, but it's frustrating, not just burdening. I resent when people take my arm and hold me up. I still want my independence because I am a proud man. I have become resigned to the fact that I am losing it and need help getting dressed, doing what I have to do. Aging progressed dramatically. It seemed so rapid, as I have pointed out before. I have remained reasonably successful and my existence is important to the people's lives for whom I play a significant role. Even that may be overstating it. My father had no significance to Emily and you. Emily could not have grasped how much I was affected by his death. I am not convinced there is a meaning to life, and I am very moved by what you have expressed to me. It feels good to know I can be that important to somebody.

Knowing that the Madoff money may come back to us is important to me because I took pride in being able to hand money over to you and Ellen. I felt responsible for that and have mentioned it to you before.

In response to Mom being part of our celebrations, I am not invested in the concept but believe the fantasy.

When I was confronting dialysis, what choice did I have? But I started functioning better because of the medication. It feels good to be diligent, and it is satisfying that I can still see patients. I am moved by how you feel about me. It feels good to have all these women looking after me, but sometimes I'd rather read the newspaper. The idea of more life lessons is a meaningful thought, so I will keep doing it. I don't know what else to do. As a result of this dialogue, I will struggle more to find the essence of life. Your questions are making me think about that. The birth of Emily's child is one of the most signicant events of my life and gives me enormous pleasure.

Love,
Dad

* * *

January 17, 2011
Dear Dad,

I will struggle more to find the essence of my life. Recently Rochester my cat died, same time of year as my old one, Milo, same illness. Now here it is January, the time Mom left this earth but back to us comes our Greyson, my first grandchild. You're officially a great-grandfather. It is wonderful and surreal, and meaningful.

Another wish of ours was granted. Jared read our book. He felt it was good to wait until he was twenty-nine. It helped him relate to it more. I never felt you accepted that reason for him waiting so long to read it. Little did I know our dinner together to discuss the book was to be the beginning of *My Father, My Son,* part two. The sign was when Jared said, "Dad, I didn't know you were such a rebel." I guess the book worked. He began to confront me about all my faults, but not in a letter. I realized we were enacting the natural flow of the life cycle—but different from our letters. With him, there was no time to pause for three weeks and digest my shock, anger, and disappointment, similar to your structure throughout these letters. I knew it was important to take the hit and remain silent, not becoming defensive. It was unexpected and I was taken off guard.

How ironic that on the way to taking you to the garage you said, "Don, this must have been a tough night." I asked you, "How did I do?" You said, "You did well, took it like a man." It was a moment for me to feel relieved, and I felt less alone, thanks to your support. Our book obviously gave Jared permission to rebel.

I finally understand what you meant in your last letter when you said Emily had no understanding of what it was like for you when you lost your father. I think you were saying she had no memory or connection to ever having a great-grandfather. Dad, I get what you were saying as you approached being a great-grandfather. Emily's son Greyson won't have a memory or connection to us when he sees me mourn your passing. If you take it one step further, when I looked at him the other day, I realized Jared and Emily could have the same experience when their kids have children. After this, I went to a place of wondering who will Greyson be when he is fifty-years-old. I will be ninety when he is at the age when we did the book together. I better take good care of myself!

We are back to my last letter with you and searching for the meaning of life. One thing we achieved beyond the past generations, is that we have written a book that allows our legacy to continue. Therefore Greyson will know you and feel connected. As you have said in the past, immortality lies in the memory we preserve for future generations. Perhaps that was the driving force behind these letters between us. If this is true, the continuation of these letters seems to serve a larger purpose. That awareness feels meaningful as we continue our search together. See you at the bris, congratulations for getting yourself there, literally and figuratively. Greyson Max will be honored and you and Mom are preserved in his middle name. I know this goes against Jewish tradition because you are still alive. How fortunate that Mom has your first initial. The son of the grey haired man, how's that for immortality?

Love,
Donald

* * *
March 6, 2011
Dear Donald,

I feel Jared reading the book gave him license to tell you off. Waiting so long to read the book must have meant he was not ready to express his anger towards you. Not reading the book was a way of getting back at you. I used to feel you pushed the sports on him when in fact he may not have wanted to do that as a child. You bugged him about reading our book, similar to when I used to try getting you to read something besides *The Mickey Mantle Story*. When he confronted you there was nowhere to go with it. He is close enough to being an adolescent trying to work out his conflicts, no use engaging in a debate. I was surprised that night; I didn't think he would take the book that way. He had an angry reaction to it. I wish the night could not have been about his rivalry with you. Although it was overwhelming, it is just the way it goes. I am glad you felt my support. You know we have been there. You handled Jared like a therapist, not taking it personally.

It upsets me when I don't feel you take care of yourself physically. I feel life is meaningful when someone you love has self-destructive tendencies and you can watch them care enough to want to turn it around.

It is incredible being a great-grandfather, I thought one had to be Methuselah. I never thought I would be around. Our book speaks to generational changes and how important it is to put things down in writing before time passes. Having a great-grandchild is as good as it gets.

I enjoyed being at the bris until it was drowned out by the humiliation of being soiled. This was the first time that ever happened; I didn't realize that it was happening. It sucks losing my balance. I don't feel like my hands are my own. With my patients, I feel like a fraud. I am depressed.

What's most important is that having a great-grandson is an emotional experience and I am pleased about his middle name being Max.

Love, Max

* * *

July 24, 2011
Dear Dad,

Happy eighty-seventh birthday. that's an amazing feat! Did you ever think you would be around for that long? You are one tough guy and you meant it when you said, "what's the alternative?" and, "I don't want to miss anything." Recently when I turned sixty, it seemed like it couldn't be. It was my most difficult birthday. I felt as if time had passed me by. I love Greyson and being a grandfather. This experience helps me understand how you have felt towards Jared and Emily. As for pushing Jared in sports, we will have to agree to disagree. One thing that stands out for me is that you hold onto your opinions. One day I will be enjoying the same activities with Greyson and smile, thinking you will be saying history repeats itself, and again we will disagree. This is the resolution to our critical exchange.

Since our last letter, my son-in-law Jeff lost his mother Barbara. It made me feel closer to him because we now shared something in common, the loss of a mother. Unfortunately for Jeff, his mom won't see Greyson grow up or take part in any of the celebrations ahead. Although Mom lived longer than Barbara, she still missed more than I had hoped. That makes me sad, and the fact is Barbara died a week before her sixtieth birthday and two weeks before mine. We were birthday soul mates.

Dad, celebrating with you makes me grateful that we still have you around to share wonderful family moments. Maybe your genes will rub off on me and be an inspiration for me to hang around. You are the oldest surviving patriarch, aren't you? You're still working, that's amazing. Why not be open with patients about Parkinson's and tremors? Last weekend, I was surprised how emotional I was when Emily, Jeff, and Greyson came to visit you in my childhood home. Upon reflection it became clear to me that Mom should have been there for that and how profound the circle of life is. For me that is what makes life meaningful. You once spoke about the circle of life. Have you thought more about what makes life meaningful for you? What was it like having your great-grandson enter your home where you raised me?

Love,
Donald

* * *

July 24, 2011
Dear Donald,

No, I didn't think I would be around. Eighty-seven seems like it would be another generation. I feel that I am the elder statesman, and have enjoyed my grandchildren. They both give me warmth and affection. I don't know how much longer I can continue to work. I am finding it more burdensome. I don't have the motivation or energy, and it is more and more difficult to multitask. It's an emotional thing giving up my practice, but it won't be long before I am forced out by poor health. It used to be the tremors, I feel uncoordinated, can't handle knife and fork, can't distinguish my hand and fingers. I have trouble writing prescriptions. I have gone longer than I thought was possible. Being truthful with my patients about Parkinson's makes me more anxious and makes the tremors worse.

I feel the circle of life more with Jared; he is my only male grandchild. He is my legacy and an admirable boy. It has created a conflict. Although I want to brag about him, I always feel it is up to other people to talk about him. I secretly enjoy when that happens. I think he is entitled to brag about himself, but when he was younger he had nothing to brag about. I am very proud of him.

When my great-grandchild came over, I felt a generation removed. When you were all there, it was difficult to handle the tumult. I am just as close to Emily, and in some ways closer because she was my first grandchild. With Emily, it was all about my first experiences. I would not want her to think I prefer Jared over her. I am proud of her. She is a terrific girl and very accomplished for her age. It doesn't seem strange seeing her as a mother. Having my grandchildren and my children is what makes life meaningful. It's about love and feeling you have an impact on others. You want to feel like you matter to the people who are important to you, and that they too have the same effect on you. At this point Donald I have nothing more to say.

Love,
Dad

My dad, Max Cohen, retired from work three weeks following this letter. He died on September 30, 2011.

Epilogue
by
Donald Cohen

As for my feelings about being cast in the role of a disappointing and fraudulent god with clay-feet, I am assuaged by the belief that however difficult it is to be the son of an imperfect and less than god-like father, to be the son of the perfect, or god-like, father would have to be infinitely harder. —MAX COHEN, 1995

My rivalry with my father was similar to Freud and Jung, but I learned to accept our differences and embrace our similarities. As the reader now knows, my father was more private than I am. I so appreciated that he agreed and was willing to write a series of letters with me that evolved into a book to share with others. We were fortunate enough to explore the dynamics of our dialogue and gain an understanding of what happened between us. What I am so grateful for, is to have had the opportunity to be part of a unique experience between father and son. We had the advantage of both being psychotherapists, which allowed us to be vulnerable and attempt to resolve our conflicts and gain a keener understanding of each other. We had insights that were at times revelations, with new discoveries about ourselves and one another.

Jung says life is paradoxical. We love and hate, we ally and protest. My father and I experienced the paradox through which we grew into one another's devotion with great recognition. This was reflected in our letters and a central ingredient of our process and struggle together.

In the end I have come to accept and celebrate being loving and passionate, without apologizing for being a man who desires beauty and creativity; and growth of all kinds. This was in my core as a child, then thought it would come through from being a basketball star. When that failed, I believed the answers could come from philosophy and my father's career, but I actually found it in the spiritual passion of another male, Carl Jung. This journey to manhood was to become the mystery of **"my inside ride**." My story with my father is that we became more than father and son. In the words of singer songwriter James Blunt, my story with my father is that we became more than father and son. In the end, it was us becoming "... two grown men learning how to love each other.

"I will always love you Dad!"

Afterword
by
Emily Cohen Nestler

I remember when my dad and my grandfather first started writing letters back and forth, and my dad told me they were going to "turn it into a book." Fourteen-year-old me could not imagine anything cooler than that. I even bought a blank journal so that my dad and I could "write our own book." I would sit on my parents' bed scrawling in that blank book whenever possible, while my dad sat next to me returning calls to his patients each night. In my memory, that was perfect. My dad was the coolest and everything he did was gold.

It is certainly not unusual that the differences between my dad and me increasingly took form as I got older. It is indeed an old trope for adults to analyze the inevitable divergence from their parents, along with the realization of their imperfections. In my case, I turned out to be a very practical person (a lawyer, no less) and very focused on efficiency, whereas I don't think *anyone* could or would describe my father that way. I also turned out to be a relatively private person. Like my dad, I'm not shy. But, while my professional life requires a fair amount of public speaking—I hate sharing personal feelings beyond a small and intimate few. I dislike public mourning, which always feels too maudlin or else to belittle my grief when it is truly deep. I am uncomfortable celebrating my own successes too much, mostly out of fear that other people will think I'm bragging. In other words, adult-me would never be a person who would want to pour my feelings into letters and then publish those letters for the world to read. It's hard enough for me to write this short piece right now— probably the reason I have been procrastinating for months. My dad shares all his feelings loudly and often. I love my father infinitely, but that is a part of him that is hard for me to understand.

My grandfather was, in many ways, much more like me. He was an intensely private person. Always appropriate. A true intellectual. He dressed up when he flew on airplanes. He taught me Yiddish nursery rhymes. He insisted on paying for my *New York Times* subscription for twenty years. He loved opera and ballet and he took me to Lincoln Center whenever possible. My grandfather was a bleeding heart liberal and a feminist before it was cool—and I wish he had seen me grow up to be a fighter, and civil rights lawyer who is quoted in the very newspapers he ordered delivered to my doorstep, all for defending the principles he taught me to believe in. I wish he had seen me grow up to be a mom.

Most of all, my grandfather loved his family. He would literally do anything for his family—no matter how extreme, no matter how bizarre, and no matter how far it landed outside his comfort zone. I can only assume that such unbounded love for his son is what propelled this book into existence—because, as a kindrid spirit, I am well aware of how hard it must have been for him. My dad needed this book, and it was an extraordinarily generous gift that my grandfather gave to him under the circumstances.

This book also is a gift to me. It is a piece of my dad and my grandfather that I get to digest anew, and a part of my grandfather that I get to know even though he's gone. While I would have described my relationship with my grandfather as very close when he was still alive, recently I've had sharp pangs of regret. Perhaps because of our shared instinct to hold back feelings, I think we somewhat loved each other from arms' length. My grandfather deserved better than that from me—because he gave me nothing but unconditional love and his constant presence my whole life up until he died. I wish I had asked him more questions, engaged him in more complex conversations, and shared more of my deepest feelings with him before it was too late. I am jealous that my dad unabashedly drew that out of him and I am grateful that we all get to reap the benefits through this book.

I also am cognizant of not repeating those same mistakes with my dad. Make no mistake, with my dad's propensity for sharing, this is a relatively low-risk situation. But, when it comes to my dad as we both get older, I want to make sure that the sharing flows both ways. I don't want to look back and regret withholding from dad—because, like my grandfather, he is extraordinary and deserves so much better. The good news is, I think we have found a clear path. I have never felt closer to my dad than I have over the past eight years, largely for two reasons: Greyson and Lucas, my sons who worship my father like he is the only true man on earth. I have never seen a more incredible grandfather than my dad. He and my older son both describe each other as their "best friend." I don't know very many men my dad's age who so readily—and so happily—will take two kids alone under his wing for entire days, and then discover adventures with them that sound like magic coming from my kids' ecstatic memories. He spends hours out in the driveway working on my son's baseball pitching, and teaching them both about sports (an area where my husband and I are both remarkably deficient). There is literally nobody my kids would rather spend time with in the entire world. Seeing my dad through my sons' eyes, I have been blessed with the important reminder that my dad is still the coolest and the most loving, and that so much of what he does is gold.

No matter how much I love my dad, I will probably never engage in a letter-writing expedition with him. It's just not my way. But something has happened over the last few years that is our own version of that journey. A few years ago, after much prodding, my dad got a smart phone, and he discovered text messaging—everything changed after that. Now, my dad and I text each other countless times every week. I can jot off an idea to him in a moment, and he can respond in kind. I can tell him something funny my kids said, and he can respond by telling me how much he adores them. We can send instant photos, tell each other if we just saw a great movie, note a piece of art we came across that the other might like. I can send articles, and we can discuss them back-and-forth over the course of our day. And all of this can happen in real time—so, it's as though my dad is by my side all the time, even though I live in DC and we both have busy lives. And those exchanges, no matter how small and shorthand they may sometimes seem are honestly *everything*. For me, the gift of constant communication with my dad is a genuine wonder of modern technology. Sure, there are lots of problems with smart phone culture, perhaps most importantly the distraction from being "present" in the time and place where we actually stand, but if the trade off is having my dad be a presence in my life every day no matter where we both are . . . I'll make that bargain every time. I love you, Dad.

A *Personal Note*

by

Emily Cohen

(Age 14, 1992)

Caring. When I hear the word caring, the first thing that comes to mind is love. Caring is so basic. You feel love and care without even realizing it. It is important not to only care for others, but to have others care for you. The only way that you can make people love for and care about you is to be kind to them. Treat them as you would want them to treat you. Tell them that you love them and that they are an important part of your life. Then and only then can you have a stable relationship with that person, no matter whether he or she is your parent, sibling, or friend. If you wait until it is too late, you will lose out.

Many years ago, my grandfather and his brother had a financial argument. They did not speak to each other for years. My entire family was split in half. I didn't speak to people with whom I had once been very close for years. One day, either my uncle or my grandfather called the other on the telephone. I am not sure who called whom, and that is not important. What is important is that they spoke and apologized to each other and once again were friends. A few months later, my grandfather's brother passed away. The moral of this story is that life is too short, so do not waste it away because of pride. Tell people how you feel about them before it is too late. Do not let petty arguments get in the way of love and caring. Nothing in the world can possibly be worth sacrificing these two important emotions for.

I feel that one of the truest forms of caring is that of parents for their children. A person's child is said to be an extension of that person's self. My father and grandfather have written a book about their relationship. To do this, they began to write letters back and forth to one another. I had the honor of reading those letters. In the letters, my grandfather and father talk about how much they love and care for each other. They express their feelings in ways that I did not know two grown men could, with much love and sensitivity. Through these letters, they discussed my grandfather's mortality. As much as we would like him to, he cannot live forever. My grandfather states in one of his letters, "My children have had children and soon their children have children. In this way I am immortal." I believe he is right.

Hello Father

Accidents waiting to happen
Many near misses
Flirtations with death
Job-like tests of faith
Leap before us
Synchronicities calling
Stars aligned
Sights to behold

Dad, another anniversary
Of your fall from earth
Can see you up there now
Summers passed
Leo the lion leading the way
Bright lights of Luna Park
Greetings from the other side
On the great divide
Your accepting hand
Dancing in the sky
Riding the carousel
All knowing eyes piercing through
Heavenly gates open up
An entrance to the garden
Rays of pearly wisdom
Welcoming passages of time
Vision of ancient ghosts
Gracefully gliding angels
Accumulations of dreams of generations
Gazing hopefulness
In the shelter of each other

Spirits riding the stagecoach
Halo full circle ahead
A Coney Island playground
Fog lifts
This father of mine
For another time around
Joy reaching out
We need you now
Save from the frenzy
For a place of peace
One not meant for mortals
Chases to see past trials of the I

No accidental accidents
See you inside living theatre in the round
An intended visit
The inside ride
Wanting for those to witness
On the other side
A hello from the founding father

Poem by Donald Cohen
From *Writings From The Ferris Wheel* (2019)

Acknowledgments

A special thanks goes to the silent partner behind this whole project, Marilyn Cohen. A wonderful person, she was the mother of one author and wife of the other. She gave us the support we needed to believe in ourselves. And Dee Cohen, wife, daughter-in-law, artist, real estate agent, (among other wonderful gifts), who patiently listened to many of our discussions. Of course, where would the book be without Jared Cohen, son and grandson, for his refreshing honesty, and enlightening foreword in the book. And Emily Cohen, loving daughter and granddaughter for her inspirational afterword at the end. I am also grateful to have the early letters that they both wrote to me. We would also like to thank the rest of our loving family: Ellen, Ron, Jeff, Rebecca, Ali, Joey, Miguel; and my five grandchildren: Greyson, Lucas, Zelda, Annabel and Ingrid . . .

I am so grateful to Jan Bassin and Clay Hughes for all their editorial support and Clay for typing all my handwritten notes. Thank you to Meryl Moss, my publicist and dear friend, always there for advice.

A special thanks to the late Dr. Rollo May, for his generous support. And to Joyce Vitali, who went searching all over the Westport Public Library to locate the Mark Twain quote that people tend to misquote. I am so grateful to Liz Marks for all her support.

I would also like to thank my close friend Jane Shapiro for her helping me to exchange thoughts that enhanced my writing. A special appreciation to Norm Zwail for his input and support. Thank you to Mimi Gross for her colorful Coney Island mural art that provided a dynamic front and back cover for the book. It was fun to have Westport artist Miggs Burroughs take the photo of the Mimi Gross mural for the cover of the book. He also took the photo of my grandson Greyson wearing the Coney Island motorcycle jacket inside the book. We are grateful to Daniel Levinson for writing *The Seasons Of A Man's Life* which provided a helpful road map during our personal journey together.

My deep appreciation to James Wasserman for being the editor who helped put this book into its final translation and cover design. And thank you to Yvonne Paglia for believing in me and this piece of work and publishing this book to share in all its humanity. And thanks as well to Angela Elgert for her meticulous work in transcribing my handwritten edits into the electronic manuscript. A special recognition goes out to the people with whom we work, whose courage to share their souls with ours has helped us grow. Their insights and words have proved to be an inspiration at various times during the process of writing this book.

As I conclude, it's my father's immortality that was the driving force to complete this book. Max Cohen is a hero to his own Coney Island, and to all who had the honor of his presence, and we will continue to know him through his letters. Hopefully this journey of ours will inspire future generations to take the inside ride.

About the Authors

DR. DONALD COHEN is a licensed Marriage and Family Therapist, in private practice for more than 40 years in Weston, Connecticut. Dr. Cohen, known for his direct approach and originality of his clinical skills, is an expert on issues of communication and relationships from childhood through adulthood, particularly with adolescents and marital and family issues.

Dr. Cohen received his B.A. from the State University of New York at Buffalo, Phi Beta Kappa; his M.S.W. from Columbia University, his Ph.D. in clinical psychology from the California School of Professional Psychology in Berkeley, California, and his post-doctoral fellowship at the Department of Psychiatry at Yale University Medical Center.

The author was the creator, producer and host of the popular weekly television and radio show, Kids Are Talking, and has published various articles, as well as lectured and conducted workshops relating to communication and family issues.

Dr. Cohen lives in Weston, CT with his wife. They have two children and five grandchildren.

DR. MAX COHEN was a practicing psychiatrist and psychoanalyst for over 50 years in Garden City, New York.

He received his B.A. from Cornell University, earned his M.D. from New York Medical College and completed psychiatric training at Columbia University. Dr. Cohen served as a training and supervising psychoanalyst at the Columbia University Center for Psychoanalytic Training and Research and was a member of the faculty at the College of Physicians and Surgeons at Columbia University.

Dr. Cohen lived on Long Island, New York where he and his wife raised two children and later enjoyed four grandchildren. He passed away in 2011 at the age of 87.

The Way of the Small: Why Less Is More

by Michael Gellert

A practical and spiritual guide to making everyday living sacred.

This book explores the principals of a sound, wholesome exisistence for both the individual and society. Addressing the search for finding true happiness, meaning and success, *The Way of the Small* gives us new perspectives based on old wisdom on what makes for a truly lived life. A practical and spiritual guide to fulfillment, it illustrates that happiness is found in "the small"—in ways to celebrate the precious small gifts of ordinary life and experiencing the sacred in all aspects of life. We are reminded that "Less Is More, Simpler Is Better."

The Way of the Small teaches ways to embrace even life's more difficult passages such as aging, failure, illness, or the loss of a loved one, making even our pain a path to the sacred that helps us find meaning in life as it happens.

"Both a zen-like meditation on the significance of insignificance and a cultural-historical tour of an idea-an 'organic way of living' rather than a 'theory, formula, or fixed belief system.' Gellert locates and celebrates the small in individual experience (including his own and those of his patients), all the major world religions and the Big Bang, among other settings. Gellert's graceful text will definitely boost readers' capacity for accepting one's predicament and finding satisfaction in the slight." —*Publishers Weekly*

About the Author

MICHAEL GELLERT is a faculty member of the C.G. Jung Institute of Los Angeles and a certified Jungian analyst in private practice. He has been a college professor and a mental health consultant to the University of Southern California and Time Magazine. He is the author of *Modern Mysticism: Jung, Zen, and the Still Good Hand of God* and *The Fate of America: An Inquiry into National Character.*

$14.95 • Paperback • ISBN: 0892541296 • 192 pp. • 5 x 6-1/2

The Spiritual Paradox of Addiction
The Call for the Transcendent

by Ashok Bedi, M.D. and Rev. Joseph H. Pereira

Addicts and alcoholics are often highly spiritualized individuals who lack the faith apparatus to make a healthy connection with their spiritual drive. As such, they turn to negative behavior patterns to fulfill that hunger: alcohol, drugs, food, sex, gambling, pornography, social media, and dysfunctional relationships. This book offers a series of insights and methods whereby faith may be restored and positively channeled into life-sustaining behaviors. It is addressed to both addicts, their families, and friends, as well as interested laypeople, government policymakers, and treatment professionals. The authors include instruction in yoga and breathing exercises, meditation, and mindfulness, and include case studies, and competent medical guidance for detoxification.

"This book will prove of inestimable value to treatment professionals and friends and families, those who share an interest in the mysteries and dynamics of successful recovery, and who often have a personal stake in that process." —From the Foreword

About the Authors

ASHOK BEDI, M.D., author of *Crossing the Healing Zone*, is a Jungian psychoanalyst and a board-certified psychiatrist. He is a member of the Royal College of Psychiatrists of Great Britain, a diplomat in Psychological Medicine at the Royal College of Physicians and Surgeons, and a Distinguished Life Fellow of the American Psychiatric Association.

REV. JOSEPH PEREIRA is the founder and managing director of the Kripa Foundation in Mumbai, India, devoted to the care, support, and treatment of those affected by chemical dependency, HIV, and AIDS. He holds a Masters in Psychology and Philosophy, is certified in Divinity and Counseling, and is a trainer in the Iyengar School of Yoga.

$18.95 • Paperback • ISBN: 978-0-89254-192-8 • 232 pp. • 5 x 7